GETTYSBURG REPLIES

The World Responds to Abraham Lincoln's Gettysburg Address

ABRAHAM LINCOLN PRESIDENTIAL LIBRARY FOUNDATION
EDITED BY CARLA KNOROWSKI, PH.D.

Guilford, Connecticut

An imprint of Rowman & Littlefield

Distributed by NATIONAL BOOK NETWORK

Copyright © 2015 by Abraham Lincoln Presidential Library Foundation

Essay by Samuel R. Harris courtesy of Illinois Holocaust Museum and Education Center

British Library Cataloguing in Publication Information Available

Library of Congress Cataloging-in-Publication Data Available

ISBN 978-1-4930-0912-1 (hard cover)
ISBN 978-1-4930-1766-9 (e-book)

∞™ The paper used in this publication meets the minimum requirements of American National Standard for Information Sciences—Permanence of Paper for Printed Library Materials, ANSI/NISO Z39.48-1992.

The views, opinions, and positions expressed by the authors who have written essays for this publication do not necessarily reflect those of the Abraham Lincoln Presidential Library Foundation.

CONTENTS

PREFACE

It is a two-page, handwritten essay on white, blue-lined paper. The paper is not unlike the standard blue-lined paper you would find in a composition book—the kind used in school—sporting a black and white marble-finished cover. The pages themselves measure seven-and-a-half by nine-and-a-half inches. The author's 19th century, right-slanted cursive fills 23 of the 25 available lines on the first page, eight on the second. The neat and even penmanship and rich, black, iron gall ink draw you in. The author's words draw you in further. His eloquence draws you in completely. The pages weigh much less than an ounce, but carry the weight of the world. It is the Gettysburg Address—Abraham Lincoln's masterpiece—one of the greatest speeches in the annals of history.

It was written on the occasion of the dedication of the National Cemetery at Gettysburg, a ceremony that took place a little more than four months after what was, and still is, the bloodiest battle ever fought on American soil. Approximately 52,000 Union and Confederate soldiers were killed, wounded, or went missing—the green rolling hills of Gettysburg, Pennsylvania, were awash in a sea of crimson blood as Union and Confederate forces fought the Civil War's tide-turning battle. When the smoke cleared and the deafening sounds of gunfire and exploding shells fell silent, all that remained was the sobering stillness of death, which continued to linger even as preparations for the dedication were taking place, even more so on that solemn day. The scars and ravages of war were still omnipresent as the civic procession was directed to "salute the President of the United States," and then "advance and occupy the area in front of the stand, the military leaving sufficient space *between them and the line of graves* for the civic procession to pass."

The program for the day was simple: A prayer, then a speech by the great orator Edward Everett—both preceded and followed by music. After that, a few "dedicatory remarks by the President of the United States" were to be delivered by Abraham Lincoln. His two-minute Address was in sharp contrast to Everett's two-hour oration, not just in length, but in outcome. Lincoln's Address stirred the soul; instilled a sense of purpose; called its audience to action; and righted a lost and faltering nation, setting its sails on course for *a new birth of freedom.*

The speech was immediately recognized for what it was, a national treasure. In May 1864, a mere six months after it was delivered, the Address was reprinted in a volume edited by Alexander Bliss, published in Baltimore by Cushings and Bailey, of the facsimile handwriting of famous Americans. While Lincoln's Address was not the first selection printed in the book—that honor was reserved for Francis Scott Key and "The Star Spangled Banner"—it immediately followed the American anthem, a tribute to the greatness of the 16th President and his "dedicatory remarks." Lincoln and the Address were followed in order by selections from Washington Irving, Oliver Wendell Holmes, John Greenleaf Whittier, and only then by Edward Everett. Lincoln's handwritten version of the Gettysburg Address originally in the Bliss book now hangs in the Lincoln Bedroom of the White House.

The occasion of the 150th anniversary of the writing and delivery of the Gettysburg

Address most certainly provided a historic opportunity for solemn commemorations and possibly, sad to say, unimaginative, well-worn, though well-meant tributes. When a person has been studied, celebrated, and commemorated for more than a century and a half, having had more than 18,000 books, long, middling, or tiny written about him, as Lincoln has, it is difficult to be original, to say or do something that hasn't been said or done before. It's easy to become complacent. After all, it is Lincoln and the Gettysburg Address—no dressing up required. Simply display the document in all its glory and have an eloquent speaker recite it at the precise moment in time that Lincoln had delivered it 150 years earlier. That sort of tribute is simple, safe, and generally meets the expectations of Lincoln-loving scholars, armchair historians, and devotees around the world. *But is it enough?* Certainly not.

While "simple" is a word which might be equated with the preferred way of life of the rail splitter from Illinois, "safe" isn't. After all, this was the man who risked the ire of many by opposing the Mexican War, pushing through Emancipation and abolition policies, and moving forward with conscription. So while displaying and reciting the Gettysburg Address was a simple and safe way for the Abraham Lincoln Presidential Library and Museum and its Foundation to commemorate the 150th, it wasn't the only path we would travel. We didn't want just to meet expectations, we wanted to exceed them. The magnitude of the man and his words deserved something more, something original, something, dare we say, larger than life. Enter 272 words.

272 words—the number of words Lincoln used in the Gettysburg Address. Challenged to speak about the enormity of Gettysburg,

Lincoln used a mere 272 words, in 10 sentences, to convey the greatest, most important message of the time—some say of *all time*. We still hold sacred its message. To commemorate its sesquicentennial, we decided to challenge people from around the world to write "272 Words" in the spirit of Abraham Lincoln.

This, for many, was daunting to grasp, let alone attempt. Many refused the challenge on the basis that they could never write anything that could approximate, let alone top, the simple yet profound eloquence of Lincoln and the Address. We found ourselves doing more than our share of explaining that the point of the 272-word challenge was not to try to "top" the Gettysburg Address, write as well as Lincoln, or change the course of history. It was simply to celebrate the 16th President and his words. It was hoped that essayists, in trying to get their message across in only 272 words, would come to realize in a deeper, more personal way the greatness of the Address and just how eloquent and gifted a communicator Lincoln was.

We asked our essayists to write about the 16th President, Gettysburg, the Gettysburg Address, or a cause that inspires them. *Gettysburg Replies* is a compilation of 100 essays selected from the more than 1,000 written by people from all walks of life—from schoolchildren to U.S. presidents. The essays are powerful, eloquent, and insightful. They are a lasting tribute not only to the greatness of Abraham Lincoln and the Gettysburg Address, but to the power of both the written and *handwritten* word.

Yes, in addition to writing 272 words, essayists were challenged to walk further in Lincoln's footsteps and write out their essays longhand on the stationery of their choice. Some essayists, faced with the challenge of both writing and handwriting, chose only the former. Others embraced the two. Many had to rediscover the seemingly lost art of applying pen to paper rather than fingers to keyboard. Some authors sheepishly revealed that it was easier to compose the essay than write it out by hand, but admitted that handwriting it made the challenge all the more appealing, while describing the process as "painful," "humbling," and in some cases "humiliating." In the end, some of our essayists chose hand lettering instead. These choices—what to write about, whether to type or write it out longhand, what stationery to use—all add to the depth and richness of the 272-word project, to the essays, and to the essayists themselves as we view the slants, curves, and styles of their very personal penmanship.

We commenced the project unsure of what the response would be. Would people find the mere suggestion of writing 272 words in the Lincoln tradition too daunting, too ridiculous, or too arrogant? We would soon find out. The first litmus test we seemed to pass came when we reached out to noted Lincoln scholar Harold Holzer. Harold does not suffer fools or foolish projects gladly. Undaunted, we sent an invitation to Harold encouraging him to write. He responded post haste. We had nothing to fear when he replied, "What a nice honor—272 words—wow—who can be as succinct as A.L.?" Who indeed? Perhaps no one on the face of the planet, but it didn't mean Harold wasn't going to give it the old college try, and as he put 272 words to paper, so too did many others.

At the Abraham Lincoln Presidential Library and Museum and its Foundation, history is our business. Every day we sail in the wake of history: collecting and preserving documents and artifacts, conducting scholarly research to uncover more of Lincoln's rich legacy. But rarely do we have the opportunity to make history. The project allowed us to do just that. Consider one essay that arrived in an oversized envelope. A peek inside revealed the treasure within: Jimmy Carter's 272-word reply. I pulled it out—gently, carefully—realizing that the essay, no less than any other item sitting in our Library's archives, was already a historic document, and I may be among the first in history privileged to read it.

It was on his personal letterhead, sporting the centered figure of an eagle outlined in blue, with four stars descending the nape of its neck. The name *Jimmy Carter*, also in blue, was set in bold, capital letters, centered and printed just beneath. The words *Gettysburg Address* were typed a few lines below and to the left. I began reading the essay, suddenly hearkening back to 1978 with the sound of the President's voice resounding in my head as if he were right in the room regaling me with an intimate story of a famous moment in history: "When I began peace talks at Camp David between Israel and Egypt, it soon became obvious . . ." The first 16 words drew me in completely. The essay, which was typed by the President himself on his office typewriter, was a historic recollection, a document not only for our nation's posterity, but the world's, a document few knew existed. We now were making history, making our own wake in which generations of readers, researchers, and scholars would sail.

In addition to President Carter's essay, *Gettysburg Replies* presents 272-word essays by Presidents George H. W. Bush, Bill Clinton, George W. Bush, and Barack Obama, as well as essays from Nobel Prize recipients, famous jurists, filmmakers, actors, scholars, poets, and people from all walks of life. There are essays from Ginny Greer and Caleb Lewis, students and members of Little Rock Central High School's Memory Project—a project that serves to record the stories and memories of Civil Rights activists like the Little Rock Nine.

And then there's an essay we received from a man named Allen Lynch. A victim of relentless bullying in both elementary and high school, Allen Lynch found his road to peace through war. Enlisting in the United States Army in 1964, Lynch volunteered to serve in Vietnam. While every day in Vietnam called for strength and courage, one particular day required Lynch to summon all he could muster as he and his comrades were ambushed. Spotting three fallen soldiers from another platoon out in the open and under attack, Lynch, with total disregard for his own personal safety, fought his way through a barrage of intense enemy fire to rescue and bring the soldiers to safety. For his actions, Lynch was presented the Medal of Honor, the award Lincoln had created in 1862 to recognize ". . . noncommissioned officers and privates as shall most distinguish themselves by their gallantry in action, and other soldier-like qualities . . ." Allen Lynch's essay speaks to that gallantry and that of the many Civil War Medal of Honor recipients who served and sacrificed to ensure the freedoms American citizens enjoy to this day.

Yes, *Gettysburg Replies* is filled with the words of the heroic and courageous. Consider Sam Harris, formerly known as Samuel Rzeznik. Sam, a Holocaust survivor, came to America as an orphan after his parents were killed in the mass genocide. He had been shuttled off to Nazi concentration camps at Deblin and Czestochowa in Poland when he was only nine years old. After being liberated, he sailed to America aboard the *Ernie Pyle* to find *a new birth of freedom*—something he found as he was adopted by Ellis and Harriet Harris.

In 1951, as a sophomore at New Trier High School in Winnetka, Illinois, he wrote an essay about his experience immigrating to America. Serendipitously, the essay was *272 words* long. Some 62 years later, Sam submitted his boyhood essay as his contribution to the project and *Gettysburg Replies*.

Or consider still, Babalwa Mhlauli, a young woman from South Africa, who in her essay recounts the story of how her father, anti-Apartheid activist Scelo Mhlauli, was assassinated with three others on a dark winter's night in 1985, because they dared speak out against oppression in their native land. They came to be known as The Cradock Four. Babalwa, a mere child at the time, lost her father to an assassin just as young Tad Lincoln had some 120 years earlier, both because they had courageous, freedom-fighting fathers. Babalwa uses her 272 words to share her personal story as a child growing up in 1980s South Africa and her family's struggle to free themselves from the shackles of Apartheid.

And some of the submissions came in pairs, like those from American singer-songwriter Pete Seeger and his nephew Bill Goodman. Their contributions are a celebration of the Address itself, Pete contributing a written version of the Address, in which the Grammy Award–winner teaches us how Lincoln's 272 word speech might be easily memorized; and nephew Bill's essay reminds us that Lincoln is more than a face on a five dollar bill. For most of their lives together, Uncle Pete and Nephew Bill would speak on the phone every November 19th on the anniversary of the commemoration of the National Cemetery and recite the Gettysburg Address together—a tradition for the ages. Their contributions convey their deep respect and admiration for both the Address and its author.

All the essays in *Gettysburg Replies*, like the Address itself, are national treasures. When we began the project, we hoped that if the response was sufficient, we could mount an exhibition of the work. This was by no means a traditional approach to exhibit curating. It would not be composed of a group of artifacts and documents already in existence. Rather, this exhibit would rely on the creation of documents—the creation of the essays. Not knowing how many essays would be written, who might write them, or whether they would be of substance presented to us a great unknown, but not for long. As essay upon essay was received, it soon became clear that the quandary wasn't whether we could mount an adequate display, but whether we had space enough to showcase the treasure trove we had received.

At the center of the exhibition, "The Power of Words," was of course the first and finest of all the essays—the inspiration for the exhibit itself, the Everett copy of Abraham Lincoln's Gettysburg Address (see pages xx–1). It was flanked on either side by the essays of four of the living U.S. Presidents. Unlike traditional exhibits contained in one gallery or series of connected galleries, "The Power of Words" was an extension of the Museum itself, as essays were displayed in the Treasures Gallery, Gettysburg Gallery, and Plaza. Guests lined the galleries to read them. Here were the words of filmmakers like Steven Spielberg, Ken Burns, and Kathy Kennedy; military heroes like Colin Powell, Tammy Duckworth, John Borling, and the sailors of USS *Abraham Lincoln*; jurists like Sandra Day O'Connor, Judith Sheindlin, and Alan Dershowitz; poets such as Billy Collins, Nikki Giovanni, and Kevin Stein; scholars such as Richard Carwardine and Allen Guelzo; astrophysicist Neal deGrasse Tyson, activist Julian Bond, astronaut James Lovell, commentators Michael Medved and Scott Simon; students such as Katherine Hitchcock, Grace Richards, and David Walser; and many, many more. This treasure trove is crowned with the beautiful visual imagery of renowned photographer Annie Leibovitz, who literally and figuratively broadened our sights by contributing her very own photo essay.

In modern society where attention spans are growing shorter, the need for constant visual stimulation and activity is growing greater, and there is a seemingly ever present need to tap, slide, or push something on a screen, *Gettysburg Replies* is a refreshing step back in time when both the written and handwritten word was the center of the cultural creative universe. Each essay is now a historic document for the ages. It is our hope that in the years to come, people will read these essays to glimpse into the thoughts of 21st century citizens of the world as they contributed their Gettysburg replies.

And now in 2015, as we commemorate the 150th anniversary of the passing of the Great Emancipator, let us read each of these essays with deep gratitude and in lasting tribute to the man who inspired them. Words cannot replace this leader lost, but dedicatory words may elevate our lives.

—Carla Knorowski, Ph.D.
Chief Executive Officer
Abraham Lincoln Presidential
Library Foundation
Springfield, Illinois

INTRODUCTION
A Nation "At Risk"—Lincoln's World and Ours

Abraham Lincoln has been studied and appreciated, rightly so, more than any other American. At Gettysburg he created the moment, the words, the lightning-bolt of memory about our origins and aspirations that stick with us today. Increasingly he is embraced as a figure of global importance and renown. Yet understanding his role in the world *of his time* has proved difficult, despite his timeless principles.

One way to attack the problem is to see how Lincoln felt his country, his world, was at risk, just as some people today see perils at every turn. We begin with his biography.

THE BACKGROUND

The main features of the world's political and social scene during Lincoln's youth barely touched him. They were locally distinctive, having mainly an indirect impact on his thinking. Napoleon was defeated at Waterloo when Lincoln was 6 years old, triggering the migration of thousands of European soldiers, chiefly from the British Isles, to the New World during the postwar slump. Lincoln grew up around a number of people with foreign accents. The volcano Tambora (in what is now Indonesia) exploded that same year, 1815, literally darkening the skies over New England and elsewhere for the next three summers, reducing the harvest in enough places that a new surge of open-land seekers—including the Lincolns—headed West, mostly into those states we now call the Midwest. Most of all, the ongoing madness of King George III in the U.K., and French stumbling between violent 'progressivism' and

African and Mexican imperialism for nearly all of 1815 to 1861, gave keen observers like Lincoln every reason to be wary of any form of government focused too largely on either an individual or on the masses. All of these events form a dim background to a "global Lincoln" during his lifetime, even if we suppose that an embrace of his presidential leadership and presidential words would be near-universal. He may have appeared on postage stamps around the world in the last two generations, but the military success of Lincoln's Union made some nations worry that they were at risk as a U.S. neighbor.

The man himself was chary of self-inflating comments, or even Big Idea pronouncements, save one: that "slavery itself . . . deprives our republican example of its just influence in the world—enables the enemies of free institutions, with plausibility, to taunt us as hypocrites," as he said in a speech given on October 16, 1854, in Peoria, Illinois. Lincoln believed most of all in the egalitarianism to be found in and fostered by a republic.

In an address given to the New Jersey senate on 21 February 1861, Lincoln expressed these feelings about the Declaration of Independence and its first defenders, including George Washington:

I recollect thinking then, boy even though I was, that there must have been something more than common that those men struggled for. I am exceedingly anxious that that thing which they struggled for; that something even more

than National Independence; that something that held out a great promise to all the people of the world to all time to come; I am exceedingly anxious that this Union, the Constitution, and the liberties of the people shall be perpetuated in accordance with the original idea for which that struggle was made, and I shall be most happy indeed if I shall be an humble instrument in the hands of the Almighty, and of this, his almost chosen people, for perpetuating the object of that great struggle.

Lincoln that day, as president-to-be, on the eve of Washington's Birthday, 1861, revealed himself as a product of some 18th-century forces. His patriotic adoration of the Founders may strike some today as antique or brittle in a 24-time-zones world. Resilient it was nonetheless. His maturing sense of a sound polity steered clear of autocrats like Andrew Jackson, anti-moral populists like Stephen Douglas, and the corrupt attachment to untutored immigrants whose votes could be had at a price. All of these types had been present in Old England, the system to be dropped.

Did Lincoln then reach immediately for the anti-slavery cause? No. Perfectionism as embodied in the abolitionists—perhaps 2 or 3 percent of the populace, mainly New Englanders, and including some free-love types—or the no-government, communal-land strongmen like Robert Owen, never attracted him at all. This should not surprise us. Those movements attracted tiny groups of people intentionally living on the margins of society whose stories now, if interesting, still remain far beyond the main path of American development.

Lincoln, on the other hand, grew up squarely on this path. He and his forebears were daily beset by discrete, practical problems, and he trained up his detail-oriented, practical mind to address them. How to help farmers sell their oats, corn, wheat, pork, and timber for sustainable prices? By clearing the rivers and building the canals that would speed their path to consumers. How to choose the best, or at least the better, candidates for election? By assembling party organizers on a statewide basis, not letting the counties be pitted one against another. How to fix the inchoate horror of Legal Slavery as deposited in our laps by the Constitution writers? That could not be fixed unilaterally, in a nation of laws. It would take debate and compromise.

The party-organization mechanism he picked up by the early 1840s from Democrats in the East. The canals and roads idea—what we now loosely call "infrastructure"—he picked up from the nonpolitical people all around him, big operators and small, trading in a dozen industries, and many of them—like his father, like his under-energetic stepbrother, like his New Salem neighbors the Kelsos and Onstotts and Hills—needing only a little greater connection to markets in order to help the pioneers in their thousands to open up the West, one free-soil farm at a time.

Lincoln saw similar versions of the same national limitations in Kentucky, which he left with his family at age 7 in 1816; in Indiana, which he left with his extended and stepfamily at age 21 in 1830; and at each little outpost in Illinois thereafter. He determined to run for public office at the age of 23, a young man in no particular hurry. "I am humble Abraham Lincoln," he said to his first public in New Salem, Illinois, and declaiming with a resounding feather-thud that "If I fail, I have known failure too often for it to affect me much." In 1832, he was also sagacious enough to apprehend that "I would not favor the passage of a law upon this subject [usury] which might be very easily evaded." No specific class of people should be harmed or aided by any law, he sincerely felt. He simply worried that the dream of the free-soil farmer, of free homes and free men no matter their color, were at risk, and needed what amounted to about 1 percent of gross state or national product to be spent by government to fix the roads and rivers.

His overall view of government was that it could, "where people themselves cannot, or cannot do as well," assist the building-out of the great national raw material: its land, waterways, minerals, and connecting points thereto. He, like Karl Marx—who got the notion from John Locke and Adam Smith—saw that labor was the essential underpinning and motive force of growth, and "preceded" capital. That is, labor creates capital; it is the *sine qua non* of economics.

That is where parallels between the thought of these two contemporaries end. One was often elected as a widely admired and hard-working man of the people; one was an underemployed dreamer, unable to grasp, or accept, or see the vast expansion of civilizational wealth in the economic and social changes around him. Lincoln felt that each man should have the right, regardless of skin color or religion, to hire himself out for wages; save his money; buy his own means of subsistence with that savings; and eventually save enough from his profits to hire another man to work with him and for him. Lincoln had seen this happen hundreds of times, and grasped how efficacious it was in uniting labor with capital in their equally contributory ways to social progress. Those "at risk" of falling behind fell victim either to bad luck (like his father), disinterest in work (like

his stepbrother), or bad laws (like the African-Americans around him). An elected official could address only one of those obstacles, the laws. Shifting money from government toward the victims of the other was untenable; this shifting he and his generation left either to insurance companies, if willing; or to God. A hundred dollars sent to his stepbrother would, he knew, be ill spent, never becoming capital nor instigating labor. Even offering double the loan, if the stepbrother would only get a job, had no effect on the man's behavior.

Expanding on this premise, in his major speech on agriculture and technology, in Milwaukee 30 September 1859, Lincoln said:

The ambition for broad acres leads to poor farming, even with men of energy. I scarcely ever knew a mammoth farm to sustain itself; much less to return a profit upon the outlay. I have more than once known a man to spend a respectable fortune upon one; fail and leave it; and then some man of more modest aims, get a small fraction of the ground, and make a good living upon it. Mammoth farms are like tools, or weapons, which are too heavy to be handled.

Speaking of tools, he laid out later in the same speech precisely how they are acquired and used:

Many independent men, in this assembly, doubtless a few years ago were hired laborers. And their case is almost if not quite the general rule. The prudent, penniless beginner in the world, labors for wages awhile, saves a surplus with which to buy tools or land, for himself; then labors on his own account another while, and at length hires

*another new beginner to help him. This,
say its advocates, is free labor—the just
and generous, and prosperous system, which
opens the way for all—gives hope to all, and
energy, and progress, and improvement of
condition to all. If any continue through
life in the condition of the hired laborer, it
is not the fault of the system, but because of
either a dependent nature which prefers it, or
improvidence, folly, or singular misfortune.*

In this speech Lincoln also predicted the invention of the steam plow. He is our only president who took out a scientific patent, a decade before that speech—an improved method for "buoying vessels over shoals." Moving goods from place to place was often on his mind, even as an attorney who often handled suits in which goods were inadequately or not quite sold and shipped as per contract. Lincoln was a logistics man, even in a policy sense.

So narrow an interpretation of the lawmaker's rights and force—narrow by modern global standards—stood at the foreground of most of his economic ideas. The "class" hurt today might not be in the same "class" tomorrow, for the American Republic offered mobility to all who would attempt it. Clearing the land was for citizens; clearing the rivers was far harder. For himself he sketched out this rule in about 1854:

*The legitimate object of government is "to
do for the people what needs to be done, but
which they can not, by individual effort, do at
all, or do so well, for themselves." . . . Making
and maintaining roads, bridges, and the like;
providing for the helpless young and afflicted;
common schools; and disposing of deceased
men's property, are instances.*

Thus, to Lincoln's mind, the limitations and fixity of simple common law were guideposts to what government at any level could do.

Why should a single person attempt to circumscribe the efforts of so vast a land and people? Thus, whatever "global" understanding Lincoln had in 1861 of the executive branch, it did *not* spring from pre-1776 models. If not European-born ideas of monarchy, mob rule, or great elegance, it had always been, rather, developments at home that struck him as vigorous, and determinative of his outlook. Like most people in the world, he had great expectations for a land blessed with free institutions, representative government, and expansive resources. The American population was growing by 30 percent each decade on average—strong natural growth, plus immigration—and the great majority of people Lincoln encountered were getting ahead, if slowly, in life.

THE PROBLEM

But what of problems beyond the law, such as slavery's social acceptance by the great majority? In 1854 he saw no mechanism whatsoever to "clear the river" of this impediment to justice in a republic. State constitutions were gradually erasing slavery from their domains, from Vermont in 1777 to California in 1850; while other states, mainly the most southern, held on against the tide. Washington, Jefferson, Clay, Lincoln, and the great swath of middle-minded men believed that slavery would fade away of its own insensibility. The colonization movement—offering the freed people a paid return to homes in Africa from which they had been kidnapped—began in 1816 and continued to gain adherents, including Lincoln, down to about 1862. Colonization was not an economically sensible idea (private money could never pay passage for 3 to 4 million people), but neither was immediate abolition a sensible policy, for people who could not read or write and were often socially defenseless; neither was the onward jackboot march of more slavery in the western lands, where free people (mostly white, but a few black) had legitimate and paid up claims to free land. In short, Lincoln saw no mechanism to end slavery; only to halt its spread.

The crux of the problem in his mind and for the nation's healthy growth was that too many Americans were "at risk." Lincoln himself never used this late-20th-century phrasing for the most vulnerable. He merely recognized precisely who they were. Hopeful prospects of a Great Republic could not rest within the hearts of that "one sixth of the population," as he described them in 1860, who were nonwhite. It is true that about 10 percent of this unfavored lot were free people, not enslaved, a figure that was about the same in the southern states as in the nation at large. The great majority of those non-slave people were mulatto.

"In New Hampshire," Lincoln said in 1857, "the State which goes farthest towards equality between the races, there are just 184 Mulattoes while there are in Virginia—how many do you think? 79,775, being 23,126 more than in all the free States together."

This was his message, in the wake of the Supreme Court's March 1857 ruling against Dred Scott, to those who feared racial amalgamation. Adverting to the same census figures in towns around Illinois as well as in his westernmost trip ever, to Leavenworth, Kansas, while he was a political candidate in 1858 and (presumptively) in 1859, he showed that Republicans like himself did not stand for racial amalgamation, which was the dirtiest charge their opposing Democrats could make of them. Rather, by

command of the data, Lincoln showed that slavery *caused* that amalgamation, that the Dred Scott ruling would only *increase* amalgamation, through the personally corrupting power of one person (male owner) over another (female slave) that it cemented.

The artificiality of this division never made economic, social, or moral sense to Lincoln, even if it was politically just about untouchable for most of his life. When Lincoln attacked the defenders of separate-race existence by examining the growth in the "Negro" population, as distinct from the mulattos (broken out by that description in the official censuses of his era), he was able to paint his opponents into a racial corner of their own making. Mulattos were nearly all children of a white master and a slave woman; their greater numbers than "Negroes" among the "free" population resulted usually from the sentiment of a master who somehow arranged for the manumission of his nonwhite children, or allowed them to buy their freedom through paid work.

But data do not often move political sentiments. In this setting, Lincoln was elected in November 1860 on 39.6 percent of the popular vote, in a four-way race; the lowest figure (by 3 points) in all presidential history. Public opinion, on top of constitutional law, blocked him from acting in the way that all other evidence shows "my oft-expressed *personal* wish that all men every where could be free," as he wrote in a letter to Horace Greeley on 22 August 1862. Coming into the presidency, just as he had observed from his youth, Lincoln knew that his role would be cooperative, instrumental.

THE OPENING
The rebels' attack on Fort Sumter on 12 April 1861 changed Lincoln's views, and

simultaneously allowed him to speak more directly about the guiding role of the Declaration of Independence in our nation's birth. "That all men are created equal" was a phrase he used repeatedly before 1860, citing Jefferson; but in the above letter to Greeley, he cast it personally. His command of data and moral suasion had not reached a majority of voters in 1860. Poetry, or powerfully inspiring words grown from simple principles, do.

For all his mastery of economic figures as a state legislator from 1834 to 1842 (Whig party spokesman on economics for most of the stint), he gradually gave himself publicly as president to literary influence. Such is the common feeling we get today from his writings, and unquestionably from his influence. In the big classroom of the national school of presidents, Lincoln takes top grade in English and Rhetoric. He was moving already, we can see in retrospect, to the point when he could deliver something like a Gettysburg Address—poetry with a political purpose.

From his earliest days he had read poetry. Some of it now forgotten snippets from the *Columbian Orator* schoolbook; some of it popular songs like "Barbara Allen"; some of it deathless, like Burns's *Tam o' Shanter*. His early memorization of large parts of the Bible helped build his bedrock sense of the uses of King James's English (and its demotic offshoots) for aesthetic and persuasive effort.

His reading, his fine ear and eye for language, developed only slightly earlier than did his eye for the problem of those people most at risk. Our best evidence about his early contact with a helpless person comes from at least 1840. Lincoln knew a little girl well. She was a mulatto named Sidney McKinstry, about 8 years old, who had arrived in Springfield that year from a

Kentucky estate as an indentured servant to the Ninian W. Edwards family, who would later be Lincoln's in-laws. (Lincoln and Edwards were already friends and fellow Whigs in the legislature.) Little Sidney served in the Edwardses' home, where Mary Todd also lived as Elizabeth Edwards's younger sister. The courting couple of Abraham and Mary may even have been waited upon by Sidney, the terms of whose indenture required her masters to train her up in "the art and mystery" of housewifery, feed her well, render her literate, then send her off at 18 with clothing and a Bible. About a year later, for reasons we do not know, Sidney moved over to another humane white household. As a free young adult she married a mulatto man in town, and they left Illinois soon after.

Although we are justified in thinking that her contented outcome was nearly the same as that of some poor whites in her situation, still, why, Lincoln evidently asked himself, was her experience legally hedged around by different laws? Why was she forever at risk of physical abuse, why was she denied access to the law, possibly subject to kidnapping and sale to the brothels of New Orleans or the fields of Alabama like so many thousands of other American-born young people? Her father had almost certainly been a free man; her legal condition was freedom in Illinois, a free state. Why was she not all that free?

Then there was William Johnson. He turns up in the historical record in early 1860, working for Lincoln in Springfield as an odd-jobs man. Probably he took care of a horse, helped in the home, swept out the office—the tasks of an unlettered and possibly fugitive young man. His origins have proved untraceable, but Lincoln made Johnson his personal attendant—his valet, or body servant—for the trip to Washington and life in the White House. Johnson was the only person outside of the family or the official political and military party to make that journey with Lincoln. Had Lincoln somehow been passively protecting this man at risk in Illinois by employing him?

The new president's expectation that Johnson could be a full-time employee in the White House was quashed by the mostly mulatto and Irish staff already present. Johnson was too dark-skinned, too rough and western, for their fashion. Lincoln instead wrote endorsements for Johnson to get him messenger jobs and the like in other federal departments, mainly Treasury and Navy. Yet Johnson still came around the White House regularly to trim the president's hair and beard, doing the job that William Florville ("Billy the Barber") had done in Springfield, and telling the President what blacks and mulattos in Washington were thinking and doing. Did Johnson have freedom papers? Was he in some way under the president's personal as well as economic protection?

Johnson traveled to Antietam with Lincoln in October 1862. He traveled to Gettysburg in November 1863. Both men had smallpox at that point—Johnson may have caught it from Tad or Abraham, or got it in the crowds in one town or the other—and while Lincoln recovered after several days sick abed after the return home, Johnson died in January 1864. He had stood in the room, tending to the president's late-night needs and early-morning routine at the Wills House in Gettysburg, as Lincoln finished composing his Address for the people on and beneath the Cemetery ground later on the 19th.

Lincoln could be said to have written the Gettysburg Address so that men like William Johnson need never again fear being "taken" by slave-nappers, by bogus bounty-hunters who grabbed and ran and sold other humans, whether they had papers to prove their "freedom" or not. Thousands had fallen victim to this contorted usage of the Fugitive Slave Law since the 1790s, and their numbers were thought to be growing each decade. Johnson, and within such a regime, every African-American, was at risk of catastrophic descent into the hands of others.

What exactly was Lincoln trying to stop in his Gettysburg Address, and what exactly to promote? He already had written, privately in a letter to General Nathaniel Banks on 5 August 1863, that he wished Louisiana's new state constitution "to adopt some practical system by which the two races could gradually live themselves out of their old relation to each other, and both come out better prepared for the new. Education for young blacks should be included in the plan."

Now, in Gettysburg, he affixed Jefferson's "all men are created equal" to his own desideratum: that "a new birth of freedom" be visited upon the young republic. The purpose of the Address, then, was to remind, in the gentlest language possible, that a Union where equality and freedom had initiated such a "grand consummation" of human effort, labor, capital, land, and ideas was not yet complete while hundreds of thousands remained "at risk." If some rebels, or if whole states, wished to fight a war to preserve the right of a few to kidnap, to sexually abuse, or to morally degrade a whole class of people in order to keep a lock on a certain profitable part of the labor supply—then Lincoln would fight. To preserve the Union was the opening that would allow the end of that slavery, and to end that slavery would preserve, nay, complete, that Union. The goals were one and same, because although the inspiration of the Founders had been rightly detected by many who volunteered to fight for the Union (in 1775 as in 1861), they were only fought out morally and militarily at the critical point, by one President, and won for all time, after 1863.

Eventually, Americans can hope that freedom will be won for all the nations of the Earth.

Can each of us speak or do something as timeless, flexible, yet as firm as the Gettysburg Address? We can draw upon the large pools of civic virtue that have always been foremost in the United States of America. We do have the ear and eye of much of the globe if we try, as Lincoln tried. Shakespeare, Burns, Byron, and the Bible remain available to just about all English speakers. So too the newspapers, and the speeches of Daniel Webster, Henry Clay, Woodrow Wilson, Franklin Roosevelt, Ronald Reagan. No sources of inspiration, nor seeds of crisis, are lacking in the 21st century. The moments, the words, are there for the taking. If it is not possible to state that Lincoln was our best president, or the Gettysburg Address the greatest statement of sorrow and encouragement ever, that is because no fixed standards exist for measuring the sublimity or the vitality of what goes into making a great president or address. Guidelines, yes; and standards for such men, we think so. Lincoln, despite his narrow, limited, non-global-mindedness, was one of those men who knew that the moment was at hand for an essay about purpose, and thus chose his words carefully.

He may have embodied more humanity than a typical person, if that is possible. But he had scarcely any advantage to make use of his thought for most of his decades until he had worked himself to a position of trust and influence. Then he could. There may have been others who made better presidents, better writers or speakers. What he achieved, however, took fellow-feeling to its greatest height—by combining self-education, religious underpinning, political conviction, concern for those at risk, and poetry. Measure no man by the humanity of Lincoln.

—James M. Cornelius, Ph.D.
Curator, Lincoln Collection, ALPLM
July 2014

THE GETTYSBURG ADDRESS IN LINCOLN'S HAND

Four score and seven years ago our fathers brought forth upon this continent, a new nation, conceived in Liberty, and dedicated to the proposition that all men are created equal.

Now we are engaged in a great civil war, testing whether that nation, or any nation so conceived, and so dedicated, can long endure. We are met on a great battle-field of that war. We have come to dedicate a portion of that field, as a final resting place for those who here gave their lives, that that nation might live. It is altogether fitting and proper that we should do this.

But, in a larger sense, we can not dedicate— we can not consecrate— we can not hallow— this ground. The brave men, living and dead, who struggled here, have consecrated it, far above our poor power to add or detract. The world will little note, nor long remember, what we say here, but it can never forget what they did here. It is for us, the living, rather, to be dedicated here to the unfinished work which they who fought here, have, thus far, so nobly advanced. It is rather for us to be here dedicated to the great task remaining before

Five versions of the Gettysburg Address (one of them incomplete) exist in Lincoln's hand. The Abraham Lincoln Presidential Library and Museum's version (above) is the one he wrote for Edward Everett, the main orator at the event, so that both men's

us— that from these honored dead we take increased devotion to that cause for which they here gave the last full measure of devotion— that we here highly resolve that these dead shall not have died in vain— that this nation, under God, shall have a new birth of freedom— and that government of the people, by the people, for the people, shall not perish from the earth.

speeches could be sold for charity in New York in 1864. It was the first handwritten copy to include "under God" near the end, a phrase Lincoln did use while speaking at the national cemetery.

Walking with Lincoln · Tom Amandes

I grew up in the cornfields and along the black mud creek banks of Illinois. I remember well the buzzing, stifling stillness of a hot, midwestern night.

On such a night a couple summers back I set out on foot from downtown Springfield, retracing Lincoln's walk home from work, hoping to tread in the great man's footsteps in preparation for my role in the film *Saving Lincoln*. It was late. I figured I wouldn't get more than a peek at the Lincoln home and surroundings.

But as I walked south on 7th, asphalt gave way to a packed dirt roadway, streetlights to gas lamps, and I was stunned to realize not only was Lincoln's lovingly restored neighborhood completely open, but on this one hushed, humid night I had it all to myself.

And as my lone footsteps echoed off that oaken boardwalk, for an instant, I was there. Walking home in the dewy air, alone in my thoughts, neighbors and family fast asleep.

First, chills. Then, wonderment, as I realized Lincoln's path wasn't so unfamiliar to me at all. I could do this. I could take on this oversized role — for hadn't Lincoln taken on tasks of staggering proportions in much the same way? One step at a time?

Later, sitting across from Lincoln's house, I was surprised by a wave of deep sadness. Lincoln was stolen from us too soon. Had he lived, to lead our battered nation through a reconstruction of true reconciliation, who can doubt that the bitterness and distrust of government that plagues us to this day would have been lessened?

Well; steps still to be taken....

June 20, 2013

WALKING WITH LINCOLN

TOM AMANDES

I grew up in the cornfields and along the black mud creek banks of Illinois. I remember well the buzzing, stifling stillness of a hot, midwestern night.

On such a night a couple summers back I set out on foot from downtown Springfield, retracing Lincoln's walk home from work, hoping to tread in the great man's footsteps in preparation for my role in the film <u>Saving Lincoln</u>. It was late. I figured I wouldn't get more than a peek at the Lincoln home and surroundings.

But as I walked south on 7th, asphalt gave way to a packed dirt roadway, streetlights to gas lamps, and I was stunned to realize not only was Lincoln's lovingly restored neighborhood completely open, but on this one hushed, humid night I had it all to myself.

And as my lone footsteps echoed off that oaken boardwalk, for an instant, I was there. Walking home in the dewy air, alone in my thoughts; neighbors and family fast asleep.

First, chills. Then, wonderment, as I realized that Lincoln's path wasn't so unfamiliar to me at all. I could do this. I could take on this oversized role—for hadn't Lincoln taken on tasks of staggering proportions in much the same way? One step at a time?

Later, sitting across from Lincoln's house, I was surprised by a wave of deep sadness. Lincoln was stolen from us too soon. Had he lived, to lead our battered nation through a reconstruction of true reconciliation, who can doubt that the bitterness and distrust of government that plagues us to this day, would have been lessened?

Well, steps still to be taken . . .

❦

Actor-director TOM AMANDES *portrayed President Abraham Lincoln in the Salvador Litvak film,* Saving Lincoln *(2013) opposite Penelope Ann Miller and Lea Coco. A graduate of the Goodman School of Drama, he has starred in theatrical productions such as* Translations, The Playboy of the Western World, *and* At Home at the Zoo. *Other film credits include* The Long Kiss Goodnight *opposite Geena Davis,* Brokedown Palace *with Claire Danes and Kate Beckinsale, and* Billboard Dad *with Mary-Kate and Ashley Olsen. A veteran of stage, film, radio, and television, he currently plays Dr. Peter Pelikan on the hit NBC series* Parenthood, *and also appears as Governor Samuel Reston on the ABC political thriller* Scandal. *Other favorite TV work includes* Big Love, Boston Legal, Spin City, Grey's Anatomy, Curb Your Enthusiasm, Just Shoot Me, ER, *and* The Larry Sanders Show.

THE MOMENT OF DISCOVERY

FOUNDED 1855

EUREKA
COLLEGE

Office of the President

"Lincoln and Eureka College"

On the evening of October 9, 1856, Abraham Lincoln spoke at Eureka College on behalf of Republican presidential nominee John C. Fremont. Unlike the brevity of the Gettysburg Address, an eyewitness account of Lincoln's Eureka remarks estimated that he spoke for well over an hour.

Eureka was an obvious site for Lincoln's campaign speech for Fremont. Founded in 1855 by abolitionists who were members of the Christian Church (Disciples of Christ) — most of whom migrated to Central Illinois from the slave state of Kentucky, the place of Lincoln's birth before his family moved to Indiana and Illinois — the young College was ideologically aligned with Lincoln.

Eureka was the first college in Illinois and the third in the nation to admit men and women on an equal basis. The College's emphasis on equality of opportunity also attracted speakers such as Susan B. Anthony and Booker T. Washington to campus.

The College's founders believed that non-sectarian liberal arts education had a higher purpose and that character should develop in concert with intellect. For nearly 160 years, Eureka's mission has focused on the inter-relationship between learning, service and leadership.

Eureka's connection to Lincoln did not end with his campus speech in 1856. The faculty and students heeded Lincoln's call for 75,000 volunteers in April 1861 with a patriotic rally underneath a stately elm tree on campus. Those assembled sang patriotic songs and flew the flag from a limb of what became known as the "Recruiting Elm." Later that year over twenty Eureka students and faculty joined Company G of the 17th Infantry of Illinois and fought together during the Civil War, including the battle of Shiloh.

9.1.2013

J. David Arnold

LINCOLN AND EUREKA COLLEGE
J. David Arnold

On the evening of October 9, 1856, Abraham Lincoln spoke at Eureka College on behalf of Republican presidential nominee John C. Fremont. Unlike the brevity of the Gettysburg Address, an eyewitness account of Lincoln's Eureka remarks estimated that he spoke for well over an hour.

Eureka was an obvious site for Lincoln's campaign speech for Fremont. Founded in 1855 by abolitionists who were members of the Christian Church (Disciples of Christ)—most of whom migrated to Central Illinois from the slave state of Kentucky, the place of Lincoln's birth before his family moved to Indiana and Illinois—the young College was ideologically aligned with Lincoln.

Eureka was the first college in Illinois and third in the nation to admit men and women on an equal basis. The College's emphasis on equality of opportunity also attracted speakers such as Susan B. Anthony and Booker T. Washington to campus.

The College's founders believed that non-sectarian liberal arts education had a higher purpose and that character should develop in concert with intellect. For nearly 160 years, Eureka's mission has focused on the inter-relationship between learning, service, and leadership.

Eureka's connection to Lincoln did not end with his campus speech in 1856. The faculty and students heeded Lincoln's call for 75,000 volunteers in April 1861 with a patriotic rally underneath a stately elm tree on campus. Those assembled sang patriotic songs and flew the flag from a limb of what became known as the "Recruiting Elm." Later that year, over twenty Eureka students and faculty joined Company G of the 17th Infantry of Illinois and fought together during the Civil War, including the battle of Shiloh.

J. David Arnold is the 26th President of Eureka College in Eureka, Illinois, where he also serves as a Professor of Psychology. Designated a National Historic District for its importance in American history, Eureka has graduated 42 college presidents, seven governors and members of Congress, and the 40th President of the United States, Ronald Reagan. Arnold is in the tenth year of his presidency. Prior to his service at Eureka, Arnold served as vice president for academic and student affairs at Missouri Western State University. He also served as provost at St. John Fisher College and as a dean and grants officer at Clarion University. He started his academic career teaching psychology and writing at St. Lawrence University. He is an Academic Trustee of The Lincoln Academy of Illinois.

In the 150th anniversary year of the Gettysburg Address and Emancipation Proclamation thoughts turn toward Abraham Lincoln's presence in our lives.

Only my father's generation stands between Julian Bond and human bondage. I am the grandson of a slave. He and his mother were property, like a horse or a chair. As a girl, she had been given to a new bride. When that bride became pregnant, her husband exercised his owner's right to take his wife's slave as his mistress.

That union produced two children, one of them my grandfather.

At 15, barely able to read and write, he hitched his tuition — a steer — to a steer — to rope and walked across Kentucky to Berea College.

His was a transcendent of black Americans, born in slavery, freed by Abraham Lincoln, determined to make their way in freedom.

When he graduated, the college asked him to deliver the commencement address.

He said:

"The pessimist from his corner looks out on the world of wickedness and sin, and blinded by all that is good or hopeful in the condition and progress

[...] present [...] ful

[...] destructive [...] across his

[...] also bring [...] hope, that lightning purifies the atmosphere, that shadow and darkness prepare for sunshine and growth, and that hardship and adversity nerve the race, as the individual, for greater efforts and grander victories."

Here's to greater efforts and grander victories.

GREATER EFFORTS, GRANDER VICTORIES

Julian Bond

In the 150th anniversary year of the Gettysburg Address and Emancipation Proclamation, thoughts turn toward Abraham Lincoln's presence in our lives.

Only my father's generation stands between Julian Bond and human bondage. I am the grandson of a slave. He and his mother were property, like a horse or chair. As a girl, she had been given to a new bride. When that bride became pregnant, her husband exercised his owner's right to take his wife's slave as his mistress.

That union produced two children, one of them my grandfather.

At 15, barely able to read and write, he hitched his tuition—a steer—to a rope and walked across Kentucky to Berea College.

His was a transcendent generation of black Americans, born in slavery, freed by Abraham Lincoln, determined to make their way in freedom.

When he graduated, the college asked him to deliver the commencement address. He said:

"The pessimist from his corner looks out on the world of wickedness and sin, and blinded by all that is good or hopeful in the condition and progress of the human race, bewails the present state of affairs and predicts woeful things for the future.

In every cloud he beholds a destructive storm, in every shadow that falls across his path a lurking foe.

He forgets that the clouds also bring life, hope that lightning purifies the atmosphere, that shadow and darkness prepare for sunshine and growth, and that hardships and adversity serve the race, as the individual, for greater efforts and grander victories."

Here's to greater efforts and grander victories.

Julian Bond is a civil rights activist, Distinguished Professor in Residence at American University in Washington DC, and Professor Emeritus in History at the University of Virginia at Charlottesville. For more than 20 years, he served in the Georgia General Assembly. Elected in 1965 as a Representative, Bond was prevented from being seated due to his opposition to the Vietnam War. Re-elected to his vacant seat, *he was unseated again and finally seated only after a third election and a unanimous decision of the United States Supreme Court. Bond was the first President and now President Emeritus of the Southern Poverty Law Center. He also served as Chairman and now Chairman Emeritus of the NAACP Board. He has narrated numerous documentaries, including the Academy Award–winning A Time for Justice and Eyes on the Prize, which received a Peabody Award and was nominated for an Academy Award. In 2002, he received the prestigious National Freedom Award and is the recipient of 25 honorary degrees.*

The Gettysburg Story

Story is integral to humans being. 150 years ago a story made by men here on ground at Gettysburg took place in 3 days and 2 minutes. This Gettysburg Story has been told and retold by tellers using the tools of their time.

First the story was told as it happened. By a soldier's pencil scrawled into a diary or a letter home moments before moving into the fight. By a general's battle report pecked by a telegraph operator. By a printer placing a reporter's words into block type and inked onto broadsheets. By a scrap of of wood carved with a name and unit, jutted into freshly dug ground covering a warrior lying beneath. By a photographer exposing a glass plate through a lens to a rotting corpse. By an illiterate dirt farmer's son's words spoken at a new cemetery.

The story is told by white granite rectangles arrayed in a half-circle inscribed with name and state unless all that is known is "unknown." By a painter brushing oils onto a giant canvas. By a sculptor's bronze statue erected by veterans marking where they fought. By a tourist's guidebook. By a child's tin metal soldiers. By a ~~network~~ silent black and white moving picture. By an author's paperback novel. By a network's television mini-series. By a programmer's video game. By a filmmaker's digital high definition camera mounted on an electronic gyro-stabilized unmanned aerial drone.

here to Gettysburg. To these ridges and fields, these woods and creeks. To this ground. Each will bring their own tools to tell this story. And it will be told forever.

THE GETTYSBURG STORY

JAKE BORITT

Story is integral to human beings. 150 years ago a story made by men here on [the] ground at Gettysburg took place in 3 days and 2 minutes. This Gettysburg story has been told and retold by tellers using the tools of their time.

First the story was told as it happened. By a soldier's pencil scrawled into a diary or a letter home moments before moving into the fight. By a general's battle report pecked by a telegraph operator. By a printer placing a reporter's words into block type and inked onto broadsheets. By a scrap of wood carved with a name and unit, jutted into freshly dug ground covering a warrior lying beneath. By a photographer exposing a glass plate through a lens to a rotting corpse. By an illiterate dirt farmer's son's words spoken at a new cemetery.

The story is told by white granite rectangles arrayed in a half-circle inscribed with name and state unless all that is known is "unknown." By a painter brushing oils on a giant canvas. By a sculptor's bronze statue erected by veterans marking where they fought. By a tourist's guidebook. By a child's tin metal soldiers. By a silent black and white moving picture. By an author's paperback novel. By a network's television mini-series. By a programmer's video game. By a filmmaker's digital high definition camera mounted on an electronic gyro-stabilized unmanned aerial drone.

Each generation will come here to Gettysburg. To these ridges and fields, these woods and creeks. To this ground. Each will bring their own tools to tell this story. And it will [be] told Forever.

JAKE BORITT is a documentary filmmaker and producer. He was raised on a Civil War farm in Gettysburg that served as a stop on the Underground Railroad and a Confederate Hospital during the battle. His films include 759: Boy Scouts of Harlem, Budapest to Gettysburg, The Internet and the Water Buffalo, Cooking to Live, *and most recently,* The Gettysburg Story, *which aired on PBS. He wrote and produced "The Gettysburg Story: Battlefield Audio Tour." In addition to his own films, Boritt has produced Rory Kennedy's Moxie-Firecracker production* The Homestead Strike, *which was part of the Emmy-winning History Channel series* 10 Days That Changed America. *He has also produced a number of short films for the United Nations Development Program. Boritt has appeared on* The Oprah Winfrey Show *and has contributed to* Vanity Fair *and* Newsweek.

A Common Path Taken

(Reflections on Gettysburg and the Quests and Costs
for Better Lives and Times)

The furrowed way in wood or plain
So deeply carved for human gain
But loss abounds and much shared pain
Attend well-trodden past terrain.

Yet, who recalls that folly rules
Though thought at home and taught in schools
The drum beat dims, the ardor cools
Imperfect world, in march the fools.

This fateful clutch of circumstance
Do gods ordain or look askance?
As sheltered shield and ready lance
Provide historical advance.

Perceptions public men implore
To rally fear and hate and more
Give Plato due, the words abhor
Dead only see the end of war.

_____,
_____ _____lon.

_____ _____ impeach,
_____ _____ to teach
_____ _____ not beseech.

_____ _____s light
_____ _____ plight
_____ _____ght
_____ _____ight.

And strewn like poppies of the field
The sons with stories who lay concealed
Their stories gone to greater yield
While silent seasons damage healed.

_____ _____uld be
_____ _____plea.

_____ _____ disguise,
_____ _____s
_____ _____rise.

_____ _____ds endure,
_____ _____ure,
A challenge vision to assure,
By fractured man, ablution pure.

John Borling
Major General (USAF-ret)
Regent, the Lincoln Academy of Illinois
6 June 2014

A COMMON PATH TAKEN

John Borling

The furrowed way in wood or plain
So deeply carved for human gain
But loss abounds and much shared pain
Attend well-trodden past terrain.

Yet, who recalls that folly rules
Though thought at home and taught in schools
The drum beat dims, the ardor cools
Imperfect world, in march the fools.

This fateful clutch of circumstance,
Do Gods ordain or look askance?
As sheltered shield and ready lance
Provide historical advance.

Perceptions public men implore
To rally fear and hate and more
Give Plato due, the words abhor
Dead only see the end of war.

The only animal is man
Idea creature, that he can
Go win the day, be better than,
Go fight and die, the battle plan.

Isaiah criticized for speech
Smooth words do not the mind impeach

But truth falls harsh and hard to teach
These words will frame but not beseech.

So nations fray and nations fight
And none escape the civil plight
Await awakening 12th night
For lamp of liberty to light.

And strewn like poppies of the field
The sons with stones who lay concealed,
Their stories gone to greater yield
While silent seasons damage healed.

That's not the case in '63
A turning point in history
The war not won, in short would be
At Gettysburg, a Lincoln plea.

An exhortation long denies
The ear and mind with dull disguise,
But Presidential skill applies
A dedication's firm reprise.

Remembered well, known words endure,
A testament, ideals de jure,
A challenge vision to assure,
By fractured man, ablution pure.

JOHN BORLING is a retired Major General in the U.S. Air Force. A highly decorated officer, his awards include: The Silver Star, two Distinguished Flying Crosses, three Bronze Stars with V for Valor, and two Purple Hearts. He was an F-15 Eagle fighter pilot and commander of the famed "Hat in the Ring" squadron. During the Vietnam War, he was shot down by ground fire and seriously injured. He was captured while trying to evade and spent six-and-a-half years as a POW in Hanoi. A poet and author, his recent book Taps on the Walls: Poems from the Hanoi Hilton *(Master Wings Publishing, LLC, 2014) received national recognition. He is a member of The Lincoln Academy of Illinois receiving the Order of Lincoln, Illinois' highest honor.*

Valediction to Earth
On the Occasion of the Great Leaving
November 19, 2063 CE

Today is the day we hoped would never come. Yet the time is here. Now we must leave the Earth, forever. We dare not call it _our_ Earth: For when it _was_ ours, we did not love her as she loved us; nor did we return her nurture in kind. And so, as we board our small fleet of starships — we, the last million or so of mankind — must humbly pray to our unknown god that our tragic mistakes of war and greed and vanity, though their painful memory cannot but go with us into the voids, will not be fatally reenacted on our long voyage thither, or in our new home, should we find one, wherever that may be in the vast cosmos.

We must believe we have learned. Our final failure on Earth was not one of freedom, but of responsibility. Freedom, a mighty good in itself, became license; license became a consuming fire; and that fire became our holocaust.

Again, we must beg forgiveness of the Earth. She can no longer sustain us, nor should she, in view of our perishing sins against her. But left to herself she may be able, in good time, to heal herself.

Our atonement must consist in doing better, if allowed the chance. We are the relicts of a colossal failure, and the deep universe does not care whether we continue to exist. _We_ alone can care.

Where shall we live? Where we deserve to live. May we know that place, and ourselves, when we reach it.

[Robert Bray]
August 19, 2013

ON THE OCCASION OF THE GREAT LEAVING

ROBERT BRAY

Today is the day we hoped would never come. Yet the time is here. Now we must leave the Earth, forever. We dare not call it <u>our</u> Earth: For when it <u>was</u> ours, we did not love her as she loved us; nor did we return her nurture in kind. And so, as we board our small fleet of starships—we, the last million or so of our kind—must humbly pray to our unknown god that our tragic mistakes of war and greed and vanity, though their painful memory cannot but go with us into the void, will not be fatally reenacted on our long voyage thither, or in our new home, should we find one, wherever that may be in the vast cosmos.

We must believe we have learned. Our final failure on Earth was not one of freedom but of responsibility. Freedom, a mighty good in itself, became license; license became a consuming fire; and that fire became our holocaust.

Again, we must beg forgiveness of the Earth. She can no longer sustain us, nor should she in view of our perishing sins against her. But left to herself she may be able, in good time, to heal herself.

Our atonement must consist in doing better, if allowed the chance. We are the relics of a colossal failure, and the deep universe does not care whether we continue to exist. <u>We</u> <u>alone</u> can care.

Where shall we live? Where do we <u>deserve</u> to live? May we know that place, and ourselves, when we reach it.

ROBERT BRAY is the R. Forrest Colwell Professor of English at Illinois Wesleyan University, where he teaches courses on 19th century American literature and continues his research and work on Abraham Lincoln. Along with several articles in the Journal of the Abraham Lincoln Association, *he has written or co-written three plays on Lincoln including* Lincoln's in Town!, *which was performed for the Lincoln bicentennial in 2009. He authored* Reading with Lincoln *(Southern Illinois University Press, 2010), which won the Russell P. Strange Memorial Book Award for the best book on an Illinois subject in 2010.*

CITY OF CHICAGO

OFFICE OF THE CHAIRMAN
COMMITTEE ON FINANCE

ALDERMAN EDWARD M. BURKE
CHAIRMAN

November 19, 2013

If not for the ingenuity of political operatives plotting for their candidate at the 1860 Republican Convention in Chicago, President Lincoln would never have delivered the immortal Gettysburg Address 150 years ago today.

Mr. Lincoln was one of our nation's early dark horse candidates, a term popularized in the 19th century to refer to candidates who emerged from relative obscurity to be selected at a political party's nominating convention.

Although he had captured some national attention following his spirited although losing, 1858 senatorial campaign against Stephen A. Douglas, few outside of Chicago considered Lincoln a major contender for the Republican nomination. New York Senator William Henry Seward was the overwhelming favorite.

In May of 1860 Chicago hosted the first of its record 25 national presidential conventions at the Wigwam, an impressive new two story wooden riverside hall constructed at the site of an old Chicago landmark, the Sauganash Tavern and Hotel.

...ay 18th and using ...by Lincoln strategists ...packed the Wigwam ...Seward delegation, ...convention hall and ...strongly in support of

...isolated between ...and into cheers whenever ...le. When Seward ...the first ballot, ...were made and, ...the underdog.

On the third ballot Lincoln was nominated and Chicago had witnessed the selection of the dark horse candidate who would later be remembered as perhaps the greatest of American presidents.

Edward M. Burke

THE DARK HORSE CANDIDATE

EDWARD M. BURKE

If not for the ingenuity of political operatives plotting for their candidate at the 1860 Republican Convention in Chicago, President Lincoln would never have delivered his immortal Gettysburg Address 150 years ago today. Mr. Lincoln was one of our nation's early dark horse candidates, a term popularized in the 19th century to refer to candidates who emerged from relative obscurity to be selected at a political party's nominating convention.

Although he had captured some national attention following his spirited, although losing, 1858 senatorial campaign against Stephen A. Douglas, few outside of Chicago considered Lincoln a major contender for the Republican nomination. New York Senator William Henry Seward was the overwhelming favorite.

In May of 1860, Chicago hosted the first of its record 25 national presidential conventions at the Wigwam, an impressive new two-story, wooden, riverside hall constructed at the site of an old Chicago landmark, the Sauganash Tavern and Hotel.

Balloting occurred on May 18th and, using counterfeit tickets provided by Lincoln strategists, thousands of Lincoln supporters packed the Wigwam. Only official members of the Seward delegation were able to gain access to the convention hall, and they were greeted with a crowd strongly in support of the local favorite.

Seward delegates were isolated between Lincoln loyalists who exploded into cheers whenever Lincoln's name was mentioned. When Seward failed to win the nomination on the first ballot, momentum began to shift. Deals were made and uncommitted delegates moved to the underdog. On the third ballot, Lincoln was nominated, and Chicago had witnessed the selection of the dark horse candidate who would later be remembered as perhaps the greatest of American presidents.

EDWARD M. BURKE is the Dean of the Chicago City Council serving as Alderman of Chicago's 14th Ward for 45 years. He is the Chairman of the City Council Committee on Finance and serves as a member of the Chicago Planning Commission. Prior to becoming Alderman, Burke was the 14th Ward Democratic Committeeman and a Chicago Police Officer. Burke is the co-author of three books, Inside the Wigwam: Chicago Presidential Conventions, 1860–1996 *(Wild Onion Books, 1996),* End of Watch: Chicago Police Killed in the Line of Duty, 1853–2006 *(Chicago Neighborhoods, Inc., 2006), and* Glory & Government, Chicago's City Hall at 100 *(2010). An attorney, Burke is a partner in the law firm of Klafter & Burke and is involved in many civic and charitable organizations, including the One Hundred Club of Cook County, the Knights of Columbus, and the Irish Fellowship Club of Chicago.*

FLORENTINE FILMS

Ken Burns

Most of us, whether we know it or not, are in the business of words, and we hope, with some reasonable expectation, that those words will last. But, alas, especially today, those words often evaporate, their precision blunted by neglect; their insight diminished by the sheer volume of their (ever increasing) brethren; their force diluted by ancient animosities that seem to set each speaker against the other.

We suffer today from what the late historian Arthur Schlesinger, Jr., said was "too much pluribus and not enough unum." Few things survive in these cynical days to remind us of the union from which so many of our personal, as well as collective, blessings flow.

And it is hard not to wonder, in an age when the present consumes and overshadows all else —our bright past and our unknown future —what finally does endure. What encodes and stores the "genetic material" of our civilization passing down to the next generation —the best of us —what we hope will mutate into "betterness" for our children and our posterity.

History holds one answer and that poet-president from a century and a half ago, Abraham Lincoln, comes closest to embodying our National DNA in his Gettysburg Address.

He started by reminding his audience that it had been only eighty-seven years since the country's founding, and went on to embolden the Union cause with some of the most stirring words ever spoken, suggesting that despite the terrible battle that had taken place at Gettysburg, his country might still have, as he put it, a new birth of freedom.

And the words would endure, as if they were medicine.

Ken Burns

THE BUSINESS OF WORDS
KEN BURNS

Most of us, whether we know it or not, are in the business of words, and we hope, with some reasonable expectation, that those words will last. But, alas, especially today, those words often evaporate, their precision blunted by neglect; their insight diminished by the sheer volume of their (ever increasing) brethren; their force diluted by ancient animosities that seem to set each speaker against the other.

We suffer today from what the late historian Arthur Schlesinger, Jr., said was "too much pluribus and not enough unum." Few things survive in these cynical days to remind us of the union from which so many of our personal, as well as collective, blessings flow.

And it is hard not to wonder, in an age when the present consumes and overshadows all else –our bright past and our unknown future—what finally does endure. What encodes and stores the "genetic material" of our civilization passing down to the next generation—the best of us—what we hope will mutate into "betterness" for our children and our posterity.

History holds one answer and that poet-president from a century and a half ago, Abraham Lincoln, comes closest to embodying our National DNA in his Gettysburg Address.

He started by reminding his audience that it had been only eighty-seven years since the country's founding, and went on to embolden the Union cause with some of the most stirring words ever spoken, suggesting that despite the terrible battle that had taken place at Gettysburg, his country might still have, as he put it, a new birth of freedom.

And the words would endure, as if they were medicine.

KEN BURNS is a director and producer, making documentary films for more than 35 years. Since the Academy Award–nominated Brooklyn Bridge *in 1981, Burns has gone on to direct and produce some of the most acclaimed historical documentaries ever made, including* The Civil War, Baseball, Jazz, The War, The National Parks: America's Best Idea, *and, most recently,* The Address. *Burns's films have been honored with dozens of major awards, including thirteen Emmy Awards, two Grammy Awards and two Academy Award nominations. In September of 2008, at the News & Documentary Emmy Awards, Burns was honored by the Academy of Television Arts & Sciences with a Lifetime Achievement Award.*

WILLIAM D. BURNS

CITY COUNCIL

CITY OF CHICAGO

——

COUNCIL CHAMBER

COMMITTEE MEMBERSHIPS
——
Committees, Rules and Ethics
——
Finance
——
Housing and Real Estate
——
Pedestrian and Traffic Safety
——
Transportation and Public Way
——
Workforce Development and Audit

October 4, 2013

There is no speech in American history like the Gettysburg Address.

Lincoln, through the Gettysburg Address, recast the purpose of the Civil War. The war was now being fought to end slavery and to usher a new birth of freedom. Absent from the Gettysburg Address were the legalistic arguments of his first inaugural address.

But even more importantly, Lincoln recast the entire purpose of the American Experiment.

In the first sentence of the speech Lincoln posited, "our fathers brought forth on this continent, a new nation, conceived in Liberty, and dedicated to the proposition that all men are created equal." In that are line Lincoln added equality to the purpose of the American Union.

The American government imagined by Lincoln in the last sentence of the address is not the Madisonian maze designed to thwart democratic impulses. It is a government of the people, by the people, and for the people.

The founding fathers feared Democracy; democracy expanded mob rule.

... le federal government ... between the ...

... the course ... and ... more than a year.

Lincoln's definition of the American experiment provided the ideological basis for a host of movements — labor, women, civil rights, LGBT and their political claims.

That's quite an achievement for a 272 word speech.

William D. Burns

THE GETTYSBURG ADDRESS:
REWRITING AMERICA'S FOUNDATIONAL NARRATIVE

William D. Burns

There is no speech in American history like the Gettysburg Address.

Lincoln, through the Gettysburg Address, recast the purpose of the Civil War. The war was now being fought to end slavery and to usher a new birth of freedom. Absent from the Gettysburg Address are the legalistic arguments of his first inaugural address.

But even more importantly, Lincoln recast the entire purpose of the American experiment.

In the first sentence of the speech Lincoln posited, "our fathers brought forth on this continent, a new nation, conceived in Liberty, and dedicated to the proposition that all men are created equal." In that one line Lincoln added equality to the purpose of the American Union.

The American government imagined by Lincoln in the last sentence of the address is not the Madisonian maze designed to thwart democratic impulses. It is a government of the people, by the people, and for the people.

The founding fathers feared democracy; democracy equaled mob rule. Therefore, the framers of the Constitution designed the federal government to stymie democratic participation, by diffusing power between the legislative, executive, and judicial branches.

These two sentences had a dramatic impact on the course of American history. Now, equality became a lodestar and democratic participation in governance the expectation, rather than a fear.

Lincoln's definition of the American experiment provided the ideological basis for a host of movements—labor, women, civil rights, LGBT, and their political claims.

That's quite an achievement for a 272-word speech.

❧

WILLIAM D. "WILL" BURNS is Alderman of Chicago's Fourth Ward, a region of the city comprised of many of the city's historic neighborhoods including Printer's Row, Museum Park, Bronzeville, and Hyde Park Kenwood. He is a former member of the Illinois House of Representatives. In addition to his work as an elected official, Burns has served various nonprofits and government agencies including the Chicago Urban League and the Metropolitan Planning Council. He also served as Deputy Chief of Staff and Senior Advisor to former Illinois Senate President, Emil Jones. An early advisor of President Barack Obama, Burns served as Community Outreach Director in Obama's State Senate office, Deputy Campaign Manager for Obama for Congress in 2000, and a consultant to the Issues Department of Obama for America in 2008.

GEORGE BUSH

The grim, uncertain reality surrounding the Gettysburg Address and its aftermath provides a sharp relief to the archetypical status which has been ascribed to the speech ever since.

To start, President Lincoln's invitation was a perfunctory afterthought by the organizers. The President had received the same printed circular as hundreds of federal, state and local officials – which declared someone else as the orator of the day. After making it known he wished to attend, Lincoln was subsequently asked to offer "a few appropriate remarks."

In the immediate aftermath, numerous critics vehemently derided the speech. "The cheek of every American must tingle with shame as he reads the silly, flat and dish-watery utterances," declared the *Chicago Times*. Indeed, President Lincoln himself harbored doubts as the ceremony drew near – and all the more so following it. "It is a flat failure and the people are disappointed," he confided to the U.S. Marshal assigned to protect him.

So what changed? From whence did spring the consensus?

In a word: truth.

Abraham Lincoln, in a mere 272 words, crystallized in plain and direct prose the essence of this grand, enduring experiment in self-governance. More than that, he gave a worth – a measure and meaning – to the freedoms conferred on us by our Constitution and Creator. And, he challenged all who would follow to do our part to help preserve this that is truly "the last best hope of earth."

In the end, it took a leader of lesser ego, fewer words, and greater action and statesmanship to hold together our Union.

G Bu

TRUTH

President George H. W. Bush

The grim, uncertain reality surrounding the Gettysburg Address and its aftermath provides a sharp relief to the archetypical status which has been ascribed to the speech ever since.

To start, President Lincoln's invitation was a perfunctory afterthought by the organizers. The President had received the same printed circular as hundreds of federal, state and local officials—which declared someone else as the orator of the day. After making it known he wished to attend, Lincoln was subsequently asked to offer "a few appropriate remarks."

In the immediate aftermath, numerous critics vehemently derided the speech. "The cheek of every American must tingle with shame as he reads the silly, flat and dish-watery utterances," declared the *Chicago Times*. Indeed, President Lincoln himself harbored doubts as the ceremony drew near—and all the more so following it. "It is flat failure and the people are disappointed," he confided to the U.S. Marshall assigned to protect him.

So what changed? From whence did spring the consensus?

In a word: truth.

Abraham Lincoln, in a mere 272 words, crystallized in plain and direct prose the essence of this grand, enduring experiment in self-governance. More than that, he gave a worth—a measure and meaning—to the freedoms conferred on us by our Constitution and Creator. And, he challenged all who would follow to do our part to help preserve this that is truly "the last best hope of earth."

In the end, it took a leader of lesser ego, fewer words, and greater action and statesmanship to hold together our Union.

George H. W. Bush is the 41st President of the United States. He was the first sitting U.S. Vice President to be elected President since 1837. Among the many laws for which he is responsible during his presidency, Bush signed into law the Americans with Disabilities Act. Since leaving office, Bush has helped to raise hundreds of millions of dollars for charity. He is a life member of the M.D. Anderson Cancer Center Board of Visitors and honorary chairman of the Points of Light Institute. He is actively involved with The George Bush Presidential Library and Museum and the George Bush School of Government and Public Service, both located at Texas A&M University. Bush has worked with President Bill Clinton to aid in the relief efforts following the tsunami in Southeast Asia. They also worked together in the aftermath of Hurricanes Katrina and Ike forming the Bush-Clinton Gulf Coast Recovery Fund to raise funds for the Gulf Coast States. The aircraft carrier USS George H. W. Bush (CVN 77) was commissioned in 2009, and two years later, he was presented the Presidential Medal of Freedom from President Barack Obama. Bush is the author of three books including his autobiography, Looking Forward *(Bantam, 1988), and the diary he wrote about his time in China,* The China Diary of George H.W. Bush—The Making of a Global President *(Princeton University Press, 2008).*

In the Oval Office, the sitting President displays a portrait of the President he believes to be most influential. As the son of a great President, George H.W. Bush, I faced a dilemma. While my father was the most influential President on me personally, Abraham Lincoln saved our country. As I told visitors, the 41st President hangs in my heart; the 16th hangs on the wall.

Abraham Lincoln firmly believed that all men are created equal under God. His position was not always popular, but it was right. Perhaps the greatest presidential decision ever made was his resolution that the Union would not be divided. We can only imagine how history would have unfolded if he had cut a deal to end the war and guarantee his re-election. Instead, thanks to his moral clarity and determination, we remain the United States of America.

In addition to his courage, President Lincoln possessed enormous compassion. He liberated the slaves, redeeming our founding promise and securing a new birth of freedom for all our people. As Commander in Chief, he developed a special bond with his troops and grieved with their families. In his writings and speeches – especially at Gettysburg – his strength and sincerity inspired the nation and set an example for all who followed him in office.

No President faced more daunting challenges than Abraham Lincoln. Yet he looked to the future with hope – with malice toward none, with charity for all. During my Presidency, seeing Abraham Lincoln's portrait in the Oval Office served as a powerful reminder that as long as America remains united and free, our best days are yet to come.

A POWERFUL REMINDER
PRESIDENT GEORGE W. BUSH

In the Oval Office, the sitting President displays a portrait of the President he believes to be most influential. As the son of a great President, George H. W. Bush, I faced a dilemma. While my father was the most influential President on me personally, Abraham Lincoln saved our country. As I told visitors, the 41st President hangs in my heart; the 16th hangs on the wall.

Abraham Lincoln firmly believed that all men are created equal under God. His position was not always popular, but it was right. Perhaps the greatest presidential decision ever made was his resolution that the Union would not be divided. We can only imagine how history would have unfolded if he had cut a deal to end the war and guarantee his re-election. Instead, thanks to his moral clarity and determination, we remain the United States of America.

In addition to his courage, President Lincoln possessed enormous compassion. He liberated the slaves, redeeming our founding promise and securing a new birth of freedom for all our people. As Commander in Chief, he developed a special bond with his troops and grieved with their families. In his writings and speeches—especially at Gettysburg—his strength and sincerity inspired the nation and set an example for all who followed him in office.

No President faced more daunting challenges than Abraham Lincoln. Yet he looked to the future with hope—with malice toward none, with charity for all. During my Presidency, seeing Abraham Lincoln's portrait in the Oval Office served as a powerful reminder that as long as America remains united and free, our best days are yet to come.

GEORGE W. BUSH is the 43rd President of the United States. He was elected to two terms, elected first in 2000 and then again in 2004. He also was elected the 46th governor of Texas—the first governor in the state's history to be elected to two consecutive four-year terms. During his first term as President, he signed into law the No Child Left Behind Act creating reforms that raised the standards and test scores in the public education system. He led the nation through the tragic events of September 11, 2001—the deadliest terrorist attack ever on American soil. In response to the attacks, Bush declared a War on Terror and initiated a reorganization of the federal government, establishing the National Counterterrorism Center, the Department of Homeland Security, and the Homeland Security Council, and creating the position of Director of National Intelligence. In January 2010, he united with President Bill Clinton to lead a major fundraising relief effort for the victims of the devastating Haitian earthquake. He continues to take an active role in the Bush Center, George W. Bush Institute, and the George W. Bush Foundation and is the author of three books, his most recent about his father, the 41st President of the United States George H. W. Bush.

Four score and thirteen years ago our great grandmothers, the Suffragettes, marched side by side and stood strong to add the voice of women to the symphony of American politics. Their dedication to the belief that not only all men, but also all women, are created equal pressured the all-male Congress to ratify the 19th amendment in 1920.

Since that time, women have been claiming and creating their personal versions of life, liberty and the pursuit of happiness. Mothers dare to dream of a world where their daughters are guaranteed equal pay for equal work; where they have power over their bodies and the decisions that affect their reproductive choices; where they are inspired by the election of female leaders to the highest offices in the land; and where they actively participate in electorates, communities, and legislatures that accurately reflect the general populace.

The desire for equality cannot be thwarted by a failure to believe in ourselves; nor can the harmful effects of stereotypes and bias be ignored. We must drown out the pernicious voices of sexism, and have the courage to hold true to our beliefs. We must not ignore our uniqueness as women; instead, we need to accept, cherish, and transcend our differences. In a world where equality is fully realized, both men and women will be celebrated and supported for their choices. As women, our duty lies in maintaining solidarity by mentoring, supporting, and bolstering one another with pure hearts and the shared knowledge that we are all sisters in the long march toward equality. Only through our fierce adherence to these principles will that dream finally become reality.

September 1, 2013

THE LONG MARCH

AMY CARLSON

Four score and thirteen years ago our great grandmothers, the Suffragettes, marched side by side and stood strong to add the voice of women to the symphony of American politics. Their dedication to the belief that not only all men, but also all women, are created equal pressured the all-male Congress to ratify the 19th Amendment in 1920.

Since that time, women have been claiming and creating their personal versions of life, liberty, and the pursuit of happiness. Mothers dare to dream of a world where their daughters are guaranteed equal pay for equal work; where they have power over their bodies and the decisions that affect their reproductive choices; where they are inspired by the election of female leaders to the highest offices in the land; and where they actively participate in electorates, communities, and legislatures that accurately reflect the general populace.

The desire for equality cannot be thwarted by a failure to believe in ourselves; nor can the harmful effects of stereotypes and bias be ignored. We must drown out the pernicious voices of sexism and have the courage to hold true to our beliefs. We must not ignore our uniqueness as women; instead, we need to accept, cherish, and transcend our differences. In a world where equality is fully realized, both men and women will be celebrated and supported for their choices. As women, our duty lies in maintaining solidarity by mentoring, supporting, and bolstering one another with pure hearts and the shared knowledge that we are all sisters in the long march toward equality. Only through our fierce adherence to these principles will that dream finally become reality.

AMY CARLSON is an actress best known for her roles as Linda Reagan on Blue Bloods, *Alex Taylor on* Third Watch, *and A.D.A. Kelly Gaffney on* Law and Order: Trial by Jury. *She was nominated for a Best Supporting Actress Daytime Emmy for her role as Josie Watts in* Another World.

Her feature film credits include the indie comedy Hits, The Green Lantern, Anamorph, The Kidnapping, Everything Put Together, The Babe, *the TV miniseries* Thanks of a Grateful Nation, *HBO's* Too Big to Fail *and* If These Walls Could Talk, *Part II. An active volunteer, she helped found her neighborhood association, SPaCE, and works with the charity Hearts of Gold, supporting homeless women and children. Amy lives in New York City with her husband and two children.*

JIMMY CARTER

GETTYSBURG ADDRESS

When I began peace talks at Camp David between Israel and Egypt, it soon became obvious that the two leaders were almost completely incompatible. For three days I tried to induce them to negotiate in good faith, but they were always diverted into expressing ancient antagonisms. For the last ten days of discussions, I kept them completely apart, with them living in separate cabins.

As the first Sunday approached, I tried to think of something that that would divert our minds from the Middle East arguments and focus our attention on something that was completely removed from our concentrated work. Finally, my wife suggested that we might drive to the nearby Civil War site at Gettysburg. We made the necessary travel arrangements for the cabinet officers and staff members from the two delegations to go in buses, and I rode in the presidential limousine, sitting between Begin and Sadat.

Once there, everyone except the Israeli prime minister was thoroughly familiar with the battlefield and what occurred there, having studied it in our military schools. I showed them where the Georgia artillery had been and recounted the terrible casualties on both sides. I soon noticed that Begin, who had never served in the military, was disturbingly aloof. He was a proud man, and I was afraid he would be both embarrassed and angry.

The group became silent when the guide announced that we were at the spot of Lincoln's address. After a few moments, Begin began to recite the words, in a clear and strong voice, and we listened with rapt attention.

It was my most unforgettable event at a memorial to war.

Jimmy Carter

GETTYSBURG ADDRESS
President Jimmy Carter

When I began peace talks at Camp David between Israel and Egypt, it soon became obvious that the two leaders were almost completely incompatible. For three days, I tried to induce them to negotiate in good faith, but they were always diverted into expressing ancient antagonisms. For the last ten days of discussions, I kept them completely apart, with them living in separate cabins.

As the first Sunday approached, I tried to think of something that would divert our minds from the Middle East arguments and focus our attention on something that was completely removed from our concentrated work. Finally, my wife suggested that we might drive to the nearby Civil War site at Gettysburg. We made the necessary travel arrangements for the cabinet officers and staff members from the two delegations to go in buses, and I rode in the presidential limousine, sitting between Begin and Sadat.

Once there, everyone except the Israeli prime minister was thoroughly familiar with the battlefield and what occurred there, having studied it in our military schools. I showed them where the Georgia artillery had been and recounted the terrible casualties on both sides. I soon noticed that Begin, who had never served in the military, was disturbingly aloof. He was a proud man, and I was afraid he would be both embarrassed and angry.

The group became silent when the guide announced that we were at the spot of Lincoln's address. After a few moments, Begin began to recite the words, in a clear and strong voice, and we listened with rapt attention.

It was my most unforgettable event at a memorial to war.

Jimmy Carter is the 39th President of the United States and the 2002 recipient of the Nobel Peace Prize. Among the significant foreign policy accomplishments of his administration was the Camp David Accords, the treaty of peace between Egypt and Israel. A 1946 graduate of the United States Naval Academy, he was a submariner in both the Atlantic and Pacific fleets rising to the rank of lieutenant. Admiral Hyman Rickover selected him for the nuclear submarine program, and he served as senior officer of the pre-commissioning crew of the Seawolf, *the second nuclear submarine. Prior to being elected President in 1977, Carter served as the 76th Governor of the State of Georgia. Post-presidency, he became University Distinguished Professor at Emory University in Atlanta, Georgia, in 1982, founding The Carter Center, which addresses national and international issues of public policy. The Center's Global 2000 programs advance health and agriculture in the developing world. He is the author of more than 20 books, including his most recent,* A Call to Action: Women, Religion, Violence, and Power *(Simon & Schuster, 2014). He also teaches Sunday school and is a deacon in the Maranatha Baptist Church of Plains and volunteers one week a year for Habitat for Humanity.*

fellow-citizens:

Seven score and ten years ago, in dedicating the American nation to a new birth of freedom, I declared, as President, that "the world will little note nor long remember what we say here." I now acknowledge, at the bar of history, that I was wrong. My address at Gettysburg - honoring government of, by, and for the people, and reasserting the principles of liberty and equality at work in the Emancipation Proclamation - did not fade from public memory, but lived on to inspire progressive forces everywhere, abroad as well as at home. Our struggle was their struggle. Even while I lived, those words at Gettysburg found foreign favor. An Oxford professor, I learnt, had urged British readers to honor the text and its claims. Karl Marx told me that our titanic struggle would shape the destiny of Europe. On that continent, for a century and more after my death, the phrases of Gettysburg entered the language of democrats, radicals and republicans of, amongst others, Britain, France, Germany, Italy and Spain, as well as the Austro-Hungarian and Soviet empires. These same cadences have sweetened the political language of hope in Argentina, Brazil, and other parts of Latin America; in Japan, China, and the wider Asia; and for Ghanaians and other Africans throwing off colonial rule. I do not claim that my words controlled these events but I rejoice that they still inspire those whose belief in human equality makes them strive for freedom and self-government. This influence cheers this former young man of New Salem, who once mistakenly expressed the unhappy thought "that when we die that is the last of us."   A.L.

Richard Carwardine

15 September 2013

Professor Richard Carwardine, MA, DPhil, FRHS, FBA **President**

Corpus Christi College Merton Street Oxford OX1 4JF

OUR STRUGGLE WAS THEIR STRUGGLE

RICHARD CARWARDINE

Fellow-citizens:

Seven score and ten years ago, in dedicating the American nation to a new birth of freedom, I declared, as President, that "the world will little note, nor long remember what we say here." I now acknowledge, at the bar of history, that I was wrong. My address at Gettysburg—honoring government of, by, and for the people, and reasserting the principles of liberty and equality at work in the Emancipation Proclamation—did not fade from public memory, but lived on to inspire progressive forces everywhere, abroad as well as at home. Our struggle was their struggle. Even while I lived, those words at Gettysburg found foreign favor. An Oxford professor, I learnt, had urged British readers to honor the text and its claims. Karl Marx told me that our titanic strife would shape the destiny of Europe. On that continent, for a century and more after my death, the phrases of Gettysburg entered the language of democrats, radicals and republicans of, amongst others, Britain, France, Germany, Italy and Spain, as well as the Austro-Hungarian and Soviet empires. Those same cadences have sweetened the political language of hope in Argentina, Brazil, and other parts of Latin America; in Japan, China, and the wider Asia; and for Ghanaians and other Africans throwing off colonial rule. I do not claim that my words controlled these events but I rejoice that they still inspire those whose belief in human equality makes them strive for freedom and self-government. This influence cheers this former young man of New Salem, who once mistakenly expressed the unhappy thought "that when we die that is the last of us."

RICHARD CARWARDINE is President of Corpus Christi College at the University of Oxford. The author of numerous books, journal articles, and chapters, his research focuses on American politics and religion in the 19th century. His biography of Abraham Lincoln won the Lincoln Prize in 2004 and was subsequently published in the United States as Lincoln: A Life of Purpose and Power *(Knopf, 2006). In July 2009, as an advisor to the Abraham Lincoln Bicentennial Commission, he convened an international conference in Oxford to examine Abraham Lincoln's global legacy, which resulted in the publication of* The Global Lincoln *(Oxford University Press, 2011). Carwardine is the recipient of numerous honors, distinctions, and awards, among them, the Lincoln Academy of Illinois elected him to the Order of Lincoln, the highest honor bestowed by the State of Illinois.*

October 1, 2013

Lincoln gave three great speeches. The first, at Cooper Union, was long, a scholarly, rational masterpiece outlining the legal and historical basis for his claim that the union could be preserved without war only by limiting slavery to the states where it already existed. The speech won him the Republican nomination and, in a deeply divided country, the Presidency.

The other two were short: Gettysburg, which put the battlefield deaths in the sweep of America's determination to see that government of, by, and for the people shall not perish from the earth; and the Second Inaugural, which told the story of the war and why it started in pained, powerful words, then gave a clarion call to bind up the nation's wounds, reunite the states in a country without slavery or malice, and build a future together.

Lincoln's genius lay in his ability to explain policy clearly and argue for it convincingly; to touch the deepest human emotions in almost biblical terms; and to advance his purposes with uncanny political skill, from playing on the mystic chords of memory to offering plans of personal advancement. He never forgot what he learned about ordinary people from his hardscrabble youth, his early jobs, and his lawyering. He understood his fellow citizens, how they felt and thought, hoped and feared.

He lived, and died, first to preserve the union, then to end slavery. He wanted "a more perfect union" and in its pursuit he was ruthless and kind, pragmatic and principled. With the war won, he wished to be firm but decent to the defeated. He knew we had to rebuild together. We still do.

Bill Clinton

REBUILD TOGETHER
President Bill Clinton

Lincoln gave three great speeches. The first, at Cooper Union, was long, a scholarly, rational masterpiece outlining the legal and historical basis for his claim that the union could be preserved without war only by limiting slavery to the states where it already existed. The speech won him the Republican nomination and, in a deeply divided country, the Presidency.

The other two were short: Gettysburg, which put the battlefield deaths in the sweep of America's determination to see that government of, by, and for the people shall not perish from the earth; and the Second Inaugural, which told the story of the war and why it started in pained, powerful words, then gave a clarion call to bind up the nation's wounds, reunite the states in a country without slavery or malice, and build a future together.

Lincoln's genius lay in his ability to explain policy clearly and argue for it convincingly; to touch the deepest human emotions in almost biblical terms; and to advance his purposes with uncanny political skill, from playing on the mystic chords of memory to offering plans of personal advancement. He never forgot what he learned about ordinary people from his hardscrabble youth, his early jobs, and his lawyering. He understood his fellow citizens, how they felt and thought, hoped and feared.

He lived, and died, first to preserve the union, then to end slavery. He wanted "a more perfect union" and in its pursuit he was ruthless and kind, pragmatic and principled. With the war won, he wished to be firm but decent to the defeated. He knew we had to rebuild together. We still do.

Bill Clinton is the 42nd President of the United States—the first Democratic president in six decades to be elected twice (1992 and 1996). Under his leadership, the country enjoyed the strongest economy in a generation and the longest economic expansion in U.S. history, including the creation of more than 22 million jobs. After leaving the White House, President Clinton established the William J. Clinton Foundation with the mission to improve global health, strengthen economies, promote healthier childhoods, and protect the environment. The Foundation has staff and volunteers around the world improving lives through several initiatives including the Clinton Health Access Initiative, Clinton Climate Initiative, Clinton Development Initiative, Clinton Giustra Sustainable Growth Initiative, and the Clinton Global Initiative. In the United States, the Foundation works to combat childhood obesity through the Alliance for a Healthier Generation. In addition to his Foundation work, President Clinton joined former President George H. W. Bush to help raise money for recovery efforts after Hurricanes Katrina and Ike, as well as for the tsunami in South Asia serving as U.N. Envoy for Tsunami Recovery. He and former President George W. Bush formed the Clinton Bush Haiti Fund to support the long-term rebuilding efforts in Haiti. In 2013, Clinton was named the 6th recipient of the Abraham Lincoln Presidential Library Foundation's Lincoln Leadership Prize.

Queen's University Belfast

As the hard hand of war thrashed its way through the grass, uprooting traditions and leaving a trail of bruised refugees, and all that remained to a scattering wind. Scared combatants foraging an unfamiliar landscape, trampling flora and fauna, disturbing any natural rhythms, as all lay bare along the banks of memory — fearful of crossing to the other side — the unknown, to perhaps defeat, and to, God forbid, retribution. The formerly proud nation was laid low, littered with the debris of reckless ego and martial pride — a Confederate nation thriving longer in commemoration than survival, those one thousand, five hundred and seventy days from secession in Charleston, from valleys to little round tops, from puddles of blood to oceans of mud — careening toward the bleak, blank surrender at Appomattox — one thousand, five hundred and seventy days, but who's counting?

Corpses strewn across rutted roads, washed upon riverbanks, overflowing with grief's ghastly crop, ruination captured in sepia for generations ever after. Who's counting the months and weeks, and days when those most vulnerable and patriotic rolled bandages, stitched sashes? As years rolled by, many chronicled poignant accounts of countless sacrifices, alongside inglorious deeds of the enemy. When snakes were driven out at last, when the disbanded soldiers gave up the ghost to traverse long roads home, it was not an afterthought but an aftermath that raised more uncomfortable truths for those not wanting to let facts get in the way of their stories. Stories that would redefine the contest for this generation, and the next, and the next after that — a rope of sand and sediment.

Abraham Lincoln amen.

THE QUEEN'S ANNIVERSARY PRIZES
FOR HIGHER AND FURTHER EDUCATION 2011

SILVER
Athena SWAN

Catherine Clinton
Queen's University Belfast 25 October 2013

ONE THOUSAND FIVE HUNDRED AND SEVENTY DAYS

CATHERINE CLINTON

As the hard hand of war thrashed its way through the grass, uprooting traditions and leaving a trail of bruised refugees, and all that remained to a scattering wind. Scared combatants foraging an unfamiliar landscape, trampling flora and fauna, disturbing any natural rhythms, as all lay bare along the banks of memory—fearful of crossing to the other side—the unknown, to perhaps defeat, and to, God forbid, retribution. The formerly proud nation was laid low, littered with the debris of reckless ego and martial pride—a Confederate nation thriving longer in commemoration than survival, those one thousand, five hundred and seventy days from secession in Charleston, from valleys to little round tops, from puddles of blood to oceans of mud—careening toward the bleak, blank surrender at Appomattox—one thousand, five hundred and seventy days, but who's counting?

Corpses strewn across rutted roads, washed up on riverbanks, overflowing with grief's ghastly crop, ruination captured in sepia for generations ever after.

Who's counting the months and weeks and days when those most vulnerable and patriotic rolled bandages, stitched sashes? As years rolled by, many chronicled poignant accounts of countless sacrifices, alongside inglorious deeds of the enemy. When snakes were driven out at last, when the disbanded soldiers gave up the ghost to traipse long roads home, it was not an afterthought, but an aftermath that raised more uncomfortable truths for those not wanting to let facts get in the way of their stories. Stories that would redefine the contest for this generation, and the next, and the next after that—a rope of sand and sentiment.

Abraham Lincoln amen.

CATHERINE CLINTON holds the Gilbert Denman Chair of American History at the University of Texas in San Antonio, and an international research association with Queen's University Belfast. She is the author and editor of more than 25 books, including Mrs. Lincoln: A Life *(HarperCollins, 2009). She served as a consultant for Steven Spielberg's Academy Award–nominated film,* Lincoln.

→ ON A POEM BY LINCOLN: "MY CHILDHOOD
                        HOME I SEE AGAIN"

In poetry, too, he spoke,
even invoking Memory with an O!
before remembering his childhood home
whose hollow rooms he rhymes with tombs
in one of a stack of quatrains
whose a-b-a-b scheme locks in its plangent sounds.

Conventional also is his opening theme
as old as the Latin _ubi_ _sunt_
where are they now, the lost and absent things?
unanswerable question we still must ask
while brooding over flowers long gone
or the snows of yesteryear.

The ones who follow poetry—
and some tail it like a private eye
through a maze of city streets—
have heard of poems that find their subjects
as they go along, exiting the sitting room
to discover a door in the dark behind the
                        pantry stairs.

and behind the public cadence of the
                                    podium
the private man, alone save
for the rhymes and common meter of his poem.

                        Billy Collins
                        20 AUGUST 2013

ON A POEM BY LINCOLN: "MY CHILDHOOD HOME I SEE AGAIN"

BILLY COLLINS

In poetry, too, he spoke,
even invoking Memory with an O!
before remembering his childhood home
whose hollow rooms he rhymes with tombs
in one of a stack of quatrains
whose a-b-a-b scheme locks in its plangent
    sounds.
Conventional also is his opening theme
as old as the Latin ubi sunt~
where are they now, the lost and absent things?
unanswerable question we still must ask
while brooding over flowers long gone
or the snows of yesteryear.
The ones who follow poetry—
and some tail it like a private eye
through a maze of city streets—
have heard of poems that find their subjects
as they go along, exiting the sitting room
to discover a door in the dark behind the
    pantry stairs.
Well, here a president shows the way,

leaving the wide path nostalgic
to face the face of a howling crazy man.
Not O, Memory! now, but Poor Matthew!
Poor Matthew! once a childhood friend
who became deranged, a man of frightening
    strength
from whom the neighbors ran
and whose limbs were fast confined.
An object more of dread, writes Honest Abe,
than ought the grave contains.
So behold Lincoln near the end of his verses
alone before dawn in some outdoor scene.
Standing in a dew of angel tears,
listening to his memory of what that man sang
when he could no longer shriek or howl.
Imagine now behind the veil of his address
this other Lincoln, cheerless and terrified
by the packed bag of reason fleeing
and behind the public cadence of the podium
the private man, alone save
for the rhymes and common meter of his poem.

BILLY COLLINS is Distinguished Professor of English at Lehman College, City University of New York, and Senior Distinguished Fellow at the Winter Park Institute of Rollins College. He is a poet having authored 10 books of poetry and edited three anthologies. His most recent book is Aimless Love *(Random House, 2013). An earlier work,* Questions About Angels *(University of Pittsburgh Press, 1999), was selected by poet Edward Hirsch for the National Poetry Series. Collins's poetry has appeared in anthologies, textbooks, and a variety of periodicals including* Poetry, *the* American Scholar, Harper's, *the* Paris Review, *and the* New Yorker. *His work appears regularly in the* Best American Poetry. *He has received fellowships from the New York Foundation for the Arts, The National Endowment for the Arts, and the Guggenheim Foundation. In 1992 he was chosen by the New York Public Library to serve as a "Literary Lion." He served as United States Poet Laureate from 2001 to 2003 and as New York State Poet Laureate from 2004 to 2006.*

ABRAHAM LINCOLN PRESIDENTIAL LIBRARY & MUSEUM

PRECISION BECOMES HARDER EVEN AS WE BECOME MORE PRESSED FOR TIME. SLOPPINESS OF EXPRESSION HURTS MY EARS, ESPECIALLY WHEN I AM THE GUILTY PARTY. OVERCOMING THE TENDENCIES THAT LEAD US TOWARD ENTROPY — SPIRITUALLY, STYLISTICALLY, POLITICALLY — IS EVERYONE'S BRIEF.

LINCOLN'S BREVITY OF UTTERANCE, BORN OF NEED AND LOGIC, INSPIRE ME. THAT HE COULD WRITE AND SPEAK SO MANY COGENT IDEAS AS WELL AS INSERT POETIC ALLUSION, BIBLICAL PHRASING, OR WRY OBSERVATION ASTONISHES TIME AND AGAIN. THAT HE COULD CHURN OUT BON MOTS AND SCARCELY EVER REPEAT HIMSELF, OVER 30 YEARS OF PUBLIC AND PRIVATE DECLARATION, SHOULD ASTOUND US ALL. HE DID NOT USE HIS BRILLIANCE OR BREVITY TO A FAULT, AS MIGHT BE EXPECTED. HE WAS CHARY WITH THE WIT AND BEAUTY, EMPLOYING THESE TOOLS ONLY WHEN THE JOB CALLED FOR THEM. OTHERWISE, IN THE MAIN, HE WAS BUSINESS.

AND THE BUSINESS AT HAND IN GETTYSBURG WAS TO CONSOLE, TO THANK, TO REMIND OF OUR PAST, AND TO STEEL FOR THE FUTURE. HE PROBABLY FINISHED TOUCHING UP HIS SPEECH IN JUDGE WILLS'S HOUSE WHILE HIS BLACK MANSERVANT, WILLIAM JOHNSON, WARMED NEARBY. LINCOLN WROTE HIS NOW-HISTORIC SPEECH FOR THAT ONE PERSON, AS HE WROTE IT FOR THE MILLIONS OF OTHERS, FREE OR NOT-YET-FREE, WHO BENEFITED FROM THE BUSINESS-LIKE RESOLVE. GREAT WRITING, AS WITH GREAT THINKING, BEGINS WHEN IT APPEALS TO A SINGLE PERSON, GRADUATES TO A LARGER GROUP, AND COMPLETES ITS TASK WHEN IT HAS INSPIRED MULTITUDES. ANYTHING DONE WITH SUCH CLARITY OF PURPOSE DESERVES OUR ADMIRATION, BUT MOST OF ALL WHEN THAT PURPOSE IS TO ENNOBLE SELF-GOVERNMENT BY FREE PEOPLE, IN A LANGUAGE THAT LINCOLN HELPED TO MAKE THE LANGUAGE OF THE WORLD.

JAMES M. CORNELIUS, Ph.D.
CURATOR, LINCOLN COLLECTION, ALPLM
NOV. 7, 2013

LINCOLN'S WORLD LANGUAGE

JAMES M. CORNELIUS

Precision becomes harder even as we become more pressed for time. Sloppiness of expression hurts my ears, especially when I am the guilty party. Overcoming the tendencies that lead us toward entropy—spiritually, stylistically, politically—is everyone's brief.

Lincoln's brevity of utterance, born of need and logic, inspire me. That he could write and speak so many cogent ideas as well as insert poetic allusion, Biblical phrasing, or wry observation astonishes time and again. That he could churn out <u>bon mots</u> and scarcely ever repeat himself, over 30 years of public and private declaration, should astound us all. He did not use his brilliance or brevity to a fault, as might be expected. He was chary with the wit and beauty, employing these tools only when the job called for them. Otherwise, in the main, he was business.

And the business at hand in Gettysburg was to console, to thank, to remind of our past, and to steel for the future. He probably finished touching up his speech in Judge Wills's house while his black manservant William Johnson worked nearby. Lincoln wrote his now-historic speech for that one person, as he wrote it for the millions of others, free or not-yet-free, who benefited from the business-like resolve. Great writing, as with great thinking, begins when it appeals to a single person, graduates to a larger group, and completes its task when it has inspired multitudes. Anything done with such clarity of purpose deserves our admiration, but most of all when that purpose is to ennoble self-government by free people, in a language that Lincoln helped to make the language of the world.

JAMES M. CORNELIUS is the Curator of the Lincoln Collection at the Abraham Lincoln Presidential Library and Museum in Springfield, Illinois, the premier repository in the world of Lincoln manuscripts, family possessions, published works and fine or popular art. He previously was an editor at Doubleday, Random House, and Collier's Encyclopedia and a visiting assistant professor working with the University of Illinois Illinois History and Lincoln Collections. *Cornelius is the author of many books, articles, and book reviews about architecture, baseball, literature, and most of all American and British history with his most recent work focusing on Lincoln, including coauthorship on the* Abraham Lincoln Presidential Library & Museum: Official Commemorative Guide *published in 2011. He has written reviews published in the* Papers of the Bibliographical Society of America, the Historian, Journal of Illinois History, For the People: Newsletter of the Abraham Lincoln Association, *and* Journal of the Abraham Lincoln Association.

USS Abraham Lincoln
Newport News, VA
August 9, 2013

A New Nation

Gettysburg, a town and a people torn apart
by war. They met on these fields in a
great battle, one that will decide the fate
of a nation. The cries for help, the shriek of
death takes hold. The bloodshed, it drenches
the ground like a hard summer's rain.
Destruction and chaos reign supreme. The shells,
the shots fill the air like seagulls by
the sea. When will this horror end, only
God knows.

Dead outnumber the living. We are confused
and we are bewildered. We wonder if these
sacrifices were in vain or would it result in
new birth. The pain of lost lives, we turn to
the heavens and ask for guidance. We are
lost as a nation, we are broken.

Who will lead us? Who will honor the
dead? Who will shine light where darkness
prevails? Abraham, we look to you for your
leadership. Please pull us up, for we have fallen.

our being.
of a new
, but you
in vain
were long
us seven

do enough
one for us.
remembered.
emembered.
teach to
people.
Perish.

Written by: CTRC Jeremy J. Crandall
Hometown: Loves Park, Ul

A NEW NATION

Jeremy T. Crandall

Gettysburg, a town and a people torn apart by war. They met on these fields in a great battle, one that will decide the fate of a nation. The cries for help, the shriek of death takes hold. The bloodshed, it drenches the ground like a hard summer's rain. Destruction and chaos reign supreme. The shells, the shots fill the air like seagulls by the sea. When will this horror end, only God knows.

Dead outnumber the living. We are confused and we are bewildered. We wonder if these sacrifices were in vain or would it result in new birth. The pain of lost lives, we turn to the heavens and ask for guidance. We are lost as a nation, we are broken.

Who will lead us? Who will honor the dead? Who will shine light where darkness prevails? Abraham, we look to you for your leadership. Please pull us up, for we have fallen.

Your words, they hit at the core of our being. You spoke of dedication and the birth of a new nation. The road was so long and hard, but you inspired us. These deaths were not in vain and we never forgot. Your words were long remembered and still resonate with us seven score and ten years later.

In a way, we as a nation can never do enough to dedicate and honor what you've done for us. These words I write will not be long remembered. But you, Abraham Lincoln, will be remembered. Your efforts, your words, inspire and teach to this day. For the people, by the people. We survive as do you. Shall not perish.

Jeremy T. Crandall is the Chief Cryptologic Technician aboard the USS Abraham Lincoln. He was born in Rockford and raised in Loves Park—both located in Illinois. He enlisted in the United States Navy in June 1999. After completing Recruit Training at Naval Station Great Lakes in Lake County, Illinois, and Cryptologic Technician "A" School in Pensacola, Florida, he reported to Naval Security Group Activity Misawa in Misawa, Japan, where he earned his Naval Aircrewman and Enlisted Aviation Warfare Specialist designation. His other assignments include National Security Agency Central Security Service at Fort Meade Maryland; Naval Expeditionary Guard Battalion at Guantanamo Bay, Cuba; Naval Air Systems Command at Patuxent River, Maryland; and his current assignment aboard the USS Abraham Lincoln (CVN 72). Chief Crandall's personal awards include the Enlisted Surface Warfare Specialist, Enlisted Aviation Warfare Specialist, Naval Aircrewman, Air Medal, Navy Commendation Medals, and the Navy Achievement Medals.

As a child in junior high school, the Gettysburg address was probably the first speech I ever attempted to memorize. There was something in those words, that gave me a sense of American pride I had previously never felt.

In the address, Mr. Lincoln states that our nation was "Conceived in liberty and dedicated to the proposition, that all men are created equal". Mesmerized by this concept, I became intrigued with observing the discrepancies in men's lofty words and their allusions to (America) being a "nation of greatness" and their inability to fulfill the concepts to which they referred.

The Gettysburg address was the first thing I heard outside of Church, that introduced the concept of accountability

I concluded that, if in fact, "we hold these truths to be self-evident, that all men are created equal...., that if we are a nation under God, born of a new freedom... and could be a government of the people, by the people and for the people". that we collectively must be accountable for making those words our reality. and if we individually took the responsibility to be accountable to the principles, that we could in fact be that great nation, Mr. Lincoln alluded to

THE CONCEPT OF ACCOUNTABILITY

KEITH DAVID

As a child in junior high school, the Gettysburg Address was probably the first speech I ever attempted to memorize. There was something in those words that gave me a sense of American pride I had previously never felt.

In the address, Mr. Lincoln states that our nation was "... conceived in liberty and dedicated to the proposition that all men are created equal." Mesmerized by this concept, I became intrigued with observing the discrepancies in men's lofty words and their allusions to (America) being a "nation of greatness" and their inability to fulfill the concepts to which they referred.

The Gettysburg Address was the first thing I heard, outside of church, that introduced the concept of accountability.

I concluded that, if in fact, "... we hold these truths to be self-evident, that all men are created equal," that "if we are a nation under God, born of a new freedom ... and could be a government of the people, by the people and for the people ..." that we collectively must be accountable for making those words our reality, and if we individually took the responsibility to be accountable to these principles, that we could, in fact, be that great nation, Mr. Lincoln alluded to.

KEITH DAVID is an Emmy Award–winning, Tony-nominated actor. Born in Harlem and raised in Queens, David is an alumnus of New York's High School of the Performing Arts and Juilliard. Multitalented, he is a mainstay in feature films, in television, and on the Broadway stage. He has had roles in more than 75 films including Platoon, Clockers, Bird, Always, Barbershop, There's Something About Mary, Armageddon, Coraline, *and* Crash. *He narrated two Ken Burns documentaries,* The War *and* Unforgivable Blackness, *receiving Emmy Awards for his work in both. He was nominated for a Daytime Emmy for his work in* The Tiger Woods Story *and for a Tony Award for his work on Broadway in* Jelly's Last Jam. *He has had recurring roles on television shows such as* Mister Rogers Neighborhood *and* ER *and starring roles on hit shows such as* Murder She Wrote *and* Hawaii Five-0.

ALAN M. DERSHOWITZ

Seven score and eight years ago, a group of terrorists brought forth on this continent a new weapon, the political assassination of a duly elected president, conceived in brutality and dedicated to the proposition that the ends justify all means and that not all people have an equal claim to life. Now we are engaged in a great conflict, testing whether our nation or any nation dedicated to the rule of law can long endure the scourge of terrorism that ranges from the shooting of President Abraham Lincoln and several of his successors to the threatened use of weapons of mass destruction against entire populations. The battlefields of this war include schools, pizza parlors, churches, synagogues and mosques. We must dedicate ourselves to preventing the murder of public officials, children and other civilians, so that our nation and other democratic nations might live in peace. It is altogether fitting and proper that we should do this. But in a larger sense, we cannot hallow all the ground on which the victims of terrorism have died. These brave men, women and children, living and dead, have consecrated it far above our poor power to add or detract. It is for us the living rather to be dedicated to the unfinished work of combatting terrorism within the rule of law and without compromising fundamental rights. It is for us to be here dedicated to the great task remaining before us -- that this nation and all nations shall be protected from the threat of nuclear terrorism, so that democratic governments of the people, by the people and for the people shall not perish from this earth.

Alan Dershowitz

UNFINISHED WORK

ALAN M. DERSHOWITZ

Seven score and eight years ago a group of terrorists brought forth on this continent a new weapon, the political assassination of a duly elected president, conceived in brutality and dedicated to the proposition that the ends justify all means and that not all people have an equal claim to life. Now we are engaged in a great conflict, testing whether our nation or any nation dedicated to the rule of law, can long endure the scourge of terrorism that ranges from the shooting of President Abraham Lincoln and several of his successors to the threatened use of weapons of mass destruction against entire populations. The battlefields of this war include schools, pizza parlors, churches, synagogues, and mosques. We must dedicate ourselves to preventing the murder of public officials, children, and other civilians, so that our nation and other democratic nations might live in peace. It is altogether fitting and proper that we should do this. But in a larger sense, we cannot hallow all the ground on which the victims of terrorism have died. These brave men, women, and children, living and dead, have consecrated it far above our poor power to add or detract. It is for us the living rather to be dedicated to the unfinished work of combating terrorism within the rule of law and without compromising fundamental rights. It is rather for us to be here dedicated to the great task remaining before us—that this nation and all nations shall be protected from the threat of nuclear terrorism so that democratic governments of the people, by the people, for the people shall not perish from this earth.

ALAN M. DERSHOWITZ is the Felix Frankfurter Professor of Law at Harvard University. A Brooklyn native, he joined the Harvard Law School faculty at age 25 after clerking for Judge David Bazelon and Justice Arthur Goldberg. Dershowitz has published more than 1,000 articles in magazines, newspapers, journals, and blogs such as the New York Times Magazine, *the* Washington Post, *the* Wall Street Journal, *the* Harvard Law Review, *the* Yale Law Journal, Huffington Post, Newsmax, Jerusalem Post, *and* Ha'aretz. *He also is the author of 30 fiction and nonfiction works including the* New York Times #1 bestseller Chutzpah *(Little Brown & Co., 1991) and five other national bestsellers. His autobiography is* Taking the Stand: My Life in the Law *(Crown-Random House, 2013). Dershowitz is the recipient of numerous awards and honors for his work on human rights including the Anti-Defamation League of the B'nai B'rith's William O. Douglas First Amendment Award for his "compassionate eloquent leadership and persistent advocacy in the struggle for civil and human rights."*

I am a foreigner.

My background comes from both slavery and indentured labor in a former colonial island in the Western Hemisphere, where both sides of my family endured racism, criticism, prejudice, malice and oppression of various forms.

This is the same background that built America.

Now that we have evolved into a global powerhouse of industrialization and technology, many people do not remember that it is that same background that forced this country to fight against each other; one half wanting to maintain this atrocious system, the other trying to eradicate it.

Even though almost 150 years ago, a president took a stand, demanding that such a derogatory inhumane system that exploits its people be abandoned against enormous political and financial pressure, I see the same system present in today's social, political and economic structure.

It gives me great hope, however, that even though some people still uphold the belief that others are not equal to them, the majority of people that I meet and that I know, do not think that way.

Abraham Lincoln's decision to keep the Union intact and dismantle the Confederate risked his career and cost him his life, but it paved the way for both the abolishment of slavery and the expansion of the economic opportunities for freedom and wealth, giving people the confidence to believe they have the right to be free in America and the world.

It is this feeling of belief that makes people reflect on the great sacrifice and diligent work that he has done, which transmits his power into the ones who read these works and recreates his eternal spirit.

MC3 DANIAN C. DOUGLAS, USS ABRAHAM LINCOLN

I AM A FOREIGNER

DANIAN C. DOUGLAS

I am a foreigner.

My background comes from both slavery and indentured labor in a former colonial island in the Western Hemisphere, where both sides of my family endured racism, criticism, prejudice, malice and oppression of various forms.

This is the same background that built America.

Now that we have evolved into a global powerhouse of industrialization and technology, many people do not remember that it is that same background that forced this country to fight against each other; one half wanting to maintain the atrocious system, the other trying to eradicate it.

Even though about 150 years ago, a president took a stand, demanding that such a derogatory inhumane system that exploits its people be abandoned against enormous political and financial pressure, I see the same system present in today's social, political and economic structure.

It gives me great hope, however, that even though some people still uphold the belief that others are not equal to them, the majority of people that I meet and that I know, do not think that way.

Abraham Lincoln's decision to keep the Union intact and dismantle the Confederate risked his career and cost him his life, but it paved the way for both the abolishment of slavery and the expansion of the economic opportunities for freedom and wealth, giving people the confidence to believe they have the right to be free in America and the world.

It is this feeling of belief that makes people reflect on the great sacrifice and diligent work that he has done, which transmits his power into the ones who read these works and recreates his eternal spirit.

———

DANIAN C. DOUGLAS is a Mass Communication Specialist 2nd Class aboard the USS Abraham Lincoln *(CVN 72). He migrated to New York from Manzanilla, Trinidad, in 1995. Douglas enlisted in the United States Navy in September 2008. He completed Recruit and Surface Common Core training at Naval Station Great Lakes in Lake County, Illinois, after which he reported to the United States Naval Academy (USNA) in Annapolis, as an undesignated seaman providing support to future Naval leaders. For his service, Douglas was selected the USNA's Blue Jacket of the Quarter and Year in 2009 and was awarded three flag letters of commendation and Navy and Marine Corps Achievement Medals. As a Mass Communication Specialist, he also served the USNA's public affairs office and attended Defense Information School at Ft. Meade, Maryland. Since reporting to the USS* Abraham Lincoln *(CVN 72), Douglas has worked with the Junior Enlisted Association and assisted on a STEM initiative with Newport News Shipbuilding and Newport News Public Schools.*

RICHARD H. DRIEHAUS

272 Words
By
Richard H. Driehaus

In 1848, Abraham Lincoln wrote, in a letter to his law partner William Herndon, "The way for a young man to rise is to improve himself in every way he can, never suspecting that anybody wishes to hinder him."

Like Lincoln, I grew up in Illinois, and though rail-splitting was never one of my occupations, I knew that hard work and improving my life through education would deliver me into the life I wanted to live.

When I was seven my father suffered a debilitating heart attack. It fell on my mother's shoulders to support our family. With limited financial resources, my parents made many personal sacrifices. We knew we would have to dig in, be tough, and learn to take care of ourselves.

Still, my parents provided my sisters and me with assets no heart attack could take away. Loving memories, a good education, self-responsibility, the value of hard work and resiliency. All qualities important to success. And we knew how to ask for help. As Lincoln advised I never suspected that anybody would wish to hinder me—the opposite was true. I had support and assistance along the way from teachers, colleagues, and my parents.

Each of us can develop these qualities, and others that lead to achievement: commitment, awareness, integrity, a positive attitude, an open mind and a willingness to learn. We just need the discipline, imagination, and determination to use them.

To paraphrase Thomas Edison, "Opportunity is often missed because it is dressed in overalls and looks like work."

I thank my parents for raising me in "overalls," and teaching me <u>not</u> to be afraid of working hard.

9/27/2013

OVERALLS

RICHARD H. DRIEHAUS

In 1848, Abraham Lincoln wrote, in a letter to his law partner William Herndon, "The way for a young man to rise is to improve himself in every way he can, never suspecting that anybody wishes to hinder him."

Like Lincoln, I grew up in Illinois, and though rail-splitting was never one of my occupations, I knew that hard work and improving my life through education would deliver me into the life I wanted to live.

When I was seven my father suffered a debilitating heart attack. It fell on my mother's shoulders to support our family. With limited financial resources, my parents made many personal sacrifices. We knew we would have to dig in, be tough, and learn to take care of ourselves.

Still, my parents provided my sisters and me with assets no heart attack could take away; loving memories, a good education, self-responsibility, the value of hard work and resiliency. These qualities are important to success and we knew how to ask for help. As Lincoln advised, I never suspected that anybody would wish to hinder me—the opposite was true. I had support and assistance along the way from teachers, colleagues, and my parents.

Each of us can develop these qualities and others that lead to achievement: commitment, awareness, integrity, a positive attitude, an open mind, and a willingness to learn. We just need the discipline, imagination and determination to use them.

To paraphrase Thomas Edison, "Opportunity is often missed because it is dressed in overalls and looks like work."

I thank my parents for raising me in "overalls" and teaching me *not* to be afraid of working hard.

RICHARD H. DRIEHAUS is founder and chairman of Driehaus Capital Management LLC. Named to Barron's *All-Century Team of All-Stars as one of the most influential money managers in the last 100 years, he was featured alongside legendary investors Warren Buffett, Sir John Templeton,* and Ben Graham in the book, The World's 99 Greatest Investors (2013). A noted philanthropist, Driehaus has focused attention and energy on philanthropy and community service, which he carries out individually and through The Richard H. Driehaus Foundation and the Richard H. Driehaus Charitable Lead Trusts. He is the recipient of many awards and honors including the Horatio Alger Award from the Horatio Alger Association and the Restore America Hero Award from the National Trust for Historic Preservation.*

TAMMY DUCKWORTH
8TH DISTRICT, ILLINOIS

COMMITTEE ON ARMED SERVICES
COMMITTEE ON OVERSIGHT
AND GOVERNMENT REFORM
www.duckworth.house.gov

Congress of the United States
House of Representatives
Washington, DC 20515–1308

info.duckworth@mail.house.gov

Barely a month before his assassination, President Lincoln defined our obligation to our Veterans, saying: "Let us strive on to finish the work we are in, to bind up the nation's wounds, to care for him who shall have borne the battle and for his widow and his orphan."

America's greatest resource is not our wealth. It's not military might or mineral deposits. Our greatest treasure is the men and women willing to die to defend the nation. War is not fought with nameless troops, but with people. They are our loved ones, our neighbors and friends. Since Lexington and Concord, our military men and women answer the call when America asks who is willing to lay down their lives for liberty and freedom. They do this not just for those they know and love, but also for strangers across the land they will never meet. These patriots serve and so do their loved ones. Our

on the streets they defended. It began with Lincoln, but it rests with all of us to care for him who has borne the battle.

OUR GREATEST TREASURE

TAMMY DUCKWORTH

Barely a month before his assassination, President Lincoln defined our obligation to our Veterans, saying: "Let us strive on to finish the work we are in, to bind up the nation's wounds, to care for him who shall have borne the battle and for his widow and his orphan."

America's greatest resource is not our wealth. It's not military might or mineral deposits. Our greatest treasure is the men and women willing to die to defend the nation. War is not fought with nameless troops, but with people. They are our loved ones, our neighbors and friends. Since Lexington and Concord, our military men and women answer the call when America asks who is willing to lay down their lives for liberty and freedom. They do this not just for those they know and love, but also for strangers across the land they will never meet. These patriots serve and so do their loved ones. Our military families time and again send their beloved to bleed for our nation.

It's easy to honor our troops when they deploy, hold parades when they return, or celebrate their memory a few holidays each year. That is not enough. How a nation treats its Veterans after their service is the true measure of all of us. Whether it's healthcare, education, or employment, we have a covenant to keep with our Veterans. And in the case of Veterans homelessness, we are all dishonored when a Veteran must lay their head to rest on the streets they defended. It began with Lincoln but it rests with all of us to care for him who has borne the battle.

TAMMY DUCKWORTH is a United States Representative serving Illinois' 8th District. In 2009, President Barack Obama appointed her Assistant Secretary of Veterans Affairs. A war veteran, in 2004, she was deployed to Iraq as a Blackhawk helicopter pilot for the Illinois Army National Guard—one of the first Army women to fly combat missions during Operation Iraqi Freedom. Duckworth continued to fly combat missions until her helicopter was hit by a rocket propelled grenade in November 2004. She lost her legs and partial use of her right arm in the explosion. She was awarded a Purple Heart for her combat injuries. Duckworth declined a military medical retirement and continues to drill as a Lieutenant Colonel in the Illinois Army National Guard.

United States Senate
WASHINGTON, D.C. 20510

RICHARD DURBIN
ILLINOIS

He told us "we cannot escape history."

And Abraham Lincoln knew he could not escape "the fiery trial" of the Civil War.

Slavery threatened to destroy a nation dedicated to the belief that all were created equal and it was slavery that had unleashed the carnage still fresh in the makeshift graves at Gettysburg.

But Lincoln said "the brave men, living and dead" who had fought on that ground were fighting for more than a single cause and more than their mortal lives. Lincoln told us they were fighting for the survival of our nation.

With his words at Gettysburg Lincoln challenged a war weary nation to honor these dead with an increased devotion, and a high resolve that they had not died in vain.

he stood was a our government for the Revolution eal and Union Army

homespun the courage ough its gine the eal a ow for all."

d throughout in that from
moment when a prairie lawyer from Springfield saved our Union and the values which inspired its creation.

Richard J. Durbin

November 19, 2013

GETTYSBURG: REBIRTH OF THE REVOLUTION

DICK DURBIN

He told us "we cannot escape history."

And Abraham Lincoln knew he could not escape "The fiery trial" of The Civil War.

Slavery threatened to destroy a nation dedicated to the belief that all were created equal and it was slavery that had unleashed the carnage still fresh in the makeshift graves at Gettysburg.

But Lincoln said, "the brave men, living and dead" who had fought on that ground were fighting for more than a single cause and more than their mortal lives. Lincoln told us they were fighting for the survival of our nation.

With his words at Gettysburg Lincoln challenged a war weary nation to honor these dead with an increased devotion and a high resolve that they had not died in vain.

The blood-soaked ground on which he stood was more than a burial place. It was a place of rebirth of the spirit of our Declaration of Independence—a government of the people, by the people and for the people. Those who fought in our Revolution gave their lives for this new ideal and their brothers-in-arms in the Union Army followed them into battle.

One can only wonder how this homespun man of the Prairie could summon the courage and the works to lead a nation through its greatest trial. One can only imagine the heart of a leader who would counsel a Union embittered by war to show "malice towards none . . . charity for all."

America has been richly blessed throughout its history but never more than in that moment when a frontier lawyer from Springfield saved our Union and the values which had inspired its creation.

Dick Durbin is the 47th U.S. Senator from the State of Illinois, the state's senior senator, and the convener of Illinois' bipartisan congressional delegation. He is a Democrat from Springfield, Illinois. Durbin also serves as the Assistant Democratic Leader/Democratic Whip, the second highest ranking position among Senate Democrats. Durbin is only the fifth Illinois Senator in history to serve as a Senate leader. He was first elected to the Senate in November of 1996. Durbin sits on the Senate Judiciary, Appropriations, Foreign Relations, and Rules Committees. He is the Chairman of the Judiciary Committee's Subcommittee on the Constitution, Civil Rights and Human Rights and the Appropriations Committee's Defense subcommittee. Durbin was cochair of the national Abraham Lincoln Bicentennial Commission and sponsored legislation creating a commemorative dollar coin honoring the 16th President.

A new American anthem

By Jason Emerson

The old saying goes that Cleopatra's nose, had it been shorter, the face of world history would have been forever altered. I often wonder what aspect of Abraham Lincoln, had it been different, would have changed American history. What if he had been handsome, been shorter, been born into aristocracy? And how would the addition or subtraction of a single word or phrase in the Gettysburg Address have transmuted such a polestar statement of the essence of America into just another presidential speech? Some 1863 newspapers, reporting on that dedicatory day in Gettysburg, simply stated, "The president also spoke." Great writers know when their writing is great, and Lincoln, though forever humble, knew he had struck a chord of union with his remarks. It is this gentle ambiguity that makes Lincoln, and his words, forever intriguing and inspiring. He was every man, and yet he stands above common men. "I happen temporarily to occupy this big White House. I am a living witness that any one of your children may look to come here as my father's child has," Lincoln once said. Robert Lincoln consistently maintained this universal promise was the enduring lesson of his father's life. Today we see the speech in Gettysburg in 1863 only in the blurred figure of a bearded man in a snowstorm of men; we read the words cold in their type, but the meaning remains, pulsing heat like a fiery heart, throbbing amid the rebellion of states, a phoenix song of a future restored to whole through freedom. At the end of that solemn day, Lincoln was America, singing a new American anthem of nation.

Sept. 20, 2013

A NEW AMERICAN ANTHEM

Jason Emerson

The old saying goes that Cleopatra's nose, had it been shorter, the face of world history would have been forever altered. I often wonder what aspect of Abraham Lincoln, had it been different, would have changed American history. What if he had been handsome, been shorter, been born into aristocracy? And how would the addition or subtraction of a single word or phrase in the Gettysburg Address have transmuted such a polestar statement of the essence of America into just another presidential speech? Some 1863 newspapers, reporting on that dedicatory day in Gettysburg, simply stated, "The president also spoke." Great writers know when their writing is great, and Lincoln, though forever humble, knew he had struck a chord of union with his remarks. It is this gentle ambiguity that makes Lincoln, and his words, forever intriguing and inspiring. He was every man, and yet he stands above common men. "I happen temporarily to occupy this big White House. I am a living witness that any one of your children may look to come here as my father's child has," Lincoln once said. Robert Lincoln consistently maintained this universal promise was the enduring lesson of his father's life. Today we see the speech in Gettysburg in 1863 only in the blurred figure of a bearded man in a snowstorm of men; we read the words cold in their type, but the meaning remains, pulsing heat like a fiery heart, throbbing amid the rebellion of states, a phoenix song of a future restored to whole through freedom. At the end of that solemn day, Lincoln was America, singing a new American anthem of nation.

Jason Emerson is a historian and journalist. He is the author or editor of multiple books about Abraham Lincoln and his family, has published numerous articles and book reviews in both scholarly and popular publications, and has appeared on Book TV, American History TV, and The History Channel. Last year Emerson had two books released, Giant in the Shadows: The Life of Robert T. Lincoln *(Southern Illinois University Press, 2013) and* Mary Lincoln's Insanity Case: A Documentary History *(University of Illinois Press, 2013). His most recent book is* Lincoln's Lover: Mary Lincoln in Poetry *(Adonis Designs Press, 2014). Emerson is a former National Park Service park ranger serving at the Lincoln Home National Historic Site in Springfield, Illinois.*

Abraham Lincoln often insightfully fused memory and mission. At Gettysburg in 1863, he urged listeners to finish the work that heroic, now-silent soldiers bequeathed them. Fifteen months later in his Second Inaugural, Lincoln told his huge audience to "bind up the nation's wounds," take care of the needy, and "achieve … a just, and a lasting peace." The pregnant memories of the past must give birth to future missions.

Lincoln's important linkages between memory and mission remain alive. Native Americans tenaciously holding to their cultures, Founding Fathers laying their lives on the line, slaves and free Blacks fighting to end slavery, women speaking for their rights, Japanese Americans suffering through relocation, millions of soldiers protecting our freedoms — these and other sustaining memories ought to spur continuing missions for social justice, economic equality, and political unity. The power of the past must move us on to address unanswered and long-lasting imbalances, as well as face new challenges.

Lincoln also tied political needs to moral imperatives. We must aim at the common good, the needs of the nation, not just the wishes of one region or coterie. Lincoln's challenge to his listeners at the Cooper Union speech in early 1860 — that they must have "FAITH THAT RIGHT MAKES MIGHT, AND IN THAT FAITH, LET US, TO THE END, DARE TO DO OUR DUTY AS WE UNDERSTAND IT" — rings down the hallways of history. The challenges remain on our doorstep. They must not be overlooked, sidestepped, or conveniently explained away. The rich, motivating memories of the past must keep us working at the several missions that Abraham Lincoln put before us a century and a half ago.

Richd W. Etulain
26 September 2013

LINCOLN IN MEMORY AND MISSION

RICHARD W. ETULAIN

Abraham Lincoln often insightfully fused memory and mission. At Gettysburg in 1863, he urged listeners to finish the work that heroic, now-silent soldiers bequeathed them. Fifteen months later in his Second Inaugural, Lincoln told his huge audience to "bind up the nation's wounds," take care of the needy, and "achieve . . . a just, and a lasting peace." The pregnant memories of the past must give birth to future missions.

Lincoln's important linkages between memory and mission remain alive. Native Americans tenaciously holding to their cultures, Founding Fathers laying their lives on the line, slaves and free Blacks fighting to end slavery, women speaking for their rights, Japanese Americans suffering through relocation, millions of soldiers protecting our freedoms—these and other sustaining memories ought to spur continuing missions for social justice, economic equality, and political unity. The power of the past must move us on to address unanswered and long-lasting imbalances, as well as face new challenges.

Lincoln also tied political needs to moral imperatives. We must aim at the common good, the needs of the nation; not just the wishes of one region or coterie. Lincoln's challenge to his listeners at the Cooper Union speech in early 1860—that they must have "FAITH THAT RIGHT MAKES MIGHT, AND IN THAT FAITH, LET US, TO THE END, DARE TO DO OUR DUTY AS WE UNDERSTAND IT"—rings down the hallways of history. The challenges remain on our doorstep. They must not be overlooked, sidestepped, or conveniently explained away. The rich, motivating memories of the past must keep us working at the several missions that Abraham Lincoln put before us a century and a half ago.

RICHARD W. ETULAIN is Professor Emeritus of History and former Director of the Center for the American West at the University of New Mexico. An author and editor, he specializes in the history and literature of the American West and the life of Abraham Lincoln having authored or edited more than 50 books including Stegner: Conversations on History and Literature *(University of Nevada Press, 1996) and* Re-imagining the Modern American West: A Century of Literature, History, and Art *(University of Arizona Press, 1996). He recently edited* Lincoln Looks West: From the Mississippi to the Pacific *(Southern Illinois University Press, 2010) and authored* Lincoln and Oregon Country Politics in the Civil War Era *(Oregon State University Press, 2013). Etulain serves as coeditor of the Concise Lincoln Library series published by the Southern Illinois University Press.*

Patron: Archbishop
Emeritus Desmond Tutu

WISE
The University of Hull

As we reflect upon the legacies of racial conflict and the evil of slavery on the sesquecentennial of the Gettysburg Address perhaps it is timely to acknowledge the enduring durability of slavery today.

Though many around the world offered moral support for President Lincoln's war time speech and his aspiration to rid America of slavery, the commercial ties between its advancing economy and her overseas trading allies were all tainted by demand for slave-grown consumables. Profit was deemed paramount to the lives blighted by bondage. Thankfully support from those who championed liberty brought opportunity for millions of African - Americans after 1863.

Yet despite Lincoln's words and the numerous wars America and her allies have fought since, slavery remains unfinished business. It remains an indelible stain on aspirations for freedom expressed by most advanced economies. However, more people now live under forms of bondage than at any time in history. Different forms of servitude blight the lives of over 30 million men, women and children in all economies of the world - affecting all races, genders and creeds. Less value is placed on such lives than at any time in the past.

Let us now hope that this anniversary of the Emancipation Proclamation reawakens consciousness within the world's largest economy that it still has a central role to play in ending slavery. The monumental task we all face is not to simply worship the words and actions of one man but instead to reflect upon his cause by asking what we are doing to help the most vulnerable members of the world today.

Nick

Dr. Nicholas J. Evans

1 / October 2013.

Funded by:

EUROPEAN REGIONAL
DEVELOPMENT FUND

Supported by

Hull
City Council

Supported by the
Heritage Lottery Fund

**Wilberforce Institute
for the study of
Slavery and
Emancipation**

WISE

THE UNFINISHED BUSINESS OF SLAVERY

NICHOLAS J. EVANS

As we reflect the legacies of racial conflict and the evil of slavery on the sesquicentennial of the Gettysburg Address perhaps it is timely to acknowledge the enduring durability of slavery today.

Though many around the world offered moral support for President Lincoln's war time speech and his aspiration to rid America of slavery, the commercial ties between its advancing economy and her overseas trading allies were all tainted by demand for slave-grown consumables. Profit was deemed paramount to the lives blighted by bondage. Thankfully support from those who championed liberty brought opportunity for millions of African-Americans after 1863.

Yet despite Lincoln's words and the numerous wars America and her allies have fought since, slavery remains unfinished business. It remains an indelible stain on aspirations for freedom expressed by most advanced economies. However, more people now live under forms of bondage than at any time in history. Different forms of servitude blight the lives of over 30 million men, women and children in all economies of the world—affecting all races, genders and creeds. Less value is placed on such lives than at any time in the past.

Let us now hope that this anniversary of the Emancipation Proclamation reawakens consciousness within the world's largest economy that it <u>still</u> has a central role to play in ending slavery. The monumental task we all face is not to simply worship the words and actions of one man but instead to reflect upon his cause by asking what we are doing to help the most vulnerable members of the world today.

NICHOLAS J. EVANS is a Lecturer in Diaspora History at the Wilberforce Institute for the study of Slavery and Emancipation and the History Department at the University of Hull in the United Kingdom. His research focuses on comparing voluntary and coerced migrations around the Atlantic during the nineteenth and twentieth centuries.

He previously has held research positions at the universities of Hull, Aberdeen and Cape Town, the Institute of Migration in Finland, the National Maritime Museum in London, and the National Archives in London. His most recent coauthored publication is "Pedagogical responses to the teaching of the transatlantic slave trade and its diasporic legacies in British schools," which may be found in Defining New Approaches for Teaching the Trans-Atlantic Slave Trade and Slavery *(UNESCO and Africa World Press, 2013), edited by Benjamin Bowser and Paul Lovejoy.*

WILL AMERICA SACRIFICE as it DID in the CIVIL WAR?

Abraham Lincoln understood the stakes in the Civil War. The immediate issue was to end the wicked national sin of slavery. However, much more was at stake: the viability and existence of democracy itself. In democracy, if the minority can pick up its marbles and go home, the institution itself is ultimately doomed. Lincoln understood this: "... and that government of the people, by the people, and for the people shall not perish from the Earth."

Our greatest leader arrived to avert the greatest crisis our nation and the institution has ever faced—in almost divine circumstance to preserve the nation. Lincoln inspired Americans to put the greater good above self to save not only the nation but also democracy.

Today's America faces the greatest crisis since Lincoln's time. In order to work, democracy demands that the people put the greater good above self. Yet, now the emphasis is to avoid sacrifice. The primary political goal of many citizens, and worse—our leaders—is the avoidance of paying taxes and seeking what government can do for them. Democracy won't work when the people are no longer asked or expected to contribute to the greater good. To be truly dedicated to any institution, its members must be held to contribute to its sustenance. Can democracy work when the leaders do not have the courage to demand sacrifice and support from the people?

The crisis is real. Where is our Lincoln who has the courage and persistence to demand the best of Americans and who will summon "the better angels of our nature."

Sept 10, 2013

WILL AMERICA SACRIFICE AS IT DID IN THE CIVIL WAR?

Guy C. Fraker

Abraham Lincoln understood the stakes in the Civil War. The immediate issue was to end the wicked national sin of slavery. However, much more was at stake: the viability and existence of democracy itself. In democracy, if the minority can pick up its marbles and go home, the institution itself is ultimately doomed. Lincoln understood this: ". . . and that government of the people, by the people, and for the people shall not perish from the Earth."

Our greatest leader arrived to avert the greatest crisis our nation and the institution has ever faced—an almost divine circumstance to preserve the nation. Lincoln inspired Americans to put the greater good above self to save not only the nation but also democracy.

Today's America faces the greatest crisis since Lincoln's time. In order to work, democracy demands that the people put the greater good above self. Yet, now the emphasis is to avoid sacrifice. The primary political goal of many citizens, and worse—our leaders—is the avoidance of paying taxes and seeking what government can do for them. Democracy won't work when the people are no longer asked or expected to contribute to the greater good. To be truly dedicated to any institution, its members must be held to contribute to its sustenance. Can democracy work when the leaders do not have the courage to demand sacrifice and support from the people?

This crisis is real. Where is our Lincoln who has the courage and persistence to demand the best of Americans and who will summon "the better angels of our nature"?

Guy C. Fraker is an attorney in Blooming-ton, Illinois, and author of Lincoln's Ladder to the Presidency: The Eighth Judicial Circuit *(Southern Illinois University Press, 2012). He has written extensively and spoken across the country about Abraham Lincoln and the Eighth Judicial Circuit. Fraker has practiced in the heart of the old Lincoln Circuit since 1962. He is Chair-man of the Looking for Lincoln Heritage Coalition, the action arm of the Abraham Lincoln National Heritage Area, a 42-county area in Illinois established by act of Congress in 2008. He consulted on the award-winning PBS documentary* Lincoln, Prelude to the Presidency, *and co-curated* Prologue to the Presidency: Abraham Lincoln on the Illinois Eighth Judicial Circuit, *an exhibit on permanent display at the David Davis Mansion, a state historic site in Bloomington, Illinois.*

Gettysburg Is Not Only In Pennsylvania
(272 words for our 16th President)

Our nation forgets the "amber waves of grain" were there because the Natives had managed, not ravaged, the land. There was no dust bowl, there were no out of control wild fires, no dead fish floating in polluted water. The shame of destroying those people is ours to bear.

Then is the awfulness of Slavery. A people torn from family and land, brought here to work sunup to sun down. But they sang a freedom song and kept hope alive.

One hundred years ago a dilemma was posed to a committed collection of college women: should they, would they, banner at the back of the Suffragettes' March? The founding group said: "No." But a smaller Sisterhood formed Delta Sigma Theta Sorority. They marched at the end. Was it fair? No. But to vote was Right and Necessary.

Fifty years later a young member of Alpha Phi Alpha who had chosen the ministry as his vocation stood at the Lincoln Memorial to declare "We are here to cash a Check." Dr. Martin Luther King, Jr. riveted the citizens with stirring oratory. And unabashed bravery.

We are here, at this point, to celebrate Dr. King but we must also celebrate the women who first stood up not knowing, or rather knowing so very well, the reception they would receive when they took to the streets of Washington DC.

A great president issued an Emancipation Proclamation that evolved into the 15th Amendment. Great women held high that banner. Dr. King gave it the cadence. And we now know, no matter what color the president, that we all must march again. For the sake of Freedom.

Department of English
Virginia Tech
Blacksburg, VA

GETTYSBURG IS NOT ONLY IN PENNSYLVANIA
NIKKI GIOVANNI

Our nation forgets the "amber waves of grain" were there because the Natives had managed, not ravaged, the land. There was no dust bowl; there were no out of control wild fires, no dead fish floating in polluted water. The shame of destroying those people is ours to bear.

Then is the awfulness of Slavery. A people torn from family and land, brought here to work sunup to sundown. But they sang a freedom song and kept hope alive.

One hundred years ago a dilemma was posed to a committed collection of college women: should they, would they, banner at the back of the Suffragettes' March? The founding group said: "No." But a smaller Sisterhood formed Delta Sigma Theta Sorority. They marched at the end. Was it fair? No. But to vote was Right and Necessary.

Fifty years later a young member of Alpha Phi Alpha who had chosen the ministry as his vocation stood at the Lincoln Memorial to declare "We are here to cash a Check." Dr. Martin Luther King Jr. riveted the citizens with stirring oratory. And unabashed bravery.

We are here, at this point, to celebrate Dr. King but we must also celebrate the women who first stood up not knowing, or rather knowing so well, the reception they would receive when they took to the streets of Washington, D.C.

A great president issued an Emancipation Proclamation that evolved into the 15th Amendment. Great women held high that banner. Dr. King gave it the cadence. And we now know, no matter what color the president, that we all must march again. For the sake of Freedom.

NIKKI GIOVANNI is a poet, writer, commentator, activist, and educator. Her first book of poetry, Black Feeling, Black Talk *(Afro-Arts, 1968) launched her award-winning career. She is a five-time NAACP Image Awards recipient. Her autobiography,* Gemini *(Viking-Penguin, 1971) was a finalist for the National Book Award.* Blues: For All the Changes *(William Morrow, 1999) reached fourth on the* Los Angeles Times *bestseller list. Her children's picture book* Rosa, *about civil rights legend Rosa Parks, was named a Caldecott Honors Book. It reached third on the* New York Times *bestseller list.* Bicycles: Love Poems *(William Morrow, 2009) ranked first on Amazon.com for Poetry. Among her many awards, Giovanni was named the first recipient of the Rosa L. Parks Woman of Courage Award and received the Langston Hughes Medal for poetry. In 2009 she took part in the Lincoln Bicentennial reading poetry at the Lincoln Memorial.*

Abraham Lincoln has a special place in my heart. He also had a special place in the heart of my Uncle Pete Seeger. Each year on Nov-19th, the day delivered and recited the Gettysburg address Uncle Pete and I tried to talk on the phone and catch up on what was going on in our lives. We would eventually get around to reciting the Gettysburg address together. Our recitation was a tradition between us.

It was something we liked to do and it was a way that we connected and bonded together. I am sure Mr. Lincoln would be surprised that 150 years after his passing death we are still reciting the words from his brief speech, but the words are important to us and to our nation, even to this very day. Which leads me to this question:

What would Mr. Lincoln think of our nation today? He might be honored that slavery ended and that the United States has its first black president and that women are allowed to vote. There have been improvements in our society.

He might be disappointed in the weakness of those in government who worship power and greed at the expense of our people. We need statespeople rather than bargain basement politicians. Our constitution is strong but our leaders are weak in character and integrity. People are homeless and hungry while the leaders waste money on projects that fail. Progress isn't building institutions its on being with people. Remember Lincoln's words "government of the people, by the people, and for the people." They shouldn't remember his picture is on the five dollar bill.

Bill Graham

WHAT WOULD MR. LINCOLN THINK?

BILL GOODMAN

Abraham Lincoln has a special place in my heart. He also had a special place in the heart of my Uncle Pete Seeger. Each year, on Nov. 19th, the day [Lincoln] delivered and recited the Gettysburg Address Uncle Pete and I tried to talk on the phone and catch up on what was going on in our lives. We eventually got around to reciting the Gettysburg address together. Our recitation was a tradition between us.

It was something we liked to do and it was a way that we connected and bonded together. I am sure Mr. Lincoln would be surprised that 150 years after his death, we are still reciting the words from his brief speech, but the words are important to us and to our nation, even to this very day. Which leads me to this question:

What would Mr. Lincoln think of our nation today? He might be honored that slavery ended and that the United States has its first black president and that women are allowed to vote. There have been improvements in our society. He might be disappointed in the weakness in those in government who worship power and greed at the expense of our people. We need statespeople rather than bargain basement politicians. Our constitution is strong but our leaders are weak in character and integrity. People are homeless and hungry while the leaders waste money on projects that fail. Progress isn't building institutions it's on being with people. Remember Lincoln's words "government of the people, by the people, and for the people." They shouldn't remember his picture is on the five dollar bill.

BILL GOODMAN is a Chicago songwriter and musician. A nephew of Pete Seeger, Goodman shares his famous late uncle's love of music. Multitalented, Goodman plays piano, banjo, guitar, autoharp, and harmonica. Each November 19th for 40 years, Uncle Pete would call Goodman and together over the phone, they would recite the Gettysburg Address in honor of its anniversary.

Ginny Greer
Equal Opportunity to Influence
June 29, 2014
[signature]

In the Gettysburg Address, Lincoln refers to the American ideal that "all men are created equal." In one sense, this promises that everyone is entitled to the same rights, guarantees and freedoms. But in this lies a deeper meaning — that all are born with an equal opportunity to influence their world.

President Lincoln, celebrated for his crucial role in the dissolution of slavery, and Orval Faubus, the Arkansas governor in 1957 who used every possible opportunity to prevent nine black teenagers from integrating Little Rock Central High School were men created equal. Both were born with great minds, both were poised for leadership.

But where Lincoln died free, Faubus died in his chains.

Lincoln's influence, rising again at Gettysburg where he urged this nation to share with...

...than idle ... with him. ...tury later ...lked through ...and hate ...ts. ...s idle as ...ese nine ...ow remarkable ...walked ...e mob and ...understanding ...beside ...t at every ...re students ...aith sit and ...their thoughts, hopes, and beliefs. Instead, he reminds us that power does not guarantee greatness.

Lincoln and Faubus were men created equal, but will be forever remembered for the difference of the influence on their world.

EQUAL OPPORTUNITY TO INFLUENCE

GINNY GREER

In the Gettysburg Address, Lincoln refers to the American ideal that "all men are created equal." In one sense, this promises that everyone is entitled to the same rights, guarantees and freedoms. But in this lies a deeper meaning—that all are born with an equal opportunity to influence their world.

President Lincoln, celebrated for his crucial role in the dissolution of slavery, and Orval Faubus, the Arkansas governor in 1957 who used every possible opportunity to prevent nine black teenagers from integrating Little Rock Central High School, were men created equal. Both were born with great minds, both were poised for leadership.

But where Lincoln died free, Faubus died in his chains.

Lincoln's influence, rising again at Gettysburg where he urged this nation to bravely move forward rather than idle in complacency, did not die with him. It was present nearly a century later as the Little Rock Nine walked through a vitriolic mob of ignorance and hate bent on breaking their spirits.

Faubus' influence today is as idle as the troops he sent to stop these nine from entering the school. How remarkable would it have been if he had walked alongside the Nine, parted the mob and demonstrated acceptance and understanding? Today, his spirit would reside beside Lincoln and Dr. King, present at every Central High lunch table where students of every race, culture, and faith sit and share with peace and pride their thoughts, hopes, and beliefs. Instead, he reminds us that power does not guarantee greatness.

Lincoln and Faubus were men created equal, but will be forever remembered for the difference of the influence on their world.

GINNY GREER *is a senior at Little Rock Central High School in Arkansas. She is a member of the Little Rock Central High School Memory Project, a school organization where students work with mentors to collect, edit, and publish oral histories from* the Little Rock community. *Greer also is a member of the student activism club, STAND, the Gay/Straight Alliance, the National Honor Society and writes for the* Tiger, *the school newspaper. Outside of school, Greer is a member of SUMMA and has participated in the National Park Foundation's Park Steward internship program for the Little Rock Central High National Historic Site.*

Abraham Lincoln understood the American Civil War as a test, "proving that popular government is not an absurdity." Ever since 1776, every aristocrat had predicted (and every liberal had feared) that democratic self-rule would founder on the inability of "the people" to govern themselves, and Lincoln was conscious that "if we fail, it will go far to prove the incapability of the people to govern themselves." But he took the Soldiers National Cemetery at Gettysburg as a silent rebuke to democracy's sceptics. Those Americans who died there had demonstrated a capacity for sacrifice in defense of democracy that easily refuted the contempt of democracy's crowned despisers. A century-and-a-half later, democracy's despisers no longer wear crowns; their complaint is now that American democracy has triumphed all-too completely, replicating a bland commercialism and indifference to injustice on every continent. But Lincoln's words at Gettysburg are a rebuke to them, too. What happened there proved that the American experiment contained the resiliency to renew itself in a "new birth of freedom." From the example of those who gave their lives in freedom's cause, Americans could highly resolve to destroy slavery and to make their Constitution a government of equal protections for all the people, and they would continue to move forward to destroy fascism, communism, and totalitarianism in all their masked forms. For democracy is the universal passion of humanity, and it cannot be decoyed by those who use its missteps to pretend that it is humanity's enemy, or that tyranny is its friend. Democracy is what ennobles us, and that ennobling ensures that government of the people, under God, shall not perish from the earth.

Allen C. Guelzo
Gettysburg, Pennsylvania
August 28, 2013

THE ENNOBLING UNIVERSAL PASSION

Allen C. Guelzo

Abraham Lincoln understood the American Civil War as a test, "proving that popular government is not an absurdity." Ever since 1776, every aristocrat had predicted (and every liberal had feared) that democratic self-rule would founder on the inability of "the people" to govern themselves, and Lincoln was conscious that "If we fail, it will go far to prove the incapability of the people to govern themselves." But he took the Soldiers National Cemetery at Gettysburg as a silent rebuke to democracy's sceptics. Those Americans who died there had demonstrated a capacity for sacrifice in defense of democracy that easily refuted the contempt of democracy's crowned despisers. A century-and-a-half later, democracy's despisers no longer wear crowns; their complaint is now that American democracy has triumphed all too completely, replicating a bland commercialism and indifference to injustice on every continent. But Lincoln's words at Gettysburg are a rebuke to them, too. What happened there proved that the American experiment contained the resiliency to renew itself in a "new birth of freedom." From the example of those who gave their lives in freedom's cause, Americans could highly resolve to destroy slavery and to make their Constitution a government of equal protections for all the people, and they would continue to move forward to destroy fascism, communism, and totalitarianism in all their masked forms. For democracy is the universal passion of humanity, and it cannot be decoyed by those who use its missteps to pretend that it is humanity's enemy, or that tyranny is its friend. Democracy is what ennobles us, and that ennobling ensures that government of the people, under God, shall not perish from the earth.

Allen C. Guelzo is the Henry R. Luce Professor of the Civil War Era, and Director of Civil War Era Studies at Gettysburg College. He is the author of Abraham Lincoln: Redeemer President *(W.B. Eerdmans Publishing Co., 1999),* Lincoln's Emancipation Proclamation: The End of Slavery in America *(Simon & Schuster, 2004), and* Lincoln and Douglas: The Debates That Defined America *(Simon & Schuster, 2008). His book on the battle of Gettysburg,* Gettysburg: The Last Invasion *(Knopf, 2013), was a* New York Times *bestseller in 2013 and earned Guelzo the Guggenheim-Lehrman Prize in Military History. He also is a three-time recipient of the Lincoln Prize.*

Always animated by the Jeffersonian ideal that _all men are created_ equal, young Abraham Lincoln had many opportunities to witness that foundational idea at work on the frontier of the State of Illinois, where virtually any Caucasian male could vote after only six months of residency. After the Black Hawk War, in which Lincoln served at the rank of Captain, having been elected by the members of his militia company, he returned home to the sleepy hamlet of New Salem and proceeded to run for the Illinois State Legislature.

Lincoln was campaigning against twelve other candidates; and, although he carried the precinct of New Salem by winning two hundred and seventy-seven of the three hundred votes cast in that tiny village, he lost in the general election, finishing eighth in a field of thirteen candidates. It was, however, the only campaign that Lincoln ever lost. Lincoln was learning the hard way to appreciate every single vote. Every vote cast was a telling gesture enacted by a free citizen. Lincoln became a passionate campaigner, a dedicated Whig politician, and a true _canvasser of votes_. Two years later, he received over fourteen hundred votes, and his political career was launched. At the end of his first presidential term, Lincoln was utterly skeptical of his chances for reelection. Yet Lincoln was easily reelected, partly because Union soldiers were given leaves to vote in their home precincts.

How would Lincoln, the great Gettysburg orator, react to the subterfuges, obfuscations, and general chicanery that characterize the voting and registration process in many states today? He worked indefatigably to open that door which is now slowly, slowly closing.

— Dan Guillory
September 19, 2013

CANVASSING THE VOTE

DAN GUILLORY

Always animated by the Jeffersonian ideal that <u>all men are created equal</u>, young Abraham Lincoln had many opportunities to witness that foundational idea at work on the frontier of the State of Illinois, where virtually any Caucasian male could vote after only six months of residency. After the Black Hawk War, in which Lincoln served at the rank of Captain, having been elected by the members of his militia company, he returned home to the sleepy hamlet of New Salem and proceeded to run for the Illinois State Legislature.

Lincoln was campaigning against twelve other candidates; and. although he carried the precinct of New Salem by winning two hundred and seventy-seven of the three hundred votes cast in that tiny village, he lost in the general election, finishing eighth in a field of thirteen candidates. It was, however, the only campaign that Lincoln ever lost. Lincoln was learning the hard way to appreciate every single vote. Every vote cast was a telling gesture enacted by a free citizen. Lincoln became a passionate campaigner, a dedicated Whig politician, and a true <u>canvasser of votes</u>. Two years later, he received over fourteen hundred votes, and his political career was launched. At the end of his first presidential term, Lincoln was utterly skeptical of his chances for reelection. Yet Lincoln was easily re-elected, partly because Union soldiers were given leaves to vote in their home precincts.

How would Lincoln, the great Gettysburg orator, react to the subterfuges, obfuscations. and general chicanery that characterize the voting and registration process in many states today? He worked indefatigably to open that door which is now slowly, slowly closing.

❦

DAN GUILLORY is Professor Emeritus of English at Millikin University in Decatur, Illinois. For 25 years, Guillory reviewed poetry for Library Journal. He has received grants and awards from the Academy of American Poets, American Library Association, Illinois Arts Council, Illinois Humanities Council, and Historical and Architectural Sites Commission of Decatur. He was a Fulbright Scholar. His poetry has appeared in many publications, including Rolling Stone and the Illinois Voices anthology edited by Illinois Poet Laureate Kevin Stein. The author of numerous articles and book reviews, Guillory's first book is Living with Lincoln: Life and Art in the Heartland (Stormline, 1989). His book, The Lincoln Poems (Mayhaven Pub, 2008), was honored during the National Bicentennial Lincoln Celebration of 2009.

Highlight spot of my life.

America is indeed the best place on earth. Most people born in America may not think of that the same way I do because all the freedoms come to them as natural as breathing. I being born in Europe and living through the war, have a different respect for Democracy as being practiced in the U.S.

Not until about three and a half years ago, did I know what democracy was. Then the day came. I moved to this free country. This was a complete change for me in the way people lived and the language they spoke. In all the countries I have been, including Poland my birth place, Austria or Germany, did the people move so freely and live in such modern countries. Then still on the harbor ship, The Ernie Pyle, I stared at all the million lights which brightened the night. Between the huge buildings and our ship on the water there lay a little island on which rested the Statute of Liberty. Even not knowing yet what this huge figure was, I stared at it with great interest. Then I questioned. When I realized what it symbolized that much more my eyes brightened with freedom and my heart

(1)

Sam Harris
Soph. Eng. Sept 1951
New Trier High School

(2)

THE BEST PLACE ON EARTH
Samuel R. Harris

America is indeed the best place on Earth. Most people born in America may not think of that the same way I do because all the freedoms come to them as natural as breathing. I, being born in Europe and living through the war, have a different respect for Democracy as being practiced in the U.S.

Not until about three and a half years ago did I know what democracy was. Then the day came. I moved to this free country. This was a complete change for me in the way people lived and the language they spoke. In all the countries I have been, including Poland, my birthplace, Austria, or Germany, did the people move so freely and live in such modern countries. Then still on the harbor ship, The Ernie Pyle, I starred [*sic*] at all the million lights which brightened the night. Between the large buildings and our ship on the water there lay a little island on which rested the Statue of Liberty. Even not knowing yet what this huge figure was, I stared at it with great interest. Then I questioned. When I realized what it symbolized that much more my eyes brightened with freedom and my heart beat like the drums of peace.

Now I have lived in this heaven for three and a half years and still I think of these first visions of real human life which all the people all over the whole world should someday experience. My heart, I should hope, will never let me forget the sight of liberty my eyes saw on the first night in America.

"God Bless America."

Samuel R. Harris is a Holocaust survivor. In 1939, when he was four years old, the Nazis took Demblin, Poland, the town in which he and his family lived. Captured, he lived out most of the war years in two concentration camps in Poland: Demblin and Czestochowa. At the age of nine, he was miraculously liberated by the Russian Army on January 17, 1945. Harris wrote the essay above—ironically 272 words in length—as a student at New Trier High School in Winnetka, Illinois, having recently emigrated as an orphan from postwar Europe. Harris has lived a rich, full life professionally, civically, and personally. Among his many accomplishments, he spearheaded the building of the Illinois Holocaust Museum and Education Center in Skokie, Illinois, where he currently serves as President Emeritus. His autobiography, Sammy, Child Survivor of the Holocaust (Blue Bird Publishing, 1999), has been published in English, Spanish, Japanese, Russian, and Polish. In 2014, Harris received the Ellis Island Medal of Honor.*

October 21, 2013

Seven score and ten years ago, Abraham Lincoln
stood amidst Gettysburg's honored dead and delivered
an address destined to endure. With the nations
future in doubt, the war weary leader enlisted
all Americans in the struggle to ensure a "new
birth of freedom."

Such moral clarity was not Lincoln's alone. It
was also the province of the 56 stars of the
Philadelphia story who risked life, fortune and sacred
honor to sign the Declaration of Independence.

It underpinned John F. Kennedy's inaugural call to
"ask what you can do for your country."

It was likewise evident 50 years ago when Martin
Luther King Jr., dared dream of the day when people
would be judged by the content of their character,
rather than the color of their skin.

It was on display in Berlin when Ronald Reagan
boldly declared, "Tear down this wall."

Indeed, it is our summons to declare independence
as much as theirs. For freedom to endure, each
must enlist in the struggle. For freedom to endure,
our call has never been more clear or more urgent.

G.A. Herbert

EACH MUST ENLIST

GARY R. HERBERT

Seven score and ten years ago Abraham Lincoln stood amidst Gettysburg's honored dead and delivered an address destined to endure. With the nation's future in doubt, the war weary leader enlisted all Americans in the struggle to ensure a "new birth of freedom."

Such moral clarity was not Lincoln's alone. It was also the province of the 56 stars of the Philadelphia story who risked life, fortune and sacred honor to sign the Declaration of Independence.

It underpinned John F. Kennedy's inaugural call to "ask what you can do for your country."

It was likewise evident 50 years ago when Martin Luther King Jr., dared dream of the day when people would be judged by the content of their character, rather than the color of their skin.

It was on display in Berlin when Ronald Reagan boldly declared, "Tear down this wall."

It is found today in the lives of those who refuse to sacrifice principle on the altars of expediency or popularity.

Such clarity is increasingly rare. Yet true personal responsibility has never been more needed.

Ours is an age of moral relativism when many call evil "good" and good "evil." In place of moral certitude, we have situational ethics and ignorance; instead of self-reliance, apathy and dependence.

However much we excuse ourselves from the fight, Lincoln's call remains—to devote ourselves to the ongoing cause our forefathers "gave their last full measure of devotion."

Indeed, it is our summons to declare independence as much as theirs. For freedom to endure, each must enlist in the struggle. For freedom to endure, our call has never been more clear or more urgent.

GARY R. HERBERT is the 17th Governor of the State of Utah. He took the Oath of Office on August 11, 2009. He currently serves on the Executive Committee, as well as the Education and Workforce Committee of the National Governors Association. Prior to becoming the state's chief executive, Governor Herbert served as Lieutenant Governor for five years. In 1990, the Governor was elected to the Utah County Commission where he served as a commissioner for 14 years, also serving as president of the Utah Association of Counties. He is a veteran of the Utah National Guard, which he served for six years.

I know rationally that I have walked in the footsteps of an ordinary man. At age eight I travel with my third grade classmates to the unpretentious Indiana hamlet where Lincoln first witnessed death up close, the loss of a beloved mother inscribing in him devotion to completing the "unfinished work" begun by those who sacrifice for us. My ninth birthday takes me to Springfield, where I participate in the good luck ritual of rubbing the nose of the Lincoln statue outside the president's tomb but also find myself sobered in the Lincoln Museum by the tableaux of what the teenage Abe witnessed his first trip down the Mississippi to New Orleans — the auctioning of human beings, regarded, due to the bad luck of birth in the early 1800s as an African-American, as being far below the level of the ordinary, impoverished observer. By my eleventh birthday I have walked in the shadows of the Daniel Chester French rendition of Lincoln, not a glorious equestrian statue of a warrior leading troops into battle but rather an oversized sculpture of an ordinary man, pensive, wearied by his constant struggle to measure up to the trials of a "great civil war" and "a great task remaining before us," the challenge of preserving a nation and rededicating "to the proposition that all men are created equal." Before my seventeenth birthday I journey to follow the footsteps of the ordinary man into a Pennsylvania cemetery and a nearby battlefield, where 272 ordinary words resonate extraordinarily today. I realize that we Americans walk together in the footsteps of an ordinary man, tried by circumstances, and made extraordinary.

Katherine Hitchcock
Signature School

FOOTSTEPS

KATHERINE HITCHCOCK

Iknow rationally that I have walked in the footsteps of an ordinary man. At age eight I travel with my third grade classmates to the unpretentious Indiana hamlet where Lincoln first witnessed death up close, the loss of a beloved mother inscribing in him devotion to completing the "unfinished work" begun by those who sacrifice for us. My ninth birthday takes me to Springfield, where I participate in the good luck ritual of rubbing the nose of the Lincoln statue outside the president's tomb but also find myself sobered in the Lincoln Museum by the tableaux of what the teenage Abe witnessed his first trip down the Mississippi to New Orleans—the auctioning of human beings, regarded, due to the bad luck of birth in the early 1800s as an African-American, as being far below the level of the ordinary, impoverished observer. By my eleventh birthday I have walked in the shadows of the Daniel Chester French rendition of Lincoln, not a glorious equestrian statue of a warrior leading troops into battle but rather an oversized sculpture of an ordinary man, pensive, wearied by his constant struggle to measure up to the trials of a "great civil war" and "a great task remaining before us," the challenge of preserving a nation and rededicating "to the proposition that all men are created equal." Before my seventeenth birthday I journey to follow the footsteps of the ordinary man into a Pennsylvania cemetery and a nearby battlefield, where 272 ordinary words resonate extraordinarily today. I realize that we Americans walk together in the footsteps of an ordinary man, tried by circumstances, and made extraordinary.

KATHERINE HITCHCOCK is a senior at Signature School, an International Baccalaureate charter high school in Evansville, Indiana, where her favorite subjects are history, political science, and English. Editor-in-Chief of the Signal, *her school's newspaper, she has also held cabinet positions in the school's French Club and Global Volunteers organization and was selected to participate in summer youth leadership conferences sponsored by the American Legion Auxiliary Hoosier Girls State and the Henry Clay Center for Statesmanship.*

How should we mark this day? This day when mourners pressed around the stage at Gettysburg. A day when, as far as the eye could see, broken bodies were dug into the battle-scarred earth. A day dedicated to honoring the dead.

How did we mark this day? With the pomp and bluster of learned men, their pronouncements now largely forgotten. And with the far simpler words of a leader grown haggard with grief and gore, with brutal necessity. These are the words we remember ~ a nation conceived in Liberty and dedicated to the proposition that all men are created equal. These are the words we cherish ~ that government of the people, by the people, for the people shall not perish from the earth. These are the words that tell us who we are and who we want to be.

On this day, Lincoln called the nation to its duty. For it was the duty of the living, he said, to dedicate themselves to the cause for which so many gave their lives ~ to nothing less than a new birth of freedom.

How do we mark this day? With words of praise and moments of silent reflection, yes. But who will take to the stage, as Lincoln did, to remind us that the struggle is not yet over? When the gap between rich and poor grows wider every day, when the rights and well-being of the most vulnerable are neglected, when social justice is an abstraction and equality a receding dream we must recognize that while many battles have been fought and won, the struggle for justice and equality remains our solemn duty.

September 12, 2013

GETTYSBURG CALLS US TO OUR SOLEMN DUTY

JACKIE HOGAN

How should we mark this day? This day when mourners pressed around the stage at Gettysburg. A day when, as far as the eye could see, broken bodies were dug into the battle-scarred earth. A day dedicated to honoring the dead.

How did we mark this day? With the pomp and bluster of learned men, their pronouncements now largely forgotten. And with the far simpler words of a leader grown haggard with grief and gore, with brutal necessity. These are the words we remember—a nation conceived in Liberty and dedicated to the proposition that all men are created equal. These are the words we cherish—that government of the people, by the people, for the people shall not perish from the earth. These are the words that tell us who we are and who we want to be.

On this day, Lincoln called the nation to its duty. For it was the duty of the living, he said, to dedicate themselves to the cause for which so many gave their lives—to nothing less than a new birth of freedom.

How do we mark this day? With words of praise and moments of silent reflection, yes. But who will take to the stage, as Lincoln did, to remind us that the struggle is not yet over? When the gap between rich and poor grows wider every day, when the rights and well-being of the most vulnerable are neglected, when social justice is an abstraction and equality a receding dream, we must recognize that while many battles have been fought and won, the struggle for justice and equality remains our solemn duty.

<hr />

JACKIE HOGAN is Associate Professor and Chair of Sociology at Bradley University in Illinois, the "Land of Lincoln." She is the author of numerous scholarly books and articles including Lincoln, Inc.: Selling the Sixteenth President in Contemporary America *(Rowman & Littlefield, 2011) and* Gender, Race and National Identity: Nations of Flesh and Blood *(Routledge, 2011).*

The Abraham Lincoln Bicentennial Foundation

c/o Harold Holzer, Chairman

Provide the essence of the Gettysburg Address in 272 words? Quite a challenge; for while Lincoln used but two sheets of paper to compose it, historians have slaughtered entire forests to expound on it. Yet the glittering essence of Lincoln's — perhaps America's — greatest speech is its magnificent economy. Invited to deliver only "a few appropriate remarks," Lincoln summoned a rhetorical discipline that revolutionized political oratory, — replaced the traditionally orotund with a new birth of simplicity, and made a virtue of brevity.

Of course it's "I can memorize this" length does not begin to explain its enduring magic. Did it "reinvent America" as some have claimed? Probably not; we've come a long way in the quest to complete Lincoln's "unfinished work," but no one can say for certain whether, if he returned to assess

[...] ... 100
[...] ... le of the
[...] ...dress
[...] ...eration
[...] ...second
[...] and much

[...] Lincoln
[...], from
[...] rebirth,
[...] relevance.

[...] The
[...]rld
[...] "what
[...] modest,
[...] This
[...]genuity,

he surely meant it to long endure.
So it has.

Harold Holzer
June 13, 2013
NYC

LONG REMEMBERED

HAROLD HOLZER

Provide the essence of the Gettysburg Address in 272 words? Quite a challenge, for while Lincoln used but two sheets of paper to compose it, historians have slaughtered entire forests to expound on it. Yet the glittering essence of Lincoln's—perhaps America's—greatest speech is its magnificent economy. Invited to deliver only "a few appropriate remarks," Lincoln summoned a rhetorical discipline that revolutionized political oratory—replaced the traditionally orotund with a new birth of simplicity, and made a virtue of brevity.

Of course its "I can memorize this" length does not begin to explain its enduring magic. Did it "reinvent America," as some have claimed? Probably not; we've come a long way in the quest to complete Lincoln's "unfinished work," but no one can say for certain whether, if he returned to assess his legacy, he might conclude we've traveled too fast or too slowly. On the opposite side of the analytical coin, was the Gettysburg Address meant to be no more than a subtle declaration of its author's intention to seek a second term as President? Too simplistic, too, and much too cynical.

Then what? In his heart, Abraham Lincoln understood Gettysburg was a place of death, from which America itself needed to summon rebirth, or die as well. Therein lies its genius and relevance.

Lincoln made one colossal error in the Gettysburg Address—suggesting the world would "little note nor long remember" what he said there. "Honest Abe" was too modest, maybe even disingenuous. He wrote this speech with such breathtaking ingenuity, he surely meant it to "long endure."

So it has.

HAROLD HOLZER is a leading authority on Abraham Lincoln and the political culture of the Civil War era and currently serves as the first Roger Hertog Fellow at The New-York Historical Society. A writer and lecturer, Holzer also serves as chairman of The Lincoln Bicentennial Foundation, successor organization to the U.S. Abraham Lincoln Bicentennial Commission, to which he was appointed by President Bill Clinton. President George W. Bush, in turn, awarded Holzer the National Humanities Medal. In 2013, he wrote an essay on Lincoln for the official program at the re-inauguration of President Barack Obama. Holzer has authored, coauthored, and edited 46 books and more than 500 articles, reviews, and chapters. Recent volumes include: The Civil War in 50 Objects *(Viking Adult, 2013);* 1863: Lincoln's Pivotal Year *(Southern Illinois University Press, 2013);* Lincoln: How Abraham Lincoln Ended Slavery in America *(HarperCollins, 2012), the official young adult companion book to the Spielberg film* Lincoln*; and* Emancipating Lincoln: The Emancipation Proclamation in Text, Context, and Memory *(Harvard University Press, 2012).*

September 6, 2013

Reading the Gettysburg address, I notice first the strong focus on the melancholy task of consecrating a mass grave. "Dedicatory Remarks" the program stated: Lincoln seizes on <u>dedicate</u> and repeats six variations of that word. To dedicate is to mark as respected or sacred, and on that clear November day he was a mourning patriarch in public and in private. His stovepipe hat still wore a blackband for his son Willie, dead of typhoid at eleven.

The shape of the Address is taut yet perfect. Lincoln exercises the power of threes, builds in parallel triplets: historical, political, spiritual; past to present to future. In 272 words he confirms the nation's birth into possibility, mourns the losses of a terrifying present, and promises future rebirth. With a catch: if freedom is worth any price, then so is Unity. He mentions the Declaration only indirectly and the Constitution not at all. He favors neither side in the ongoing, bloody war. His new compact with the dead and living is intensely personal, an oath of private conscience made national.

Applause interrupted the President's address five times, remarkable in part because his text is so brief. Not many voices from 1863 sound modern to us, but he speaks hard thoughts stripped to the line as if for the telegraph, or a jury summation. <u>Multum in parvo</u>, saying much in little, is the hardest effect to achieve. Thoreau and Dickinson distill the language of feeling. Sherman and Grant remade the work of war. Lincoln's heartbreaking gravity, in that late autumn graveyard where the stench of death still hovered, is our greatest voice, and rightly so.

William Howarth

SAYING MUCH IN LITTLE
WILLIAM HOWARTH

Reading the Gettysburg Address, I notice first the strong focus on the melancholy task of consecrating a mass grave. "Dedicatory Remarks," the program stated: Lincoln seizes on <u>dedicate</u> and repeats six variations of that word. To dedicate is to mark as respected or sacred, and on that clear November day he was a mourning patriarch in public and in private. His stovepipe hat still wore a black band for his son Willie, dead of typhoid at eleven.

The shape of the Address is taut yet perfect. Lincoln exercises the power of threes, built in parallel triplets: historical, political, spiritual; past to present to future. In 272 words he confirms the nation's birth into possibility, mourns the losses of a terrifying present, and promises future rebirth. With a catch; if Freedom is worth any price, then so is Unity. He mentions the Declaration only indirectly and the Constitution not at all. He favors neither side in the ongoing, bloody war. His new compact with the dead and living is intensely personal, an oath of private conscience made national.

Applause interrupted the President's address five times, remarkable in part because his text is so brief. Not many voices from 1863 sound modern to us, but he speaks hard thoughts stripped to the core as if for the telegraph, or a jury summation. <u>Multum in parvo</u>, saying much in little, is the hardest effect to achieve. Thoreau and Dickinson distill the language of feeling. Sherman and Grant remake the words of war. Lincoln's heartbreaking gravity, in that late autumn graveyard where the stench of death still hovered, is our greatest voice, and rightly so.

WILLIAM HOWARTH is a professor emeritus at Princeton University. A native of Springfield, Illinois, his career has spanned five decades. He has published widely on history, literature, and environmental issues, and served for many years as editor-in-chief of The Writings of Henry D. Thoreau. *His books include* Walking with Thoreau *(Beacon Press, 2001) and* The John McPhee Reader *(Farrar, Straus & Giroux, 1981). Under the pen name Dana Hand, he collaborates with Anne Matthews on fiction and film.*

One hundred and fifty years ago, Abraham Lincoln said, "the world will little note, nor long remember what we say here." He was wrong. Just as the great battle that raged on these fields stands at the vortex of American history, Lincoln's words stand at the vortex of our national consciousness. Hearing them, we are reminded of the sacrifice of so many for our freedom. We are likewise reminded of our long journey, still on-going, to fulfill the fundamental proposition that indeed all men and women are created equal and deserve the full benefit of the freedom that has been purchased at such great price.

The steps on this journey are marked by the eloquence of many. The patriot who regretted he had but one life to give for his country. The president who affirmed our country's resolve on a day that will live in infamy. The passenger in an aircraft above another Pennsylvania field, who declared "Let's Roll," giving voice to a Nation battered by terrorism.

But no words are greater than those spoken here by a simple man, born in a log cabin in Kentucky, who not only saved the American union but also came to symbolize its greatest virtues of humility, honesty, and decency. His words, chiseled on the walls of his memorial in Washington, are likewise chiseled onto our hearts. They tell us what it means to be an American. They call us to the unfinished work, not just to win a war, but to continue to perfect our Nation and a government that is truly "of the people, by the people, and for the people."

Sally Jewell

NO GREATER WORDS

SALLY JEWELL

One hundred fifty years ago, Abraham Lincoln said, "the world will little note, nor long remember what we say here." He was wrong. Just as the battle that raged on these fields stands at the vortex of American history, Lincoln's words stand at the vortex of our national consciousness. Hearing them, we are reminded of the sacrifice of so many for freedom. We are likewise reminded of our long journey, still on-going, to fulfill the fundamental proposition that indeed all men and women are created equal and deserve the full benefit of this freedom that has been purchased at such great price.

The steps on this journey are marked by eloquence. The patriot who regretted he had but one life to give for his country. The president who affirmed our resolve on a day that will live in infamy. The courageous woman whose simple "No" on an Alabama bus gave birth to choruses of "We Shall Overcome." The passenger above another Pennsylvania field, who declared "Let's Roll," giving voice to a nation battered by terrorism.

But no words are greater than those spoken here by a simple man, born in a log cabin, who not only saved the American union but also came to symbolize its greatest virtues of humility, honesty, and decency. His words, chiseled on the walls of his memorial, are likewise chiseled on our hearts. They tell us what it means to be an American. They call us to unfinished work, not just to win a war, but to continue to perfect our nation and a government that is truly "of the people, by the people, for the people."

Sally Jewell is the 51st U.S. Secretary of the Interior. She was appointed by President Barack Obama and took the oath of office in 2013. As Secretary of the Interior she oversees approximately 20 percent of the nation's lands, including national wildlife refuges and national parks like Gettysburg National Military Park. Prior to her confirmation as Secretary, she served in the private sector, most recently as President and Chief Executive Officer of Recreation Equipment, Inc. (REI). Trained as a petroleum engineer, Jewell began her career with Mobil Oil Corp. An avid outdoorswoman, Jewell has scaled Mount Rainier seven times and climbed Vinson Massif, the highest mountain in Antarctica.

Gary T. Johnson
President

History is a cause.

History is not confined to the halls of universities and the temples we build for our national archives. Ask a family member to recall a childhood memory, and that's history. Invite a community group to tell its story, and that's history. Volunteer for a local museum, and that's history. We are in it together for the cause of history.

Without sharing a story, it will be lost forever. Without meticulous care, an artifact will deteriorate. Without setting a document aside, the content will disappear. There is no way to recover from the loss of evidence and stories, if we fail to do our part in our own time and place. History is a call to action.

In every age, we have witnessed how superior powers suppresses stories and wipes records clean. We have seen the publication of official versions and approved texts. We even have heard of family members afraid to share their own stories with each other. We need to stand up for history.

Sometimes we have nobody to blame but ourselves. We lose our curiosity. We do not seek out the lessons. We must resolve that we will never forget.

Learning where you came from gives you an identity. Knowing you are heard gives you a voice. Deciding where you are bound gives you a mission. History transforms lives.

"Four score and seven years ago...." "Now we are engaged...." "[We] here highly resolve....," All of us who wonder how we got here, what we are doing, and where we are going, have a tie that binds us together. We all know that history is a cause.

Gary T. Johnson

HISTORY IS A CAUSE

GARY T. JOHNSON

History is a cause.

History is not confined to the halls of universities and the temples we build for our national archives. Ask a family member to recall a childhood memory, and that's history. Invite a community group to tell its story, and that's history. Volunteer for a local museum, and that's history. We are in it together for the cause of history.

Without sharing a story, it will be lost forever. Without meticulous care, an artifact will deteriorate. Without setting a document aside, the content will disappear. There is no way to recover from the loss of evidence and stories, if we fail to do our part in our own time and place. History is a call to action.

In every age, we have witnessed how superior power suppresses stories and wipes records clean. We have seen the publication of official versions and approved texts. We even have heard of family members afraid to share their own stories with each other. We need to stand up for history.

Sometimes we have nobody to blame but ourselves. We lose our curiosity. We do not seek out the lessons. We must resolve that we will never forget.

Learning where you came from gives you an identity. Knowing you are heard gives you a voice. Deciding where you are bound gives you a mission. History transforms lives.

"Four score and seven years ago . . ." "Now we are engaged . . . " "[W]e here highly resolve . . ." All of us who wonder how we got here, what we are doing, and where we are going, have a tie that binds us together. We all know that history is a cause.

GARY T. JOHNSON is the eighth President of the Chicago History Museum appointed in 2005. Prior to joining the museum, he had a 28-year career in the private practice of law, admitted to practice both in the United States and as a solicitor in England. His civic commitments included serving as Co-Chair of the Lawyers' Committee for Civil Rights Under Law, Washington, DC; president of both the Legal Assistance Foundation of Metropolitan Chicago and Museums in the Park, a coalition of eleven of Chicago's major museums on Park District property; and chair of Museums Work for Chicago, a collaboration of 15 of Chicago's major museums. Johnson is a Rhodes Scholar.

On November 19, 1863, President Abraham Lincoln dignified the principles of republicanism in his Gettysburg Address. He had initially sought in the Civil War to preserve the Union of 1861, but he had broadened his objective to that of forming a more perfect Union. The Union he envisioned would rest on the natural rights principles incorporated into the Declaration of Independence by the Founding Fathers. The death of slavery was crucial to a nation that welcomed all peoples. The Civil War Lincoln realized, provided a critical transition between slavery and freedom and thereby highlighted the principle so eloquently stated some thirty years earlier by his longtime favorite in history, Daniel Webster: "Liberty and Union, now and forever, one and inseparable!" Guiding Lincoln's thinking was the ideal of universal freedom, a revolutionary concept that required Americans to be "born again" after undergoing a crucible of fire on the battlefield. Out of the death and destruction of Gettysburg arose a renewed spirit of liberty that became the foundation of an improved Union and an example for all countries to follow. Lincoln recognized that republicanism was at stake not only in the United States but throughout the world. He believed that mid-19th century Americans were engaged in an epic struggle to determine whether they could establish what their forefathers had wanted their grand experiment to become — a republic "conceived in Liberty, and dedicated to the proposition that all men are created equal." Only with "a new birth of freedom" could they construct what Lincoln's words had magnificently captured as the essence of a republic: a government "of the people, by the people, for the people."

Howard Jones   September 19, 2013

REPUBLICANISM RENEWED

HOWARD JONES

On November 19, 1863, President Abraham Lincoln dignified the principles of republicanism in his Gettysburg Address. He had initially sought in the Civil War to preserve the Union of 1861, but he had broadened his objective to that of forming a more perfect Union. The Union he envisioned would rest on the natural rights principles incorporated into the Declaration of Independence by the Founding Fathers. The death of slavery was crucial to a nation that welcomed all peoples. The Civil War, Lincoln realized, provided a critical transition between slavery and freedom and thereby highlighted the principle so eloquently stated some thirty years earlier by his longtime favorite in history, Daniel Webster: "Liberty <u>and</u> Union, now and forever, one and inseparable!" Guiding Lincoln's thinking was the ideal of universal freedom, a revolutionary concept that required Americans to be "born again" after undergoing a crucible of fire on the battlefield. Out of the death and destruction of Gettysburg arose a renewed spirit of liberty that became the foundation of an improved Union and an example for all countries to follow. Lincoln recognized that republicanism was at stake not only in the United States but throughout the world. He believed that mid-19th century Americans were engaged in an epic struggle to determine whether they could establish what their forefathers had wanted their grand experiment to become—a republic "conceived in Liberty, and dedicated to the proposition that all men are created equal." Only with "a new birth of freedom" could they construct what Lincoln's words had magnificently captured as the essence of a republic: a government "of the people, by the people, for the people."

HOWARD JONES is University Research Professor of History Emeritus at the University of Alabama, where he chaired the Department of History in Tuscaloosa for eight years. He is the recipient of both the John F. Burnum Distinguished Faculty Award for teaching and research and the Blackmon-Moody Outstanding Professor Award. Jones is the author or editor of more than a dozen books, including Union in Peril: The Crisis over British Intervention in the Civil War *(University of North Carolina Press, 1992)—a History Book Club Selection and winner of the Phi Alpha Theta Book Award;* Abraham Lincoln and a New Birth of Freedom: The Union and Slavery in the Diplomacy of the Civil War *(University of Nebraska Press, 1999)— nominated for both the Lincoln and Bancroft Prizes; and* Blue and Gray Diplomacy: A History of Union and Confederate Foreign Relations *(University of North Carolina Press, 2010)—an Honorable Mention for the Lincoln Prize.*

19 SEPTEMBER 2013

MY CAREER-LONG PASSION HAS BEEN TEACHING STUDENTS ABOUT THE INHERENT JOY OF UNDERSTANDING AND MAKING MUSIC. I AM ALWAYS SEEKING INSPIRATION THAT WILL YIELD IDEAS FOR A NEW COMPOSITION AND FOUND ONE IN THE UNLIKELY SOURCE OF OUR SIXTEENTH PRESIDENT'S POETRY, LETTERS, AND SPEECHES. OF THE PEOPLE, BY THE PEOPLE AND FOR THE PEOPLE EDITED BY DR. GABOR BORITT PROVIDED THE FODDER FOR MY ORATORIO CREATED TO CELEBRATE THE LINCOLN BI-CENTENNIAL IN 2009.

WHY AN ORATORIO? ORATORIOS BECAME MORE SECULAR AT THE TURN OF THE 18TH CENTURY WITH THEMATIC IDEAS THAT INCLUDED MYTHOLOGICAL FIGURES AND CLASSICAL HEROES. ARIAS AND RECITATIVES ARE INDISPENSABLE ELEMENTS OF THE ORATORIO FORM. LINCOLN'S LETTERS AND POETRY ARE MUSICAL BY NATURE AND WERE EASY TO SET TO MUSIC AS ARIAS. SPEECHES SELECTED WERE MORE DECLARATORY AND ENGAGE THE LISTENER BETTER AS SPOKEN RECITATIVE. MOREOVER, WE KNOW THAT LINCOLN LOVED MUSIC. ATTENDING CONCERTS AND OPERAS BROUGHT HIM MUCH PLEASURE DURING FOUR TUMULTUOUS YEARS IN OFFICE AND HE OFTEN INVITED TRAVELING MUSICIANS TO PERFORM AT THE WHITE HOUSE.

SETTING LINCOLN'S WORDS TO MUSIC ALLOWED ME TO ILLUMINATE TOPICS SUCH AS HOPE, DEATH, EMANCIPATION, MELANCHOLY, AND RECONCILIATION THAT, IN TURN, EDUCATED LISTENERS ABOUT HIS STRENGTHS, FEARS, AND FOIBLES. ONE PERVASIVE THOUGHT WAS ALWAYS WITH ME AS I COMPOSED THE ORATORIO — "WOULD PRESIDENT AND MRS. LINCOLN ENJOY THE MUSIC AS PART OF AN EVENING'S ENTERTAINMENT."

I AM INDEED GRATEFUL FOR ABRAHAM LINCOLN'S IMMENSE GIFT FOR WRITING INSPIRING SPEECHES, CREATING POETRY FILLED WITH YOUTHFUL VIGOR, AND COMPOSING PERSONAL CORRESPONDENCE THAT COULD BE REPLETE WITH ANGUISH. HIS MEMORABLE WORDS CLEARLY AIDED ME IN SATISFYING MY PASSION FOR TEACHING THROUGH MUSIC.

JOAN WILLIAM JONES DMA
PROFESSOR OF MUSIC

WORDS TO MUSIC

John William Jones

My career-long passion has been teaching students about the inherent joy of understanding and making music. I am always seeking inspiration that will yield ideas for a new composition and found one in the unlikely source of our sixteenth president's poetry, letters, and speeches. <u>Of The People, By The People and For The People</u> edited by Dr. Gabor Boritt provided the fodder for my oratorio, created to celebrate the Lincoln bicentennial in 2009.

Why an oratorio? Oratorios became more secular at the turn of the 18th century with thematic ideas that included mythological figures and classical heroes. Arias and recitatives are indispensable elements of the oratorio form. Lincoln's letters and poetry are musical by nature and were easy to set to music as arias. Speeches selected were more declaratory and engage the listener better as spoken recitative. Moreover, we know that Lincoln loved music. Attending concerts and opera brought him much pleasure during four tumultuous years in office and he often invited traveling musicians to perform at the White House.

Setting Lincoln's words to music allowed me to illuminate topics such as hope, death, emancipation, melancholy, and reconciliation that, in turn, educated listeners about his strengths, fears, and foibles. One pervasive thought was always with me as I composed the oratorio—"would President and Mrs. Lincoln enjoy the music as part of an evening's entertainment?"

I am indeed grateful for Abraham Lincoln's immense gift for writing inspiring speeches, creating poetry filled with youthful vigor, and composing personal correspondence that could be replete with anguish. His memorable words clearly aided me in satisfying my passion for teaching through music.

John William Jones is Professor of Music at Gettysburg College, where he served as Director of Bands, Music Department Chair, Director of the Sunderman Conservatory of Music, and Director of the Gettysburg College England Program. Jones is a member of ASCAP and has earned ASCAP Standard Awards in composition annually since 1996. He has written commissioned works for concert band, jazz ensemble, and orchestra including For The People, *an oratorio for brass band and soloists celebrating the Abraham Lincoln bicentennial, which premiered in 2009 with Stephen Lang (*Avatar, Gods and Generals*) as narrator.* Voices from the Hill *is a recent (2013) Jones composition for wind quintet and baritone commemorating the sesquicentennial of the Battle of Gettysburg.*

September 11th 2013

We spend much — if not all — of our lives in search of our reason for being. And the harder we look, the more the hidden meaning of our own existence seems to elude us. Abraham Lincoln, on the other hand, had an enviable clarity of purpose that resulted in his many great achievements. He recognized the part he was to play in American history, and wasted no time in accomplishing all that he could. Though seemingly insurmountable obstacles were put in his path, his understanding of how he fit into his time and place, coupled with his ambition, vision, inner strength and strong moral compass, always gave him the will to overcome them. But that personal prescience, we often fail to recognize, comes at a serious cost. The responsibility to fulfill one's destiny, once it has been revealed, is an enormous burden that demands tremendous sacrifice. The cost required of Lincoln to save the union, put an end to slavery, and preserve the very idea of democracy could not have been higher. It is difficult to imagine that someone would rise to that challenge; it is even more difficult to imagine the kind of person that would rise so wholly, so selflessly and with unconditional dedication. It is for that very reason that, often in the same breath, we refer to his story as both an incredible triumph, and a terrible tragedy. But because this man was exactly who was meant to be, and just at the right time, he has left an indelible mark on our history, our country and our lives. For that, President Abraham Lincoln will always be remembered.

Kathleen Kelly

CLARITY OF PURPOSE

KATHLEEN KENNEDY

We spend much—if not all—of our lives in search of our reason for being. And the harder we look, the more the hidden meaning of our own existence seems to elude us. Abraham Lincoln, on the other hand, had an enviable clarity of purpose that resulted in his many great achievements. He recognized the part he was to play in American history, and wasted no time in accomplishing all that he could. Though seemingly insurmountable obstacles were put in his path, his understanding of how he fit into his time and place, coupled with his ambition, vision, inner strength, and strong moral compass, always gave him the will to overcome them.

But that personal prescience, we often fail to recognize, comes at a serious cost. The responsibility to fulfill one's destiny, once it has been revealed, is an enormous burden that demands tremendous sacrifice. The cost required of Lincoln to save the Union, put an end to slavery, and preserve the very idea of democracy could not have been higher. It is difficult to imagine that someone would rise to that challenge; it is even more difficult to imagine the kind of person that would rise so wholly, so selflessly and with unconditional dedication. It is for that very reason that, often in the same breath, we refer to his story as both an incredible triumph, and a terrible tragedy. But because this man was exactly who was meant to be, and just at the right time, he has left an indelible mark on our history, our country, and our lives. For that, President Abraham Lincoln will always be remembered.

KATHLEEN KENNEDY is the President of Lucasfilm. An eight-time Academy Award nominee, she is one of the most successful and respected producers and executives in the film industry. She is Vice President and serves on the Board of Governors of the Academy of Motion Pictures Arts and Sciences. Among her credits are four of the highest grossing films in motion picture history: Jurassic Park, E.T. The Extra-Terrestrial, Indiana Jones and the Kingdom of the Crystal Skull, *and* The Sixth Sense. *Prior to joining Lucasfilm, Kennedy headed The Kennedy/Marshall Company, which she founded with director/producer Frank Marshall, and cofounded Amblin Entertainment with both Steven Spielberg and Marshall. Recent Kennedy/Marshall projects include Steven Spielberg's critically acclaimed* Lincoln. *Among her many honors, Kennedy has received the Producers Guild of America's Charles Fitzsimmons Service Award, as well as its David O. Selznick Award for Career Achievement.*

He paces his office, weighed down by heavy thoughts. He wonders how he is supposed to honor those who have fallen. How he was supposed to reassure his fellow Americans. His eyes tear up as he thinks of the 51,000 Confederate and Union soldiers, husbands, fathers and sons who were dead, wounded or missing. He slams his fist on his desk before sinking into his chair. The battle was won but he still felt at war. He begins to contemplate the Declaration of Independence and what the United States of America stands for as he picks up his pen. 'Our fathers brought forth on this continent a new nation, conceived in liberty, and dedicated to the proposition that all men are created equal.' Only a few short moments later he is done. He hopes it is enough, but for the first time in a long time he feels at peace. He knows that words cannot dry up tears. Money cannot close wounds left behind by missing loved ones. Those who fought for the freedom of all Americans needed more. Dedicating a portion of the battlefield to them seemed fitting and honorable. 'The world will little note, nor long remember what we say here, but it can never forget what they did here.' As he steps out to face the growing crowd and feels a calm wash over him. It was time to honor all the brave men who gave their lives for their country. That they would always continue to fight for their rights 'and that government of the people, by the people, for the people, shall not perish from the earth.'

A L

MC2 Amanda L. Kilpatrick, USS Abraham Lincoln

LINCOLN WALKING AT NIGHT

Amanda L. Kilpatrick

He paces his office, weighed down by heavy thoughts. He wonders how he is supposed to honor those who have fallen. How he was supposed to reassure his fellow Americans. His eyes tear up as he thinks of the 51,000 Confederate and Union soldiers, husbands, fathers, and sons who were dead, wounded or missing. He slams his fist on his desk before sinking into his chair. The battle was won but he still felt at war. He begins to contemplate the Declaration of Independence and what the United States of America stands for as he picks up his pen. "Our fathers brought forth on this continent a new nation, conceived in liberty, and dedicated to the proposition that all men are created equal." Only a few short moments later he is done. He hopes it is enough, but for the first time in a long time he feels at peace. He knows that words cannot dry up tears. Money cannot close wounds left behind by missing loved ones. Those who fought for the freedom of all Americans needed more. Dedicating a portion of the battlefield to them seemed fitting and honorable. "The world will little note, nor long remember what we say here, but it can never forget what they did here." As he steps out to face the growing crowd and feels a calm wash over him. It was time to honor all the brave men who gave their lives for their country. That they would always continue to fight for their rights "and that government of the people, by the people, for the people, shall not perish from the earth."

Amanda L. Kilpatrick is a Mass Communication Specialist 2nd Class in the United States Navy. Born in Corona, California, and raised in San Diego, Kilpatrick enlisted in June 2008. After completing Recruit Training at Naval Station Great Lakes in Lake County, Illinois, she reported to Mass Communication Specialist "A" training school at Fort Meade, Maryland. She first served aboard the USS Ronald Reagan (CVN 76), was deployed around the world advancing from Seaman Recruit to Petty Officer Third Class. She then transferred to Naval Medical Center San Diego followed by service aboard the USS Abraham Lincoln (CVN 72). Kilpatrick was again deployed around the world advancing to Petty Officer Second Class, earning her designation as Enlisted Surface Warfare Specialist and becoming Work Center Supervisor, Safety Petty Officer, and temporary Leading Petty Officer. Kilpatrick is now assigned to Headquarters Supreme Allied Command Transformation where she serves as Leading Petty Officer of the Visual Information Section. She has earned two Navy Marine Corps Achievement Medals and numerous individual, campaign, and unit awards.

The Gettysburg Address: 272 words masterfully woven together resulting in the extraordinary. The brevity of the Address, the multiple pre-delivery drafts over which he labored, paint a picture of Abraham Lincoln, a man who clearly understood the power of words and who was deeply committed to his message. It conjures up an image of the thoughtful wordsmith, pen in hand, toiling over paper, considering the effect each word would have upon the next and how the sum of those words contributed to the whole -- no less than da Vinci, brush in hand, stroking his canvas, or Mozart sitting at his piano pouring notes upon paper. There stands Lincoln exhorting a nation with words and voice, thought and reason. He speaks 272 words -- no more, no less; each word or series of words building upon those which came before, all clearly calculated for the integrity of the message and the integrity of the man. None are extraneous. All are purposeful. And so, I ask you to consider just two: "Under God." Lincoln's insertion of these words was a proclamation that while a wall of separation between church and state existed, as founding father Thomas Jefferson illuminated, the United States of America was still a nation based on spiritual principles. Lincoln reminded us that it was God in whom we placed our trust when building our Nation, and it was God to whom both the North and the South should turn to lead them spiritually through the "mighty scourge of war." Separation of church and state does not mean separating ourselves from our spiritually enriched history -- our collective national soul. In God We Trust.

Carla Knorowski
November 7, 2013

ABRAHAM LINCOLN
PRESIDENTIAL LIBRARY
FOUNDATION

www.PresidentLincoln.org

HOME OFFICE
SPRINGFIELD

500 E. Madison Street
Suite 200
Springfield, Illinois 62701

Phone: (217) 557-6251
Fax: (217) 558-6041

"IN GOD WE TRUST"

CARLA KNOROWSKI

The Gettysburg Address: 272 words masterfully woven together resulting in the extraordinary. The brevity of the Address, the multiple predelivery drafts over which he labored, paint a picture of Abraham Lincoln, a man who clearly understood the power of words and who was deeply committed to his message. It conjures up an image of the thoughtful wordsmith, pen in hand, toiling over paper, considering the effect each word would have upon the next and how the sum of those words contributed to the whole—no less than da Vinci, brush in hand, stroking his canvas, or Mozart sitting at his piano pouring notes upon paper. There stands Lincoln exhorting a nation with words and voice; thought and reason. He speaks 272 words—no more, no less. Each word or series of words building upon those which came before, all clearly calculated for the integrity of the message and the integrity of the man. None are extraneous. All are purposeful. And so, I ask you to consider just two: "Under God." Lincoln's insertion of these words was a proclamation that while a "wall of separation between church and state" existed, as founding father Thomas Jefferson illuminated, the United States of America was still a nation based on spiritual principles. Lincoln reminded us that it was God in whom we placed our trust when building our Nation, and it was God to whom both the North and the South should turn to spiritually lead them through the "mighty scourge of war." Separation of church and state does not mean separating ourselves from our spiritually enriched history—our collective national soul. "In God We Trust."

CARLA KNOROWSKI is Chief Executive Officer of the Abraham Lincoln Presidential Library Foundation. She conceived and co-curated The Power of Words *(2013), an exhibit at the Abraham Lincoln Presidential Museum that commemorated the 150th Anniversary of the Gettysburg Address, featuring essays compiled in this book. A writer, her work appears in* Lincoln: An Intimate Portrait *(Life Books, 2014). The Points of Light Foundation, founded by President George H. W. Bush, named her a Daily Point of Light for her work and commitment to civic engagement and active and purposeful citizenship.*

THE LIBRARY OF CONGRESS
101 INDEPENDENCE AVENUE, S.E.
WASHINGTON, D.C. 20540–4680

MANUSCRIPT DIVISION

"Touch any aspect of the [Gettysburg] address and you touch a mystery," David Mearns of the Library of Congress said in 1964. It remains true in 2013. There are still so many questions about the Gettysburg cemetery dedication and Lincoln's address that we cannot answer with certainty. Was Abraham Lincoln informally asked to participate in the cemetery dedication before David Wills wrote the official invitation on November 2, 1863? When did he begin working on the address? Had he finished the address in Washington? Did he make further amendments in Gettysburg? Did he have the Nicolay copy with him at the dedication? The Hay copy? Another copy that no longer exists? Did he speak from memorized text, or read from a manuscript, or a combination of the two? Did the audience applaud during and after the speech, or remain silent? We do know, at least, that he did not write it on the back of an envelope on the train to Gettysburg. The rest, however, remains shrouded in mystery and the fallible memories of witnesses, and gives historians fodder for endless interpretation and argument.

Does any of this touch on the enduring qualities of the Gettysburg Address itself? No. Lincoln's eloquent words are what truly draw us to the document. They speak to the value of American lives lost on all battlefields in ensuring that "government of the people, by the people, for the people, shall not perish from the earth." That ... of freedom" ... "that all ...3, 1963

... or 2013.

Michelle A. Krowl
Civil War and Reconstruction specialist
Manuscript Division
Library of Congress

September 16, 2013

MYSTERY IN THE HISTORY OF THE GETTYSBURG ADDRESS

MICHELLE A. KROWL

"Touch any aspect of the [Gettysburg] address and you touch a mystery," David Mearns of the Library of Congress said in 1964. It remains true in 2013. There are still so many questions about the Gettysburg cemetery dedication and Lincoln's address that we cannot answer with certainty. Was Abraham Lincoln informally asked to participate in the cemetery dedication before David Wills wrote the official invitation on November 2, 1863? When did he begin working on the address? Had he finished the address in Washington? Did he make further amendments in Gettysburg? Did he have the Nicolay copy with him at the dedication? The Hay copy? Another copy that no longer exists? Did he speak from memorized text, or read from a manuscript, or a combination of the two? Did the audience applaud during and after the speech, or remain silent? We do know, at least, that he did not write it on the back of an envelope on the train to Gettysburg. The rest, however, remains shrouded in mystery and the fallible memories of witnesses, and gives historians fodder for endless interpretation and argument.

Does any of this touch on the enduring qualities of the Gettysburg Address itself? No. Lincoln's eloquent words are what truly draw us to the document. They speak to the value of American lives lost on all battlefields in ensuring that "government of the people, by the people, for the people, shall not perish from the earth." That out of conflict can spring "a new birth of freedom" for the nation, moving closer to the dream "that all men are created equal," whether in 1863, 1963, or 2013.

~ ~

MICHELLE A. KROWL, Ph.D., is the Civil War and Reconstruction specialist in the Manuscript Division at the Library of Congress. She is the author of several articles and books including Women of the Civil War *(Pomegranate Communications, 2006) as part of the* Women Who Dare *series and* The World War II Memorial: Honoring the Price of Freedom *(Donning Company Publishers, 2007). She has worked as a library assistant at the Historical Society of Washington, DC, an assistant professor at Northern Virginia Community College, and as a research assistant for historian Doris Kearns Goodwin.*

PHOTO ESSAY
ANNIE LEIBOVITZ

This photo submitted by American photographer Annie Leibovitz for *Gettysburg Replies* is of a plaster model created by American renaissance sculptor Daniel Chester French for his sculpture of a seated Lincoln at the center of the Lincoln Memorial located on the Mall in Washington, DC. The model is on display at French's Chesterwood studio located in Glendale, Massachusetts, where Leibovitz took the photo. The photo originally appeared in the traveling exhibition *Pilgrimage*, a compilation of the photographer's work, which was exhibited at a number of cultural institutions across the United States including the Abraham Lincoln Presidential Museum in Springfield, Illinois. It was submitted to *Gettysburg Replies* by the photographer who chose to speak through her lens, rather than her pen.

—◆—

ANNIE LEIBOVITZ is an American photographer, who has captured iconic images of celebrities from John Lennon to Johnny Depp. She has trained her camera on famous places and objects, revealing more of herself in the process. She began her career as a photojournalist for Rolling Stone *in 1970, while she was still a student at the San Francisco Art Institute. Her pictures have appeared regularly on magazine covers ever since. Leibovitz's large and distinguished body of work encompasses some of the most well-known portraits of our time. Her most recent compilation of work is* Pilgrimage, *an exhibition organized by the Smithsonian Institution of more than 70 stunning photographs, including those of Abraham Lincoln's stovepipe hat and the gloves Lincoln carried with him on the night of his assassination, a handwritten copy of the Gettysburg Address, the Lincoln Memorial, Gettysburg, and photographic negatives of Lincoln. The exhibit companion book is* Pilgrimage *(Random House, 2011).*

D Leroy

DAVID H. LEROY   ATTORNEY AT LAW

FOUR SCORE AND SEVEN LINCOLNS

A man drove his Lincoln Town Car from Lincoln Park in San Francisco along the Lincoln Highway through the Lincoln Tunnel into New York City. Along the way, he passed 24 Lincoln Counties, 28 Lincoln Cities and stopped at a Lincoln park, Lincoln tavern, Lincoln theatre, Lincoln statue, Lincoln shrine, Lincoln zoo, Lincoln bridge, Lincoln barbershop, Lincoln hospital and Lincoln College in Illinois. People offered him Lincoln Peas, Lincoln Roses, Lincoln Welders, Lincoln Windows and a Lincoln Grease Gun. He passed children at a Lincoln School playing with Lincoln Logs and some senior citizens watching Lincoln, the movie, at a Lincoln nursing home. When he ran short of Lincoln pennies and Lincoln five dollar bills, he replenished at a Lincoln bank. At a Lincoln library, he perused one of 17,000 Lincoln books.

The Lincoln brand is alive and well in America.
Yet his best "product" is not sold in stores.

This month I debated a noted Lincoln detractor upon the topic "Abraham Lincoln: Friend or Foe of Freedom?" Eleven hundred citizens attended. When I argued that Lincoln was the greatest advocate of liberty the world has ever known, many in the crowd applauded. When my opponent called

... politician,

... reflective,

Was not our Lincoln, for whom a grease gun is named, just such a man?

David H Leroy
Boise, Idaho
November 19, 2013
272 words

FOUR SCORE AND SEVEN LINCOLNS

David H. Leroy

A man drove his Lincoln Town Car from Lincoln Park in San Francisco along the Lincoln Highway through the Lincoln Tunnel into New York City. Along the way, he passed 24 Lincoln Counties, 28 Lincoln Cities and stopped at a Lincoln park, Lincoln tavern, Lincoln theatre, Lincoln statue, Lincoln shrine, Lincoln zoo, Lincoln bridge, Lincoln barbershop, Lincoln hospital and Lincoln college in Illinois. People offered him Lincoln Peas, Lincoln Roses, Lincoln Welders, Lincoln Windows, and a Lincoln Grease Gun. He passed children at a Lincoln School playing with Lincoln Logs and some senior citizens watching Lincoln, the movie, at a Lincoln nursing home. When he ran short of Lincoln pennies and Lincoln five dollar bills, he replenished at a Lincoln bank. At a Lincoln library, he perused one of 17,000 Lincoln books.

The Lincoln brand is alive and well in America.
Yet his best "product" is not sold in stores.

This month I debated a noted Lincoln detractor upon the topic "Abraham Lincoln: Friend or Foe of Freedom?" Eleven hundred citizens attended. When I argued that Lincoln was the greatest advocate of liberty the world has ever known, many in the crowd applauded. When my opponent called Lincoln a dictator, despot, racist, war monger and corrupt politician, a like number clapped.

But all of the attendees were silent, respectful, even reflective, after I said these words:

"Freedom is not an abstract concept.
It can be lost. It can be chained.
It can be sold.
And under the right circumstances,
with the right leader,
it can be gained."

Was not our Lincoln, for whom a grease gun is named, just such a man?

David H. Leroy is chairman of the Idaho Abraham Lincoln Bicentennial Commission and Chairman of the Governor's Council of the United States Lincoln Bicentennial Commission. A former prosecutor, Attorney General, and Lt. Governor, Dave has been lecturing on Lincoln since 1976. He is the author of many articles and a book on the sixteenth president, and he has a collection of historic artifacts relating to Lincoln's life, which he uses to enhance his talks. His interpretations and comments tell of the unknown, the unusual, and the "real animal" as Lincoln called himself.

Caleb Lewis
"A Look at a People"
July 14, 2014
Caleb Lewis

Five decades and seven years ago, a
people stood together, but yet were divided. Divided,
misconstrued, lampooned — they were segregated.
A people criticized by the color that also bound
them together. It was the color that gave them
their names "My Brother" and "My Sister". It was
a color so beautiful; a color so powerful that it
brought forth nine youth and made them one.
Through this, a color which was meant to "un-dignify" a people, actually came to unify a people.

Five decades and seven years We fast forward
to the present. We find a people with interral
division, obscure minds, and adolescent, convinced
that they are nothing more than inadequate of
world's expectations. A people who subclass one
another by the complexity and hue of their own
skin. Five decades and seven years we fast forward
into the present, beautiful bodacious brown skin
rivals gorgeous illuminating cadescent light skin.
Here, a people who would rather wage war with
their brothers and disown their sisters, rather
then embrace each other with an open arm.

Five decades and seven years ago a people
stood unified. They walked hand in hand singing
hymns dear to their souls and with hope in

_...walk on. Let Jesus
...song rang through
...gh the streets of
..." hymns sung
so far and fair. Here, a people stood together.
It was a beautiful sight — a historical sight.

Five decades and seven years we fast
forward to the present. Are we not disturbed?
Together, we all shall unify a people.

A LOOK AT A PEOPLE

CALEB LEWIS

Five decades and seven years ago, a people stood together, but yet were divided. Divided, miscon-strued, lampooned—they were segregated. A people criticized by the color that also bound them together. It was the color that gave them their names "My Brother" and "My Sister." It was a color so beautiful; a color so powerful that it brought forth nine youth and made them one. Through this, a color which was meant to "un-dignify" a people, actually came to unify a people.

Five decades and seven years we fast forward to the present. We find a people with internal division, obscure minds, and adolescent, convinced that they are nothing more than inadequate of world's expectations. A people who subclass one another by the complexity and hue of their own skin. Five decades and seven years we fast forward into the present, beautiful bodacious brown skin rivals gorgeous illuminating candescent light skin. Here, a people who would rather wage war with their brothers and disown their sisters, rather than embrace each other with an open arm.

Five decades and seven years ago a people stood unified. They walked hand in hand singing hymns dear to their souls and with hope in their hearts. "Walk on. Walk on. Let Jesus be your rock," their voices and song rang through the air. "We will walk through the streets of the city with our loved ones . . ." hymns sung so far and fair. Here, a people stood together. It was a beautiful sight—a historical sight.

Five decades and seven years we fast forward to the present. Are we not disturbed? Together, we all shall unify a people.

CALEB LEWIS is a senior at Little Rock Central High School in Arkansas. He is a member of the Little Rock Central High School Memory Project, a school organization where students work with mentors to collect, edit, and publish oral histories from the Little Rock community. He also is a member of the National Park Service Little Rock Central High School Youth Leadership Academy. He enjoys writing and poetry.

I am one of the few people who heard Abraham Lincoln deliver the Gettysburg Address in person. My time machine was the set of Saving Lincoln - the true story of our 16th President and his closest friend, U.S. Marshal Ward Hill Lamon. Lamon introduced Lincoln at the dedication of the National Cemetery in Gettysburg, and reported the President's own assessment of his address: "Lamon, that speech won't scour! It is a flat failure and the people are disappointed."

Others agreed, including Secretary of State Seward and Lamon himself. The speech was simply too short for an audience that had just heard two hours from the great orator, Edward Everett. Lincoln's prose was too packed with meaning, and the audience could not absorb it in one hearing. The passage of time has unpacked that meaning.

In a country of 30 million people, the Civil War exacted the ultimate price from 750,000 soldiers. In today's numbers, that would be 7.5 million. A holocaust. My grandfather was murdered in the Holocaust, his life taken at Dachau. I honored him by making my first film, when Do we Eat?, in which a survivor's family is challenged to transform grudges into healing during the festival of freedom known as Passover.

Abraham Lincoln died during Passover. His 272 words at Gettysburg challenge us to create meaning from the tragic loss of every American soldier who died in the Civil War. Their sacrifice will not be in vain if we continue their work of extending freedom to those who are not free. This is the mission of the American Experiment, once entrusted to Abraham Lincoln, and now entrusted to us. Sol Lilith 6-19-2013

I HEARD LINCOLN DELIVER THE GETTYSBURG ADDRESS

SALVADOR LITVAK

I am one of the few people who heard Abraham Lincoln deliver the Gettysburg Address in person. My time machine was the set of <u>Saving Lincoln</u>—the true story of our 16th President and his closest friend, U.S. Marshal Ward Hill Lamon. Lamon introduced Lincoln at the dedication of the National Cemetery in Gettysburg, and reported the President's own assessment of his address: "Lamon, that speech won't scour! It is a flat failure and the people are disappointed."

Others agreed, including Secretary of State Seward and Lamon himself. The speech was simply too short for an audience that had just heard two hours from the great orator Edward Everett. Lincoln's prose was too packed with meaning, and the audience could not absorb it in one hearing. The passage of time has unpacked that meaning.

In a country of 30 million people, the Civil War exacted the ultimate price from 750,000 soldiers. In today's numbers, that would be 7.5 million. A holocaust. My grandfather was murdered in the Holocaust, his life taken at Dachau. I honored him by making my first film, <u>When Do We Eat?</u>, in which a survivor's family is challenged to transform grudges into healing during the festival of freedom known as Passover.

Abraham Lincoln died during Passover. His 272 words at Gettysburg challenge us to create meaning from the tragic loss of every American soldier who died in the Civil War. Their sacrifice will not be in vain if we continue their work of extending freedom to those who are not free. This is the mission of the American Experiment, once entrusted to Abraham Lincoln, and now entrusted to us.

Salvador Litvak is an independent filmmaker and screenwriter. He was born in Santiago, Chile, and moved to New York at age five. His first film was the Passover comedy and cult hit When Do We Eat? *which he cowrote with his wife, Nina Davidovich Litvak.*

Their second film, Saving Lincoln, *examines Abraham Lincoln's crisis of faith during the darkest hours of the Civil War, as witnessed by his close friend and bodyguard, Ward Hill Lamon. The film introduced and featured a new visual style called CineCollage, which visually places actors within actual Civil War photographs. Litvak shares a bit of ancient Jewish wisdom with an audience of over 100,000 fans at Facebook.com/ AccidentalTalmudist and is developing a television show based on this rapidly growing community.*

Horseshoe Bay, Texas

One hundred fifty three years ago, Abraham Lincoln, a newly inaugurated president of the United States committed our military to restore a divided nation.

The legislative leaders of seven southern states had already voted to secede from the Union and military assets were being seized throughout the south. South Carolina was demanding the surrender of Fort Sumter. Lincoln's own advisors suggested that by giving up Fort Sumter might modify southern thinking and preserve the Union.

The Union army consisted of only about sixteen thousand troops scattered throughout the country and most of Lincoln's military commanders were southern.

But Lincoln realized to give into South Carolina only embolden the southern states governments. Lincoln was committed to preserve the Union and ordered Fort Sumter to hold fast.

On April 15, 1861 Lincoln summoned 75,000 militia to quell the rebellion and once again the American serviceman rallied to the Stars and Stripes.

our military
ur enemies.
harged and our
t, but the
our military
y to
ghanistan the
ceman permeates

Gettysburg
n who died
t spirit was

53 under a
gave our
unforgettable tribute in just 272 words to honor
Gettysburg's fallen heros.

Dave Lowe
June 2 2014

FALLEN HEROES

JAMES LOVELL

One hundred fifty three years ago, Abraham Lincoln, a newly inaugurated president of the United States committed our military to restore a divided nation.

The legislative leaders of seven southern states had already voted to secede from the Union and military assets were being seized throughout the south. South Carolina was demanding the surrender of Fort Sumter. Lincoln's own advisors suggested that by giving up Fort Sumter might modify southern thinking and preserve the Union.

The Union army consisted of only about sixteen thousand troops scattered throughout the country and most of Lincoln's military commanders were southern.

But Lincoln realized to give into South Carolina only embolden the southern states governments. Lincoln was committed to preserve the Union and ordered Fort Sumter to hold fast.

On April 15, 1861, Lincoln summoned 75,000 militia to quell the rebellion and once again the American serviceman rallied to the Stars and Stripes.

For more than 230 years our military has provided a bastion against our enemies. In that time our world has changed and our arm forces have changed with it, but the valor, dignity and courage of our military remains the same. From Valley Forge to Gettysburg, from Pearl Harbor to Afghanistan, the fighting spirit of the American serviceman permeates the history of our nation.

The brave men who fell at Gettysburg represented a sameness of all men who died for the liberty of our nation. That spirit was deeper than the uniform they wore.

And so, on 19 November 1863 under a cloudless sky, President Lincoln gave an unforgettable tribute in just 272 words to honor Gettysburg's fallen heroes.

Among America's heroic astronauts, JAMES LOVELL is regarded as a leader of near mythic proportion, maintaining calm and discipline aboard Apollo 13 *while the mission experienced monumental equipment failures that threatened to leave the crew stranded in outer space. Commander Lovell and his crew successfully modified their lunar module into an effective lifeboat, assuring their survival in space and their safe return to Earth.*

Lovell, an experienced U.S. Navy aviator and test pilot prior to being selected for the Gemini program, also served in various command positions during four space missions including pilot and navigator on Apollo 8's *6-day journey to the Moon, backup commander to Neil Armstrong for* Apollo 11, *and commander of* Apollo 13. *In 1994 Lovell and Jeff Kluger wrote* Lost Moon, *which was re-released as* Apollo 13 *and filmed in 1995 with Tom Hanks playing the role of Jim Lovell.*

In two hundred seventy-two words Lincoln's Gettysburg Address speaks to the conscience of America. Lincoln drew from the Declaration of Independence, which states, "We hold these truths to be self-evident, that all men are created equal, that they are endowed by their Creator with certain unalienable rights, among these are Life, Liberty and The pursuit of Happiness." We are a nation founded upon the principles of Liberty and Equality.

Dedicating the Cemetery for all those who fought and died here, Lincoln reminds us that they were in the service of our nation. The greatest honor of my life was being awarded the Medal of Honor. Sixty-three Medals of Honor were earned in the Battle of Gettysburg. To win the honor to take my place alongside such men is humbling, I believe I must do my best to honor the Medal because of what it represents. Lincoln calls on all Americans to complete the unfinished work not only of maintaining the Union but also our Founding principles of Liberty and Equality. These are National Principles worth defending with our lives; principles well worth enduring Great hardship to Advance.

Lincoln inspires us to ensure that those who, "gave the last full measure of devotion ooo shall not have died in Vain." It is for us who remain to pledge; "that his nation — under God, shall not perish from the earth." Lincoln ends with a reference to God that at the Declaration of Independence declares that our Equality and Liberty — our unalienable rights — are not given to us by men, for men can take away what they give, but are given by our Creator.

Allen J Lynch
Medal of Honor

FREEDOM: GIVEN BY GOD, DEFENDED BY MAN

ALLEN J. LYNCH

In two hundred seventy-two words, Lincoln's Gettysburg Address speaks to the conscience of America. Lincoln draws from the Declaration of Independence, which states, "We hold these truths to be self-evident, that all men are created equal, that they are endowed by their Creator with certain unalienable rights, among these are Life, Liberty and the pursuit of Happiness." We are a nation founded upon the principles of Liberty and Equality.

Dedicating the cemetery for all those who fought and died there, Lincoln reminds us that they were in the service of our nation. The greatest honor of my life was being awarded the Medal of Honor. Sixty-three Medals of Honor were earned in the Battle of Gettysburg. Given the honor to take my place alongside such men is humbling. I believe I must do my best to honor the Medal because of what it represents. Lincoln calls on all Americans to complete the unfinished work not only of maintaining the Union but also our founding principles of Liberty and Equality. These are national principles worth defending with our lives; principles well worth enduring great hardship to advance.

Lincoln inspires us to ensure that those who, "gave the last full measure of devotion . . . shall not have died in vain." It is for us who remain to pledge "that this nation, under God, shall not perish from the earth." Lincoln ends with a reference to God just as the Declaration of Independence declares that our Equality and Liberty—our unalienable rights—are not given to us by men, for men can take away what they give, but are given by our Creator.

ALLEN J. LYNCH is a Medal of Honor recipient. He enlisted in the United States Army in November 1964, completing Basic Training at Fort Knox, Kentucky. He volunteered to serve in Vietnam, arriving there in May 1967. In December, Lynch's unit was sent to provide relief for an ambushed company, but his company, too, was ambushed en route. In the midst of a firefight, Lynch spotted three wounded soldiers out in the open, who were under intense enemy fire. He went to their aid, carrying them one by one to a trench that offered some protection, then moving them to another location leading to their evacuation. He was honorably discharged from the Army in April 1969, and on June 14, 1970, President Richard Nixon presented the Medal of Honor to him. He completed 21 years of service in the Army Reserve and National Guard and served the Veterans Administration for more than 35 years. Lynch now volunteers for the Vietnam Veterans of America and Lake County Illinois Veterans Assistance Commission. He is a cofounder of the Allen J. Lynch Medal of Honor Veterans Foundation, which assists veterans and their families.

It is surely among the greatest paradoxes of the human condition that liberty attains its clearest meaning at its most imperiled hour. At its safest moments, liberty is lived and acted upon and enjoyed and praised, and yet largely unrecognized. It is the threat of loss, or indeed the realization that occurs when liberty has been extinguished, that attests its worth; not the many vacuous appeals to its name for political ends in less threatening times. We accordingly shudder at the incongruities of a government 'conceived in Liberty' while denying its blessings to an entire race and asserting by force of law that which nature cannot sanction. We reconcile ourselves to its architects in hopeful attachment to the notion that they tolerated this internal contradiction that it might be later eclipsed. So too do we stake the legitimacy of our entire civic order to the promise of consent and an absolute liberty to withdraw it, yet the occasion of our present commemoration indulged a "consent" by force against those who would claim the mantle of self determination while denying its most basic exercise to a captive brethren in their midst. As we remember the Civil War, we do so under the shadows of impenetrable complexity, discomforting contradiction, and an unfathomable toll in lives. While we see liberty betrayed all around — at the whipping post of the plantation, though the destructive force of clashing armies and in the halls of governments that sanctioned each and sanction such other predations as we know today — when lost, human nature yearns for its recovery, as a few distant words at Gettysburg so plainly attest.

Phillip W. Magness

CONCEIVED IN LIBERTY

Phillip W. Magness

It is surely among the great paradoxes of the human condition that liberty attains its clearest meaning at its most imperiled hour. At its safest moments, liberty is lived and acted upon and enjoyed and praised, and yet largely unrecognized. It is the threat of loss, or indeed the realization that occurs when liberty has been extinguished that attests to its worth; not the many vacuous appeals to its name for political ends in less threatening times. We accordingly shudder at the incongruities of a government 'conceived in Liberty' while denying its blessings to an entire race and asserting by force of law that which nature cannot sanction. We reconcile ourselves to its architects in hopeful attachment to the notion that they tolerated this internal contradiction that it might be later eclipsed. So too do we stake the legitimacy of our entire civic order to the promise of consent and an absolute liberty to withdraw it, yet the occasion of our present commemoration indulged a "consent" by force against those who would claim the mantle of self-determination while denying its most basic exercise to a captive brethren in their midst. As we remember the Civil War, we do so under the shadows of impenetrable complexity, discomforting contradiction, and an unfathomable toll in lives. While we see liberty betrayed all around—at the whipping post of the plantation, through the destructive force of clashing armies, and in the halls of governments that sanctioned each and sanction such other predations as we know today—when lost, human nature yearns for its recovery, as a few distant words at Gettysburg so plainly attest.

Phillip W. Magness is a policy historian specializing in slavery and economic policy in the 19th century United States, as well as Academic Program Director at the Institute for Humane Studies at George Mason University. He is the coauthor of Colonization after Emancipation: Lincoln and the Movement for Black Resettlement *(University of Missouri Press, 2010) and the text* The Rules of the Game: How Government Works and Why It Sometimes Doesn't *(The Modern Scholar, 2011). He is also a specialist in the black colonization and emigration movements during the Civil War era.*

President Lincoln delivered The Gettysburg Address
in about two minutes and precisely 272 words.

In today's world the equivalent of a commercial break.

I wonder, as a journalist, having had the opportunity
to interview our last five American Presidents,
how Lincoln would be covered today in the age of
teleprompter, TMZ, and TMI?

150 years ago Lincoln was tasked to give meaning and
make moral sense of our country's Civil War
to a war-weary public.

He framed the battle as one of ideals,
challenging the nation to live up to the founding principle
"that all men are created equal."

The immediate media reaction ran the gamut.
The Springfield Republican called the address "a perfect gem."
The Chicago Times declared it "silly, flat and dish-watery utterances."

I am struck by its timeless call to action,
"for us the living...to be dedicated...to the unfinished work."

That "unfinished work" took more than 100 years
and a Civil Rights Movement to end segregation for blacks in 1964,

A TIMELESS CALL TO ACTION

SUZANNE MALVEAUX

President Lincoln delivered the Gettysburg Address in about two minutes and precisely 272 words.

In today's world the equivalent of a commercial break.

I wonder, as a journalist, having had the opportunity to interview our last five American presidents, how Lincoln would be covered today in the age of teleprompters, TMZ, and TMI?

One hundred and fifty years ago Lincoln was tasked to give meaning and make moral sense of our country's Civil War to a war-weary public.

He framed the battles as one of ideals, challenging the nation to live up to the founding principle "that all men are created equal."

The immediate media reaction ran the gamut. The <u>Springfield Republican</u> called the address "a perfect gem." The <u>Chicago Times</u> declared it "silly, flat and dish-watery utterances."

I am struck by its timeless call to action, "for us the living . . . to be dedicated . . . to the unfinished work."

That "unfinished work" took more than 100 years and a Civil Rights Movement to end segregation for blacks in 1964, 57 years for women to be granted the right to vote, and 141 years for the first gay couples to legally marry.

My parents, growing up in segregated Louisiana, were barred from using schools, pools, restrooms, and fountains set aside for whites only.

I, however, have benefitted from their sacrifices, living a life abundant with opportunity—-to be educated at Harvard, honored to cover the White House, blessed to have a family, but cognizant there is still "unfinished work."

If I could interview Lincoln today, I'd ask him about his assertion "that this nation under God shall have a new birth of freedom . . ." Mr. President, how'd you know?

Suzanne Malveaux is an award-winning journalist and CNN's national correspondent, covering politics, national news, international events and culture. Previously, she co-anchored CNN's Around the World. She also co-anchored the network's Emmy-winning coverage of the revolution in Egypt and Peabody Award-winning coverage of the Arab Spring. Malveaux served as White House correspondent for more than ten years—covering Presidents Bill Clinton, George W. Bush, and Barack Obama. In September 2011, Malveaux embedded with U.S. troops in Afghanistan for the 10th anniversary of 9/11 where she led breaking news coverage of the Taliban's terrorist attack on the U.S. Embassy there. She was part of the coverage teams that earned CNN a Peabody Award for its Katrina reporting and a duPont Award for CNN's coverage of the tsunami disaster in Southeast Asia. Malveaux is an Aspen Institute Henry Crown Fellow, an Aspen Global Leadership Network fellow and holds four honorary degrees.

ULYSSES S. GRANT PRESIDENTIAL LIBRARY
ULYSSES S. GRANT ASSOCIATION

Mitchell Memorial Library
Mississippi State University

Since this nation's beginnings, our forefathers have trekked over land and sea to reach refuge on the North American continent.

When they arrived, they did not find those already here greeting them with arms open in welcome. They found themselves disdained, with obstacles placed in their paths. Their purpose was questioned, and their capabilities ridiculed. Those already here viewed the newcomers as threats to the American nation; laws were purposefully passed to try to exclude them.

Despite such seemingly ceaseless and hard travails, these immigrants have kept coming. Their hearts filled with hope, they have populated the cities and the country-sides and, over time, they have overcome. They have become a part of those already here.

The 21st century newcomers are following this same difficult path. Like the earlier travelers, they too want inclusion. Like previous pilgrims, they throw themselves into this great democracy. To come here and to be here is their dream.

All immigrants to America have shared and continue to share the desire for inclusion. They want to hear the whisper of the American dream and sense the throb of

[...] steady passage [...] footsteps [...] land to benefit, [...] more than they [...] this nation [...] today.

It is a never ending course, this refreshment of the promise of American life, the continued new birth of freedom. May this movement of immigrant feet never cease. May the last great hope of mankind survive for ever more.

John F. Marszalek

September 10, 2013

IMMIGRATION TO AMERICA

JOHN F. MARSZALEK

Since this nation's beginnings, our forefathers have trekked over land and sea to reach refuge on the North American continent.

When they arrived, they did not find those already here greeting them with arms open in welcome. They found themselves disdained, with obstacles placed in their paths. Their purpose was questioned, and their capabilities ridiculed. Those already here viewed the newcomers as threats to the American nation; laws were purposely passed to try to exclude them.

Despite such seemingly ceaseless and harsh travails, these immigrants have kept coming. Their hearts filled with hope, they have populated the cities and the countrysides and, over time, they have overcome. They have become a part of those already here.

The 21st-century newcomers are following this same difficult path. Like the earlier travelers, they too want inclusion. Like previous pilgrims, they throw themselves into this great democracy. To come here and to be here is their dream.

All immigrants to America have shared and continue to share the desire for inclusion. They want to hear the whisper of the American dream and sense the throb of its equality. In time with the steady passage of the years, the immigrants' determined footsteps push forward. They come to this land to benefit, but, in the end, they contribute more than they receive. It is they who have made this nation great, and they continue to do so today.

It is a never-ending course, this refreshment of the promise of American life, the continued new birth of freedom. May this movement of immigrant feet never cease. May the last great hope of mankind survive for ever more.

JOHN F. MARSZALEK is Giles Distinguished Professor of History Emeritus and Executive Director and Managing Editor of the Ulysses S. Grant Presidential Library, Mississippi State University. He has published 13 books and more than 300 articles and book reviews on the Civil War, Jacksonian America, and Race Relations. He is best noted for his biography: Sherman, A Soldier's Passion for Order *(Southern Illinois University Press, 2007). He is executive director and managing editor of the Ulysses S. Grant Association, coexecutive director of the Historians of the Civil War Western Theater, and a member of the Board of Advisors of the Lincoln Forum, the Lincoln Prize, and the Lincoln Bicentennial Commission.*

LINCOLN'S WORLD AND GETTYSBURG

In his Gettysburg Address, America's sixteenth president rallied the Union to its best angels. Summarizing America's traditions and the Union war effort in a few uncompromisingly idealistic phrases, Abraham Lincoln posited that Union soldiers died at Gettysburg to perpetuate their nation's promise of human equality.

Clearly, Lincoln played cheerleader, prodding and inspiring countrymen on site and those reading his remarks to stay the course—to bear all necessary sacrifices until Confederates surrendered. No wonder. As he spoke, Union troops remained besieged in Chattanooga and Lee's army was regrouping from its summer's thrashing by Meade. The New York City draft riots were more recent history than the fighting on Gettysburg's Cemetery Ridge.

Yet two of Lincoln's nine sentences struck international themes. Lincoln imagined foreign peoples judging the American conflict and humbly predicted that "the world" would remember the deeds of brave Union soldiers on Gettysburg's fields—not what he and other orators said about it. By arguing that humanity needed America's mixed republican and democratic government ("of the people, by the people, for the people") to persist in the family of nations, his address globalized the war. Even Lincoln's opening sentence, recalling the emergence "on this continent" of a new nation dedicated to liberty and equality implied international contexts. What kinds of governments existed on other continents in 1776?

The Gettysburg Address reminds us that the war of 1861-1865 concerned foreign countries and implies the role of Lincoln's Emancipation Proclamation—freedom's rebirth—in winning foreign approval for the Union cause. Have successor administrations kept the faith? Is today's United States a beacon of liberty? Would Abraham Lincoln be satisfied with America's image abroad?

9/28/2013

DISTINGUISH *yourself*

LINCOLN'S WORLD AND GETTYSBURG

ROBERT E. MAY

In his Gettysburg address, America's sixteenth president rallied the Union to its best angels. Summarizing America's traditions and the Union war effort in a few uncompromisingly idealistic phrases. Abraham Lincoln posited that Union soldiers died at Gettysburg to perpetuate their nation's promise of human equality.

Clearly, Lincoln played cheerleader, prodding and inspiring countrymen on site and those reading his remarks to stay the course—to bear all necessary sacrifices until Confederates surrendered. No wonder. As he spoke, Union troops remained besieged in Chattanooga and Lee's army was regrouping from its summer thrashing by Meade. The New York City draft riots were more recent history than the fighting on Gettysburg's Cemetery Ridge.

Yet two of Lincoln's nine sentences struck international themes. Lincoln imagined foreign peoples judging the American conflict and humbly predicted that "the world" would remember the deeds of brave Union soldiers on Gettysburg's fields—not what he and other orators said about it. By arguing that humanity needed America's mixed republican and democratic government ("of the people, by the people, for the people") to persist in the family of nations, his address globalized the war. Even Lincoln's opening sentence, recalling the emergence "on this continent" of a new nation dedicated to liberty and equality implied international contexts. What kinds of government existed on other continents in 1776?

The Gettysburg Address reminds us that the war of 1861–1865 concerned foreign countries and implies the role of Lincoln's Emancipation Proclamation—freedom's rebirth—in winning foreign approval for the Union cause. Have successor administrations kept the faith? Is today's United States a beacon of liberty? Would Abraham Lincoln be satisfied with America's image abroad?

ROBERT E. MAY is a Professor of History at Purdue University. He is the author of four books, most recently Slavery, Race, and Conquest in the Tropics: Lincoln, Douglas, and the Future of Latin America *(Cambridge University Press, 2013), which was a finalist selection for the 2014 Gilder-Lehrman Lincoln Prize. He is also the editor of* The Union, the Confederacy, and the Atlantic Rim *(University Press of Florida, 2013) and the author of articles in many journals including* Civil War History, North and South, *and* Lincoln Lore. *His side interest is U.S. art history, and he has coauthored* Howard Pyle: Imagining an American School of Art *(University of Illinois Press, 2011) with his wife Jill P. May.*

August 26, 2013

Matthew H. MEAD
Governor
of
Wyoming

150 Anniversary
of the
Gettysburg Address

When Lincoln spoke at Gettysburg, the battlefield lay before him. The wounds opened by the Civil War were raw. The graves were fresh. The war was not over. Looking over that Pennsylvania field and contemplating the loss, Lincoln gave the speech of a lifetime — perhaps the greatest speech in America's history.

The Gettysburg Address was written in the way the best speeches always are — from the head and from the heart. It showed depth of thought and emotion. Although Lincoln wrote that his words would soon be forgotten, they have not been. When we read the Address today, it still moves us, bringing tears to our eyes and sadness to our souls for the thousands who fell during the three day battle at Gettysburg.

Soldiers have fought for America throughout our Nation's history. Many have died fighting or come home injured in body or spirit.

[...] day's battlefields [...]y. We may [...]s of distant [...] with hidden [...]eacherous places [...]iends may actually [...]d our soldiers [...]dom, but the [...] of sight.

[...] different eras, [...] constant. Now [...] the 150th [...]sburg Address, we are reminded that those who make sacrifices to keep America strong — the men and women in our armed forces — must be ever in our prayers. God Bless them.

Governor
of
Wyoming

150TH ANNIVERSARY OF THE GETTYSBURG ADDRESS

Matthew H. Mead

When Lincoln spoke at Gettysburg, the battlefield lay before him. The wounds opened by the Civil War were raw. The graves were fresh. The war was not over. Looking over that Pennsylvania field and contemplating the loss, Lincoln gave the speech of a lifetime—perhaps the greatest speech in America's history.

The Gettysburg Address was written in the way the best speeches always are—from the head and from the heart. It showed depth of thought and emotion. Although Lincoln wrote that his words would soon be forgotten, they have not been. When we read the Address today, it still moves us, bringing tears to our eyes and sadness to our souls for the thousands who fell during the three day battle at Gettysburg.

Soldiers have fought for America throughout our nation's history. Many have died fighting or come home injured in body or spirit.

Unlike in Lincoln's time, today's battlefields are often half a world away. We may imagine the rugged mountains of distant lands, the barren turf filled with hidden dangers, and the perils of treacherous places where persons thought to be friends may actually be foes. We may imagine what our soldiers go through to protect our freedom, but the battlefields are far away, out of sight.

The years 2013 and 1863 are different eras, centuries apart, yet there is a constant. Now as then, freedom has a cost. On the 150th commemoration of the Gettysburg Address, we are reminded that those who make sacrifices to keep America strong—the men and women in our armed forces—must be ever in our prayers. God bless them.

—◆—

Matthew H. Mead is the 32nd Governor of the State of Wyoming. He took the oath of office on January 3, 2011. In addition to his leadership at the state level, he serves on the Council of Governors, the U.S. Homeland Security Advisory Council, and the Natural Resources Committee of the National Governors Association and is cochair of the State and Federal Sage Grouse Task Force, which brings together federal officials and representatives of 11 western states for a regional conservation effort. Prior to becoming the state's chief executive, Mead served as a county and federal prosecutor, practiced in a private firm, and was appointed by President George W. Bush as United States Attorney for Wyoming, serving from October 2001 to June 2007.

In this sour season of division and disillusionment, Lincoln's example matters more than ever. Americans need inspiration from his up-from-the-bottom rise, but must also learn lessons from his means of ascent. Lincoln reached the pinnacle of power through his two great loves: politics and prose.

He spent his entire adult life as a proud, practicing politician. Unlike his common modern counterparts, he didn't go from a legal career to public office; he only earned his law license five years after his first run for the Illinois legislature (at age 23). To him, the process of vote-seeking and coalition-building counted as ennobling, not demeaning. He also unashamedly embraced partisanship, remaining one of the last of the loyal Whigs until the party he had always cherished suffered complete collapse in the 1850's.

By that time Lincoln had become a national figure not through achievements or electoral victories (there were few of those) but through the force of his words. His love of language shines through even the earliest letters and transcriptions of stump speeches and debates. Consider his spectacularly wrong prediction in the Gettysburg Address: "The world will little note, nor long remember what we say here, but it cannot forget what they did here." The words resonate with the music of poetry; they count as not only memorable, but easy to memorize.

If our culture could follow Lincoln in exalting, rather than shunning, the grubby business of practical politics; if more of our leaders learned to deploy prose with the precision and dignity of the Emancipator, then we might yet enjoy an American revival and perhaps, even, a new birth of freedom.

Michael Medved

LEARNING FROM LINCOLN
MICHAEL MEDVED

In this sour season of division and disillusionment, Lincoln's example matters more than ever. Americans need inspiration from his up-from-the-bottom rise, but must also learn lessons from his means of ascent. Lincoln reached the pinnacle of power through his two great loves: politics and prose.

He spent his entire adult life as a proud, practicing politician. Unlike his common modern counterparts, he didn't go from a legal career to public office; he only earned his law license five years after his first run for the Illinois legislature (at age 23). To him, the process of vote-seeking and coalition-building counted as ennobling, not demeaning. He also unashamedly embraced partisanship, remaining one of the last of the loyal Whigs until the party he had always cherished suffered complete collapse in the 1850s.

By that time Lincoln had become a national figure not through achievements or electoral victories (there were few of those) but through the force of his words. His love of language shines through even the earliest letters and transcriptions of stump speeches and debates. Consider his spectacularly wrong prediction in the Gettysburg Address: "The world will little note, nor long remember what we say here, but it cannot forget what they did here." The words resonate with the music of poetry; they count as not only memorable, but easy to memorize.

If our culture could follow Lincoln in exalting, rather than shunning, the grubby business of practical politics; if more of our leaders learned to deploy prose with the precision and dignity of the Emancipator, then we might yet enjoy an American revival and perhaps, even, a new birth of freedom.

—◦—

MICHAEL MEDVED is a nationally syndicated radio talk show host and bestselling author on everything from politics to feature films. The Michael Medved Show, *his daily three-hour show, reaches 200 stations across the United States and has an audience of 4.7 million listeners placing him, for ten years in a row, on the* Talkers Magazine *list of the top ten political talk shows in the United States. Former cohost of the syndicated film review show,* Sneak Previews, *Medved was also chief film critic for the* New York Post *and is a frequent contributor to the* Wall Street Journal, *the* Daily Beast, *and* USA Today. *The author of twelve books, his first,* What Really Happened to the Class of '65 *(Random House, 1976) was a bestseller.*

The log cabin of Lincoln's youth reminds me of my own childhood home in South Africa, which was one room, divided in half by a curtain for privacy. Ironically, that was the very best of times for our family. We did everything together, and it was where I learned about the history of our country.

Our father, Scelo Mhlauli, always spoke with reverence and gratitude about the leaders of our African National Congress freedom movement, and their work to overthrow apartheid. When I was six years old, my parents traveled to Johannesburg for a rally, trusting me with where and why they were going, even though they knew their lives were in danger. I felt I was a part of something much bigger than myself. Had I said so much as a single word about their journey to my friend, who's father was a policeman for the apartheid government, my parents could have been assassinated. Years later, my father and three of his comrades were indeed murdered by the oppressor's regime.

When I was 19, I asked the South African Truth and Reconciliation Commission to let me testify about my experience. It was broadcast worldwide, made headline news in the oppressor's newspaper, and referenced in many books, including one by Hillary Clinton, and Archibishop Desmond Tutu's, "No Future Without Forgiveness," a little inspired by my testimony. The greatest honor was Nelson Mandela

Cradock, ther and ing, "The death of these gallant freedom fighters marked a turning point in the history of our struggle. They were the true heroes..."

Babalwa Mhlauli

TRANSITION IN SOUTH AFRICA

BABALWA MHLAULI

The log cabin of Lincoln's youth reminds me of my own childhood home in South Africa, which was one room, divided in half by a curtain for privacy. Ironically, that was the very best of times for our family. We did everything together, and it was where I learned about the history of our country.

Our father, Scelo Mhlauli, always spoke with reverence and gratitude about the leaders of our African National Congress freedom movement, and their work to overthrow apartheid. When I was six years old, my parents traveled to Johannesburg for a rally, trusting me with where and why they were going, even though they knew their lives were in danger. I felt I was a part of something much bigger than myself. Had I said so much as a single word about their journey to my friend, whose father was a policeman for the apartheid government, my parents could have been assassinated. Years later, my father and three of his comrades were indeed murdered by the oppressor's regime.

When I was 19, I asked the South African Truth and Reconciliation Commission to let me testify about my experience. It was broadcast worldwide, made headline news in the oppressor's newspaper, and referenced in many books, including one by Hillary Clinton, and Archbishop Desmond Tutu's "No Future without Forgiveness," a title inspired by my testimony. The greatest honor was Nelson Mandela coming to our hometown of Cradock, to pay tribute to my late father and his martyred comrades, stating, "The death of these gallant freedom fighters marked a turning point in the history of our struggle. They were true heroes . . ."

BABALWA MHLAULI is an artist and poet. She is a native South African currently residing on the West Cape. Her father, activist Scelo Mhlauli, was one of the group dubbed the Cradock Four, all of whom were assassinated for their outspoken antiapartheid views.

Babalwa Mhlauli was nine years old at the time of her father's assassination, and a decade later, she became the youngest person ever to testify before the South African Truth and Reconciliation Commission. Archbishop Desmond Tutu and South African Presidents Nelson Mandela and Jacob Zuma each paid tribute to her father and she in turn pays tribute to him and other civil rights activists through her paintings, the subjects of which have included Abraham Lincoln and his stovepipe hat.

At a Springfield church Lincoln said alcohol abusers' neighbors should offer help rather than condemnation, and that abstainers are no better than alcoholics.

Today righteous drug warriors encourage fear about drugs. Sufficient panic will destroy civil liberties that impede authoritarians from implementing a broader agenda of social control, one determining who we may love and how to love them, whether we may or must pray to a deity. War on drugs masks war on democracy.

Some authoritarians seek to rule. Many more simply yearn to be followers because, as Lincoln taught, democracy involves accepting personal responsibility for what goes wrong, as well as what goes right. Many citizens welcome politicians willing to lift that burden and to regiment us. Followers who never reach far enough to touch walls of their cage will feel free.

Change is inherent to life. Only death brings stillness. Even morality changes. To demand that everyone, for all time, accept one person's concept of morality is to call forth the forces of death. It is no coincidence that moral zealots kill people.

Lincoln used democracy to deal with change rather than avoid it. Democracy celebrates life. Democracy promotes adventure by questioning cherished notions. Democracy is a universal antidote to problems, a single solution but not a simple one, a solution as rich and complex as life itself.

The approaching future is unnerving. Survival, let alone prosperity, is not assured. Nonetheless, if we welcome the future as an opportunity to once again test our nation's ideals of democracy, rather than abandon them, they will see us through. If we are faithful to them, they will be faithful to us.

Richard Lawrence Miller
September 10, 2013

DEMOCRACY PERSISTS

RICHARD LAWRENCE MILLER

At a Springfield church Lincoln said alcohol abusers' neighbors should offer help rather than condemnation, and that abstainers are no better than alcoholics.

Today righteous drug warriors encourage fear about drugs. Sufficient panic will destroy civil liberties that impede authoritarians from implementing a broader agenda of social control, one determining who we may love and how to love them, whether we may or must pray to a deity. War on drugs masks war on democracy.

Some authoritarians seek to rule. Many more simply yearn to be followers because, as Lincoln taught, democracy involves accepting personal responsibility for what goes wrong, as well as what goes right. Many citizens welcome politicians willing to lift that burden and to regiment us. Followers who never reach far enough to touch walls of their cage will feel free.

Change is inherent to life. Only death brings stillness. Even morality changes. To demand that everyone, for all time, accept one person's concept of morality is to call forth the forces of death. It is no coincidence that moral zealots kill people.

Lincoln used democracy to deal with change rather than avoid it. Democracy celebrates life. Democracy promotes adventure by questioning cherished notions. Democracy is a universal antidote to problems, a single solution but not a simple one, a solution as rich and complex as life itself.

The approaching future is unnerving. Survival, let alone prosperity, is not assured. Nonetheless, if we welcome the future as an opportunity to once again test our nation's ideals of democracy, rather than abandon them, they will see us through. If we are faithful to them, they will be faithful to us.

RICHARD LAWRENCE MILLER is a historian and author of several books. He chose to be an independent scholar, without any university affiliation.

Having the freedom to study any subject, in 1990 he began researching Lincoln's prepresidential years resulting in Miller's four-volume series, Lincoln and His World. *Volumes from the series were published in 2006, 2008, 2011, and 2012. Active in public affairs, Miller is a recognized authority on addictive drugs and on policy about their control.*

Two score and six years after the death of Abraham Lincoln, he was first portrayed in the brand-new medium of film. 102 years and over 300 films later, Lincoln has appeared on screen more than any other historical figure and more than any other character except for Sherlock Holmes. In 2013 alone there were three feature films about Abraham Lincoln, one with an Oscar-winning performance by Daniel Day-Lewis, directed by Steven Spielberg. In another one, he was a vampire slayer. He has been portrayed by Henry Fonda (John Ford's "Young Mr. Lincoln"), Raymond Massey ("Abe Lincoln in Illinois"), Walter Huston (D.W. Griffith's "Abraham Lincoln"), and Bing Crosby - in blackface ("Holiday Inn"). The movies have shown us Lincoln defending clients, mourning Ann Rutledge, courting Mary Todd, and serving as President. We have also seen him traveling through time with a couple of California teenagers in "Bill and Ted's Excellent Adventure" and granting amnesty to Shirley Temple's Confederate family in "The Littlest Rebel."

Lincoln is appealingly iconic as a movie character, instantly recognizable as a symbol of America's most cherished notion of ourselves: unpretentious but aspiring for a better world and able to find both the humor and integrity in troubled times. In every

[...] d most
[...]. The
[...]ntial in the
[...]

[...]us outdoors
on a frozen January 1 to view the Emancipation Proclamation on its 150th anniversary. When I saw it, I wept. A security guard whispered, "I know how you feel."

Nell Minow
September 24, 2013
McLean, Virginia

VISIONS OF LINCOLN: A CENTURY ON SCREEN

NELL MINOW

Two score and six years after the death of Abraham Lincoln, he was first portrayed in the brand new medium of film. One hundred and two years and over three hundred films later, Lincoln has appeared on screen more than any other historical figure and more than any other character except for Sherlock Holmes. In 2013 alone there were three feature films about Abraham Lincoln, one with an Oscar-winning performance by Daniel Day-Lewis, directed by Steven Spielberg. In another one, he was a vampire slayer. He has been portrayed by Henry Fonda (John Ford's "Young Mr. Lincoln"), Raymond Massey ("Abe Lincoln in Illinois"), Walter Huston (D.W. Griffith's "Abraham Lincoln"), and Bing Crosby—in black face ("Holiday Inn"). The movies have shown us Lincoln defending clients, mourning Ann Rutledge, courting Mary Todd, and serving as President. We have also seen him traveling through time with a couple of California teenagers in "Bill and Ted's Excellent Adventure" and granting amnesty to Shirley Temple's Confederate family in "The Littlest Rebel."

Lincoln is appealingly iconic as a movie character, instantly recognizable as a symbol of America's most cherished notion of ourselves: unpretentious but aspiring for a better world and able to find both the humor and integrity in troubled times. In every film appearance, even the silliest and most outlandish, he reminds us, as he did in the Gettysburg Address, of what is most essential in the American character, the search for justice.

P.S. My husband and I waited for two hours outdoors in a frozen January to view The Emancipation Proclamation on its 150th anniversary. When I saw it, I wept. A security guard whispered, "I know how you feel."

NELL MINOW is a writer specializing in corporate governance, movies, and culture. She is the former editor, chair, and cofounder of The Corporate Library (later GMI Ratings) and has been published in the Wall Street Journal, *the* Chicago Tribune, *the* New York Times, *and* USA Today. *Minow is the author of several books including* The Movie Mom's Guide to Family Movies *(iUniverse, Inc., 2d ed., 2004),* 101 Must-See Movie Moments *(Miniver Press, 2013), and the* 50 Must-See Movies *series of e-books.*

NEWTON N. MINOW

June 25, 2013

If Abraham Lincoln gave his Gettysburg Address today, he would look into a crowd checking its email, updating Facebook, texting on iPhones and iPads and tweeting with the hashtag #g-address# more talk from Lincoln. Most people in the immediate audience would not be paying full attention, and they would miss one of the great messages in American History. Ironically, at the same time, men, women and children throughout the world would see and hear Lincoln through radio, television, streaming the internet, cable, satellites, and Google. A paradox of our time.

Lincoln redefined American ideals of freedom and equality. His dedication to the "unfinished work" of seeking justice set a goal we are still trying to achieve seven score and ten years later.

2

... Gettysburg ... in the Declaration ... men are created ... re hundred and ... e with disabilities, ... statement ... big strides, but we ... in Lincoln's words ... am "that this ... g freedom, and that ... and for the people

... Access to ... r Human History. But we have less understanding. The power of the Gettysburg Address reminds us that we have so much more to learn and that we should listen more carefully to each other.

Newton N. Minow
June 25, 2013

MORE INFORMATION, LESS UNDERSTANDING

Newton N. Minow

If Abraham Lincoln gave his Gettysburg Address today, he would look into a crowd checking its email, updating Facebook, texting on iPhones and iPads, and tweeting with the hashtag #g-address# more talk from Lincoln. Most people in the immediate audience would not be paying full attention, and they would miss one of the great messages in American History. Ironically, at the same time, men, women, and children throughout the world could see and hear Lincoln through radio, television, streaming the internet, cable, satellites, and Google. A paradox of our time.

Lincoln redefined American ideals of freedom and equality. His dedication to the "unfinished work" of seeking justice set a goal we are still trying to achieve seven score and ten years later.

What Lincoln gave us at Gettysburg was his vision of equality. Jefferson, in the Declaration of Independence, wrote that "all men are created equal." But in the past one hundred and fifty years, women, blacks, people with disabilities, gays, and lesbians all argued that statement includes all people. We've made big strides, but we have not yet fully succeeded. Abraham Lincoln's words continue to inspire us with his dream "that this nation shall have a new birth of freedom, and that government of the people, by the people, and for the people shall not perish from the earth."

Today's technology gives us access to more information than ever before in human history. But we have less understanding. The power of the Gettysburg Address reminds us that we have so much more to learn and that we should listen more carefully to each other.

Newton N. Minow is Senior Counsel to the law firm of Sidley Austin LLP. His career includes service as Law Clerk to U.S. Supreme Court Chief Justice Fred M. Vinson and Assistant Counsel to Governor Adlai E. Stevenson. In 1961, President John F. Kennedy appointed him Chairman of the Federal Communications Commission. He served in the Kennedy Administration until 1963 when he became Executive Vice President and General Counsel of Encyclopaedia Britannica, Inc. In 1965, he joined the law firm of Leibman, Williams, Bennett, Baird & Minow, which merged with Sidley & Austin in 1972 where he remained a partner until 1991. Minow has been a director of many companies and is trustee emeritus of the Mayo Clinic and a life trustee of Northwestern University and the University of Notre Dame. A World War II veteran, Minow was a U.S. Army Sergeant in the China-Burma-India Theater. He is the author of five books and has written numerous magazine articles.

THE WHITE HOUSE

WASHINGTON

In the evening, when Michelle and the girls have gone to bed, I sometimes walk down the hall to a room Abraham Lincoln used as his office. It contains an original copy of the Gettysburg Address, written in Lincoln's own hand.

I linger on these few words that have helped define our American experiment: "a new nation, conceived in liberty, and dedicated to the proposition that all men are created equal."

Through the lines of weariness etched in his face, we know Lincoln grasped, perhaps more than anyone, the burdens required to give these words meaning. He knew that even a self evident truth was not self executing; that blood drawn by the lash was an affront to our ideals; that blood drawn by the sword was in painful service to those same ideals.

He understood as well that our humble efforts, our individual ambitions, are ultimately not what matter; rather, it is through the accumulated toil and sacrifice of ordinary men and women — those like the soldiers who consecrated that battlefield — that this country is built, and freedom preserved. This quintessentially self made man, fierce in his belief in honest work and the striving spirit at the heart of America, believed that it falls to each generation, collectively, to share in that toil and sacrifice.

Through cold war and world war, through industrial revolutions and technological transformations, through movements for civil rights and women's rights and workers rights and gay rights, we have. At times, social and economic change have strained our union. But Lincoln's words give us confidence that whatever trials await us, this nation and the freedoms we cherish can, and shall, prevail.

REPLY

President Barack H. Obama

In the evening, when Michelle and the girls have gone to bed, I sometimes walk down the hall to a room Abraham Lincoln used as his office. It contains an original copy of the Gettysburg Address, written in Lincoln's own hand.

I linger on these few words that have helped define our American experiment: "a new nation, conceived in liberty, and dedicated to the proposition that all men are created equal."

Through the lines of weariness etched in his face, we know Lincoln grasped, perhaps more than anyone, the burdens required to give these words meaning. He knew that even a self-evident truth was not self-executing; that blood drawn by the lash was an affront to our ideals; that blood drawn by the sword was in painful service to those same ideals.

He understood as well that our humble efforts, our individual ambitions, are ultimately not what matter; rather it is through the accumulated toil and sacrifice of ordinary men and women—those like the soldiers who consecrated that battlefield—that this country is built, and freedom preserved. This quintessentially self-made man, fierce in his belief in honest work and the driving spirit at the heart of America, believed that it falls to each generation, collectively, to share in that toil and sacrifice.

Through cold war and world war, through industrial revolutions and technological transformations, through movements for civil rights and women's rights and worker's rights and gay rights, we have. At times, social and economic change have strained our union. But Lincoln's words give us confidence that whatever trials await us, this nation and the freedoms we cherish can, and shall, prevail.

Barack H. Obama is the 44th President of the United States and the first African American to be elected to the office. He is the 2009 recipient of the Nobel Peace Prize. The product of a middleclass upbringing, Obama worked his way through college with the help of scholarships and student loans. Upon graduation, he moved to Chicago, where he worked with a group of churches to rebuild communities devastated by the closure of local steel plants. Obama went on to attend Harvard Law School, where he served as editor of the Harvard Law Review, *eventually becoming the first African-American president of the publication. Upon graduation, he returned to Chicago to help lead a voter registration drive, teach constitutional law at the University of Chicago, and remain active in his community. He was elected to the Illinois State Senate in 1996 and the U.S. Senate in 2004 representing the state of Illinois. He was elected to the presidency in 2008 and to a second term in 2012. During his presidency, among other things, the President signed the Affordable Care Act for healthcare reform and shepherded the nation through the Sandy Hook Elementary School and Boston Marathon tragedies. The author of three books, his second,* The Audacity of Hope: Thoughts on Reclaiming the American Dream *(Crown Publishers, 2006) reached the top of the* New York Times *list of bestsellers.*

Leadership can be very difficult and the most rewarding experience. When you stand up for what you believe in, you ruffle some feathers. Today a country, we can't seem to agree on anything - it's Republicans versus Democrats, business versus government, and state versus state. We think our problems are just too big and nothing can be done. We can't make everyone happy with each critical decision, so instead, we do nothing. But sometimes we need to step back and look how far we've come. We need to look back at a leader whose situation

unmountable. truly divided years ago. at war battling for at our very freedom. today Lincoln stood right. At the country hated to violently that they lines on the line to fight against what he believed. But he was steadfast. Today he is one of the most beloved leaders in our country's history - he's certainly my favorite here in Illinois.

I'd like all what leadership and dream. Stand up We need make the with make but we can We can continue to build on Lincoln's legacy and make our state and country great for years to come.

Doug Oberhelman

BUILDING ON LINCOLN'S LEGACY

DOUGLAS R. OBERHELMAN

Leadership can be very difficult and the most rewarding experience.

When you stand up for what you believe in, you ruffle some feathers. Today as a country, we can't seem to agree on anything—it's Republicans versus Democrats, business versus government, and state versus state. We think our problems are just too big and nothing can be done. We can't make everyone happy with each critical decision, so instead we do nothing. But sometimes we need to step back and look how far we've come. We need to look back at a leader whose situation had to seem insurmountable.

Our country was truly divided one hundred and fifty years ago. We were literally at war with each other and battling for something that is at our very core as Americans—freedom. We are a great country today because President Lincoln stood up for what's right. At the time, half the country hated him. Half the country so violently disagreed with him, that they literally put their lives on the line to fight against what he believed. But he was steadfast. Today he is one of the most beloved leaders in our country's history—he's certainly my favorite here in Illinois.

Today, in 2013, I'd like all leaders to remember what President Lincoln's leadership provided all Americans and what other countries dream about. Be brave. Stand up for what's right. We need leaders who can make the tough decisions with integrity. We can't make everyone happy, but we can make a difference. We can continue to build on Lincoln's legacy and make our state and country great for years to come.

DOUGLAS R. OBERHELMAN is chairman of the Board of Directors and chief executive officer of Caterpillar Inc. He was named vice chairman and CEO-elect in October 2009 and immediately began to develop the company's future strategic plan. Since becoming CEO and chairman, he has led the successful implementation of that plan. Oberhelman joined Caterpillar in 1975 and, since then, has worked in or led a wide variety of businesses across the company in North and South America and Asia. He serves on the Board of Directors of Eli Lilly and Company and is chairman of the National Association of Manufacturers, vice chairman of The Business Council, and chairman of the Business Roundtable's International Engagement Committee where he serves on its executive committee. Additionally, he is a member of The Nature Conservancy's Latin America Conservation Council, vice president of the Wetlands America Trust, and chairman of the Board of Trustees for the Easter Seals Foundation of Central Illinois.

Abraham Lincoln and the vital importance
of Civic Education

A great man once wrote that, in his view,
education is "the most important subject which we as
a people can be engaged in." [1] He went on to designate
as "an object of vital importance" that "every man
may receive at least a moderate education, and
thereby be enabled to read the history of his own and
other countries, by which he may duly appreciate
the value of our free institutions." [2] That great
man was Abraham Lincoln. He was not yet the
magnificent President that we celebrate today.
Indeed, he was just a 23-year-old clerk in a
small town in Illinois. It was his first
noteworthy public meeting in his first campaign
for political office, a race that he would lose.

I once wrote that "no speaker can find words
to compete with those spoken by Abraham Lincoln
at Gettysburg." [3] To this day, the Gettysburg address

... is Lincoln's
... read so early
... home. In those
... and brilliance
... civic education
... Court I have
... the decline of
... schools. I
... in education,
... such array of
... and video
... a website
called iCivics. You can find the website as
www.icivics.org. Please join me in this effort
to restore civic education to its rightful place.
It is an object of vital importance.

Sandra Day O'Connor
8/21/2013

ABRAHAM LINCOLN AND THE VITAL IMPORTANCE OF CIVIC EDUCATION

SANDRA DAY O'CONNOR

A great man once wrote that, in his view, education is "the most important subject which we as a people can be engaged in." He went on to designate as "an object of vital importance" that "every man may receive at least, a moderate education, and thereby be enabled to read the histories of his own and other countries, by which he may duly appreciate the value of our free institutions." That great man was Abraham Lincoln. He was not yet the magnificent President that we celebrate today. Indeed, he was just a 23-year-old clerk in a small town in Illinois. It was his first noteworthy public writing in his first campaign for political office, a race that he would lose.

I once wrote that "no speaker can find words to compete with those spoken by Abraham Lincoln at Gettysburg." To this day, the Gettysburg Address renders me speechless. But it is Lincoln's first public words of note composed so early in life that now hit closest to home. In those words, Lincoln captured with trademark brilliance and succinctness how critical civic education is to our nation.

Since retiring from the Supreme Court, I have made it my goal to help reverse the decline of civic education in our nation's schools. I have been working with experts in education, law, and technology to develop a rich array of curriculum units, lesson plans, and video games for students and teachers on a website called iCivics. You can find the website at www.icivics.org. Please join me in this effort to restore civic education to its rightful place. It is an object of vital importance.

SANDRA DAY O'CONNOR is the first woman appointed to the United States Supreme Court. A graduate of Stanford Law School, where she served on the Stanford Law Review, she chose a life of public service as Arizona Assistant Attorney General followed by an appointment to the Arizona State Senate, becoming the first woman in the United States to serve as a state majority leader. She next was elected as superior court judge and then to the Arizona Court of Appeals. In 1981, she was appointed by President Ronald Reagan to the United States Supreme Court on which she served as an associate justice for 25 years. After her retirement, O'Connor continued her judicial service hearing cases in the U.S. Courts of Appeals. Later that year, she was named the first recipient of the Abraham Lincoln Presidential Library Foundation's Lincoln Leadership Prize and in 2009, President Barack Obama presented her the Presidential Medal of Freedom. Justice O'Connor has authored several books, including a memoir Lazy B: Growing up on a Cattle Ranch in the Southwest *(Random House, 2002) and the* New York Times *bestseller* Out of Order: Stories from the History of the Supreme Court *(Random House, 2013).*

Proud Disciples

Daily in Washington DC I am surrounded by the American dream. There are those who say it is fading and in peril. Others choose to roil the waters to create rancor & division, but every day the ideas fought for on the hallowed ground of Gettysburg still manifest themselves— the young Colombian whose father was kidnapped by FARC guerillas, who came here,

2

put himself through school and today runs a thriving restaurant & catering business. The once penniless Turkish hairdressers who arrived without knowing English who now cut and color famous heads. The hardworking Korean dry cleaners, the Kenyan cab driver whose son is a lawyer and whose daughter is a professor.

They tell me their stories & I like to listen. It warms me to hear them sometimes say, that by watching my late husband, Tim Russert, on television, "I learned politics,

3

...ed how to be a ...he more pleasing ...to communicate ...that he had taught ...zenship from others. ...Corps I learned that ...a monopoly in ...d in the world, but ...ers we enrich our— ...n lead by example. ...mass card ring

4

...the human ...to help someone ...coln fought for ...ves like to the marble of his magnificent monument.

Maureen Orth

Washington D.C.   November 24, 2014

PROUD DISCIPLES

MAUREEN ORTH

Daily in Washington DC I am surrounded by the American dream. There are those who say it is fading and in peril. Others choose to roil the waters to create rancor & division, but every day the ideas fought for on the hallowed ground of Gettysburg still manifest themselves—the young Colombian whose father was kidnapped by FARC guerillas, who came here, put himself through school and today runs a thriving restaurant & catering business; the once penniless Turkish hairdressers who arrived without knowing English who now cut and color famous heads; the hardworking Korean dry cleaners, the Kenyan cab driver whose son is a lawyer and daughter a professor.

They tell me their stories & I love to listen. It warms me to hear them sometimes say, that by watching my late husband, Tim Russert, on television, "I learned politics, I learned civics, I learned how to be a citizen." What could be more pleasing for someone who chose to communicate for a living than hearing that he had taught citizenship?

And we too learn citizenship from others. While serving in the Peace Corps I learned that we Americans do not have a monopoly on what is right or just or good in the world, but by providing service to others we enrich ourselves enormously. We can lead by example. The words on Tim's funeral mass card ring as true as ever. "The best exercise for the human heart is to reach down to help someone else up."

The wonder that Lincoln fought for is all around us; it gives life to the marble of his magnificent monument.

———

MAUREEN ORTH is a Special Correspondent for Vanity Fair Magazine. *An award-winning journalist, Orth began her career at* Newsweek *in the 1970s, where she wrote cover stories on such music icons as Bob Dylan, Stevie Wonder, and Bruce Springsteen. She has interviewed heads of state such as Russian President Vladimir Putin, British Prime Minister Margaret Thatcher, Argentine President Carlos Menem, Irish President Mary Robinson, and the First Lady of France Carla Bruni. Her investigative work includes pieces on Michael Jackson, Tom Cruise and Scientology, and Woody Allen and Mia Farrow. Orth has been nominated twice for a National Magazine Award, receiving it for group coverage of the arts at* Newsweek. *Her late husband, Tim Russert, was Washington bureau chief of NBC News and moderator of* Meet the Press *and the 2011 recipient of the Abraham Lincoln Presidential Library Foundation's Lincoln Leadership Prize.*

What do we owe the past? What do we offer those who gave their bones and their blood to build America?

This was the first country to believe people from the four corners of the Earth — people who spoke different languages, people who prayed to God in different ways — could come together & build a nation. Partnerships forged here between those who might have warred elsewhere would not only strengthen the new nation, but might help ease the discord on other soil. In a world where people from different backgrounds were too often at one another's throats, America would exemplify pluralism.

Nothing about America was ever inevitable, it was all painstakingly built — built by poets and presidents, by slaves and immigrants, by nobles and vagrants. Our inheritance, America, is an unfinished masterpiece.

October 11, 2013.

Chicago

AN UNFINISHED MASTERPIECE
EBOO PATEL

What do we owe the past? What do we offer those who gave their bones and their blood to build America?

This was the first country to believe people from the four corners of the earth—people who spoke different languages, people who prayed to God in different ways—could come together and build a nation. Partnerships forged here between those who might have warred elsewhere would not only strengthen the new nation, but might help ease discord on other soil. In a world where people from different backgrounds were too often at one another's throats, America would exemplify pluralism.

Wherever your ship sailed from, the Statue of Liberty would guide you into harbor, Woody Guthrie and Walt Whitman would sing you a welcome, Martin Luther King Jr., would fight for your rights, Jane Addams would build spaces that respected your identity and cultivated your humanity. Behind it all, Abraham Lincoln would gravely say: I knew it would never be easy, but I believed it could be done.

Nothing about America was ever inevitable, it was all painstakingly built—built by poets and presidents, by slaves and immigrants, by nobles and vagrants. Our inheritance, America, is an unfinished masterpiece.

America, like no other nation, allows you to participate in its progress, carve a place in its promise, play a role in its possibilities. This is both a privilege for Americans, and a necessity for the nation. A government of the people, by the people, and for the people requires people who commit and contribute to the health of the whole. People who aspire to the high office of citizen.

EBOO PATEL *is the Founder and President of Interfaith Youth Core, a Chicago-based organization building the interfaith movement on college campuses. Named by* US News & World Report *as one of America's Best Leaders of 2009, Patel is author of the book* Acts of Faith: The Story of an American Muslim, the Struggle for the Soul of a Generation *(2007), which won the Louisville Grawemeyer Award in Religion,* Sacred Ground: Pluralism, Prejudice, and the Promise of America *(2012), and the forthcoming book* Interfaith Leadership: A Primer. *Patel is a regular contributor to the* Washington Post, USA Today, Huffington Post, *NPR, and CNN. He served on President Barack Obama's inaugural Advisory Council of the White House Office of Faith-based and Neighborhood Partnerships. He holds a doctorate in the sociology of religion from Oxford University, where he studied on a Rhodes scholarship.*

September 22, 2013

Dear Mr. Lincoln,

In 1912, after overthrowing the Qing dynasty in China, Sun Yat-sen developed a political philosophy for his new nation. Sun later acknowledged that "The Three Principles of the People correspond with the principles stated by President Lincoln – government of the people, by the people, for the people."

As World War II came to a close those looking to rebuild their nations again found inspiration in your words. From Bulgaria to Brazil to San Marino, politicians and world leaders pointed their nations towards the ideal you had established a century earlier: government of, by, and for the people.

In 1958, France formally incorporated your words into its constitution, noting "Son principe est: gouvernement du peuple, par le peuple, et pour le peuple." Quite a turnaround from your day when they considered allying with the Confederacy!

Our own country has also changed, Mr. Lincoln. Though it took nearly a hundred years we finally came to grips with your message: that a democracy could only persist with equality at its core, and for the last half-century we have moved

[...] you honored that day

Did you know when you wrote "a few appropriate remarks" to be delivered at Gettysburg that the speech would become, in Dwight Eisenhower's words, "The inspiration for movements toward free and responsible government the world over?" We have "long remembered" your words, and they have become perhaps the most important in our nation. Maybe in the world. As Giuseppe Garibaldi said, you, and your words, have truly been the "pilot of liberty."

Sincerely,
Jared Peatman

THE LONG SHADOW OF LINCOLN'S GETTYSBURG ADDRESS

Jared Peatman

Dear Mr. Lincoln,

In 1912, after overthrowing the Qing dynasty in China, Sun Yat-sen developed a political philosophy for his new nation. Sun later acknowledged that "The Three Principles of the People correspond with the principles stated by President Lincoln—government of the people, by the people, for the people."

As World War II came to a close, those looking to rebuild their nations again found inspiration in your words. From Bulgaria to Brazil to San Marino, politicians and world leaders pointed their nations toward the ideal you had established a century earlier: government of, by, and for the people.

In 1958, France formally incorporated your words into its constitution, noting "Son principle est: gouvernement du peuple, par le peuple, et pour le peuple." Quite a turnaround from your day when they considered allying with the Confederacy!

Our own country has also changed, Mr. Lincoln. Though it took nearly a hundred years we finally came to grips with your message: that a democracy could only persist with equality at its core, and for the last half-century we have moved ever closer to a nation worthy of the men you honored that day at Gettysburg.

Did you know when you wrote "a few appropriate remarks" to be delivered at Gettysburg that the speech would become, in Dwight Eisenhower's words, "The inspiration for movements toward free and responsible government the world over?" We have "long remembered" your words, and they have become perhaps the most important in our nation. Maybe in the world. As Giuseppe Garibaldi said, you, and your words, have truly been the "pilot of liberty."

Sincerely,

Jared Peatman

Jared Peatman is director of curriculum for the Lincoln Leadership Institute at Gettysburg and a faculty member at the George Washington University Center for Excellence in Public Leadership. His first book is The Long Shadow of Lincoln's Gettysburg Address *(Southern Illinois University Press,* 2013). *The book was based on an earlier monograph by Peatman for which he was named the 2009 Organization of American Historians/Abraham Lincoln Bicentennial Commission Doctoral Fellow. In 2012, he received the Hay-Nicolay Dissertation Prize for the best work on Abraham Lincoln or the Civil War. Peatman also has written articles on the Boston Port Act of 1774, the role of Daniel Sickles in shaping President Lincoln's early perceptions of the Battle of Gettysburg, and a chapter in* Virginia at War, 1863, *titled "Lincoln acted the clown': Virginia's Newspapers and the Gettysburg Address."*

"In the Throes of Democracy"

Seven score + ten years ago, on a bleak Pennsylvania landscape pockmarked by death + desolation, Abraham Lincoln reforged the nation's creed of popular sovereignty in the crucible of Civil War, pledging Americans' fidelity to human equality in service of liberty. This he urged, + this we have largely done.

In so doing, we have memorialized his words as both national emblem + patriotic boast -- the marvelous fruits of backwoods genius risen to greatness in the world's citadel of hope + opportunity. It is a creed to be inscribed on marble, to be admired + beheld, + invoked didactically throughout the globe.

Yet his words were not a celebration.

His tongue found voice in the throes of democracy, straining to comprehend the catastrophic results of America's revolutionary experiment : the carnage of the world's first democratic war -- a people's conflict spawned by freedom, spurred by righteousness, + sanctioned by the ballot box -- in which volunteers devoted to hearth + home + armored by God threw themselves into the teeth of bayonets + watered battlefields with their blood, dying crushed, pierced, + shattered, in hundreds of thousands, forever mingling broken bones in nameless graves.

American celebrants of popular sovereignty must ask why.

It was not due to the political virtues of the people : wisdom, restraint, + self-sacrifice were in characteristically short supply.

Nor was conflict unavoidable, for the problem was well-known, + the solution judged impracticable.

The true reason is with us still : the tentative, incomplete, + unrealized human commitment to freedom, which binds us equally profoundly today, + calls out insistently, everywhere, for a new birth in service of human dignity.

Abraham A. Peck

November 19, 2013

IN THE THROES OF DEMOCRACY

GRAHAM A. PECK

Seven score and ten years ago, on a bleak Pennsylvania landscape pockmarked by death and desolation, Abraham Lincoln forged the nation's creed of popular sovereignty in the crucible of civil war, pledging Americans' fidelity to human equality in service of liberty. This he urged, and this we have largely done.

In so doing, we have memorialized his words as both national emblem and patriotic boast—the marvelous fruits of backwoods genius risen to greatness in the world's citadel of hope and opportunity. It is a creed to be inscribed on marble, to be admired and beheld, and invoked didactically throughout the world.

Yet his words were not a celebration.

His tongue found voice in the throes of democracy, straining to comprehend the catastrophic results of America's revolutionary experiment: the carnage of the world's first democratic war—a peoples' conflict spawned by freedom, spurred by righteousness, and sanctioned by the ballot box—in which volunteers devoted to hearth and home and armored by God threw themselves into the teeth of bayonets and watered battlefields with their blood, dying crushed, pierced, and shattered, in hundreds of thousands, forever mingling broken bones in nameless graves.

American celebrants of popular sovereignty must ask why.

It was not due to the political virtues of the people: wisdom, restraint, and self-sacrifice were in characteristically short supply.

Nor was conflict unavoidable, for the problem was well-known, and the solution judged impracticable.

The true reason is with us still: the tentative, incomplete, and unrealized human commitment to freedom, which binds us equally profoundly today, and calls out insistently, everywhere, for a new birth in service of human dignity.

<hr />

GRAHAM A. PECK is an associate professor of history at Saint Xavier University in Chicago. Specializing in antebellum American politics, in 2003 he was awarded the Abraham Lincoln Institute's Hay-Nicolay Scholars Prize for his dissertation, "Politics and Ideology in a Free Society: Illinois from Statehood to Civil War." *He has since published three articles on Abraham Lincoln and Stephen A. Douglas in the* Journal of the Abraham Lincoln Association, *and his book manuscript,* Abraham Lincoln, Stephen A. Douglas, and the Coming of the Civil War, *is under contract with the University of Illinois Press. He is a member of the Illinois Abraham Lincoln Bicentennial Commission.*

KEVIN PERAINO

Sept. 20, 2013

Abraham Lincoln is rightly honored as the president who led the nation through a devastating Civil War at home. Yet he is only rarely appreciated for his deft maneuvering on the WORLD STAGE.

The scholar James Randall has observed that when compared to Theodore Roosevelt, a Woodrow Wilson, a Franklin Roosevelt, Lincoln was only minimally involved in international relations. Still the things that Lincoln did do in the global arena ended up being vitally important. As a young congressman, Lincoln challenged President James K. Polk over his conduct of the Mexican War. Once in the Executive Mansion, he reined in his occasionally impetuous secretary of state, William Seward. During the Trent Affair of 1861, Lincoln lured the calls of doves in his cabinet to conciliate the British — a decision that may well have averted a destructive trans-Atlantic war. Perhaps most importantly, Lincoln issued the Emancipation Proclamation, which he viewed at least in part as an appeal to the sympathies of British liberals. Finally, Lincoln and Seward together crafted a ⟶

shrewd and effective policy aimed at the French emperor, Napoleon III. French armies had invaded Mexico at the height of the Civil War, taking advantage of the North American chaos. While Lincoln and Seward ruthlessly prosecuted the war against the Confederate forces at home, they also cleverly placated Napoleon, doing everything in their power to avert French intervention.

We all learn in GRADE SCHOOL that Lincoln had a broad vision for America, which he viewed as the world's "LAST, BEST HOPE." Yet by looking at his presidency through the prism of GLOBAL AFFAIRS, we discover that there is far more to the story.

Kevin Peraino

LINCOLN IN THE WORLD

KEVIN PERAINO

Abraham Lincoln is rightly honored as the president who led the nation through a devastating civil war at home. Yet he is only rarely appreciated for his deft maneuvering on the world stage.

The scholar James Randall has observed that when compared to Theodore Roosevelt, or Woodrow Wilson, or Franklin Roosevelt, Lincoln was only minimally involved in international relations. Still, the things that Lincoln did do in the global arena ended up being vitally important. As a young congressman, Lincoln challenged President James K. Polk over his conduct of the Mexican War. Once in the Executive Mansion, he reined in his occasionally impetuous secretary of state, William Seward. During the Trent Affair of 1861, Lincoln heeded the calls of doves in his cabinet to conciliate the British—a decision that may well have averted a destructive trans-Atlantic war. Perhaps most importantly, Lincoln issued the Emancipation Proclamation, which he viewed at least in part as an appeal to the sympathies of European liberals. Finally, Lincoln and Seward together crafted a shrewd and effective policy aimed at the French emperor Napoleon III. French armies had invaded Mexico at the height of the Civil War, taking advantage of the North American chaos. While Lincoln and Seward ruthlessly prosecuted the war against the Confederate forces at home, they also cleverly placated Napoleon, doing everything in their power to avert French intervention.

We all learn in grade school that Lincoln had a broad vision for America, which he viewed as the world's "last, best hope." Yet by looking at his presidency through the prism of global affairs, we discover that there is far more to the story.

❦

Kevin Peraino is the author of Lincoln in the World: The Making of a Statesman and the Dawn of American Power *(Crown, 2013). He is a veteran foreign correspondent who has reported throughout the world, including Syria, Libya, Yemen, Lebanon, Israel, and Iraq. He has written for the* Wall Street Journal, Newsweek, Foreign Policy, *and other publications, and was a finalist for the Livingston Award for his global-affairs coverage. Peraino is a term member at the Council on Foreign Relations.*

Dickinson

None of Abraham Lincoln's famous words at Gettysburg involved individual names. The president actually went out of his way to avoid mentioning anybody, because he feared "I might do wrong to those I might forget."

Yet people who encountered Lincoln's speech in 1863 could never forget their own friends and family who had already given "the last full measure of devotion." Those grieving Americans knew names. They cherished letters. They saw faces.

It is difficult for us the living to recreate the full power of the Gettysburg Address without experiencing these emotions. We struggle to recall the stories of heroic individuals along with the solemn phrases.

Bayard Wilkeson should be first among these hallowed figures. He was a 19-year-old Union officer whose leg was shattered on the battle's first day. He conducted his own amputation, according to eye-witnesses and later died from the shock. His father, Samuel, a correspondent for the New York Times, was present on the battlefield. After Sam Wilkeson finally recovered his son's dead body, on Saturday evening, July 4, 1863, he penned one of the most stirring newspaper dispatches of the war which concluded that the dead at Gettysburg had "baptised" with their blood, a second birth of freedom in America."

Matthew Pinsker
Dickinson College
November 19, 2013

REMEMBERING A SECOND BIRTH OF FREEDOM

Matthew Pinsker

None of Abraham Lincoln's famous words at Gettysburg involved individual names. The president actually went out of his way to avoid mentioning anybody, because he feared "I might do wrong to those I might forget."

Yet people who encountered Lincoln's speech in 1863 could never forget their own friends and family who had already given "the last full measure of devotion." These grieving Americans knew names. They cherished letters. They saw faces.

It is difficult for us the living to re-create the full power of the Gettysburg Address without experiencing these emotions. We struggle to recall the stories of heroic individuals along with the solemn phrases.

Bayard Wilkeson should be first among these hallowed figures. He was a 19-year-old Union officer whose leg was shattered on the battle's first day. He conducted his own amputation, according to eye-witnesses, and later died from the shock. His father, Samuel, a correspondent for the New York Times, was present on the battlefield. After Sam Wilkeson finally recovered his son's dead body, on Saturday evening, July 4, 1863, he penned one of the most stirring newspaper dispatches of the war, which concluded that the dead at Gettysburg had "baptised" with their blood, "a second birth of Freedom in America." An anguished father's phrase thus became immortalized several months later by President Lincoln as "a new birth of freedom." This might be the most powerful evocation within Lincoln's great address and yet it is almost unknown today. Clearly, our "unfinished work" is to remember the lives of those "honored dead," and use them, as Lincoln once urged, to rededicate ourselves to this great national experiment in self-government.

Matthew Pinsker is Associate Professor of History and holds the Brian Pohanka Chair of Civil War History at Dickinson College in Carlisle, Pennsylvania. He also serves as Director of the House Divided Project at Dickinson, which builds digital resources on the Civil War era. He is the author of two books, Abraham Lincoln, *a volume in the* American Presidents Reference Series *(Congressional Quarterly Press, 2002) and* Lincoln's Sanctuary: Abraham Lincoln and the Soldiers' Home *(Oxford University Press, 2003). Pinsker has held visiting fellowships at the US Army War College, New America Foundation, and the National Constitution Center and currently serves the Organization of American Historians as a "Distinguished Lecturer." Pinsker is an advisory board member of Ford's Theatre Society, Gettysburg Foundation, National Civil War Museum in Harrisburg, and President Lincoln's Cottage at the Soldiers' Home among others.*

Should fate and circumstance collide in a most cerebral manner, and should you find yourself smack-dab in the middle of America, then take a moment, won't you, to survey your surroundings, breathe deeply, and if you're not en route to a business meeting or a wedding or some other engagement that demands decorum, stick your hand in some Midwestern soil. Plant your fingers in there firmly and clench. Feel the minerals and the loess grip your digits as you slowly squeeze. Let the moist, black, nourishing components engulf your hand until you extract it. Close your eyes. Save for the dirt under your fingernails - a symbolic nod to generations of agrarians who lived their lives and plied their trades on these hallowed grounds - your hand will feel rejuvenated. Collectively, these parts constitute nothing less than the cradle of American civilization. Were it not for the Midwestern farmer and the crops and livestock he purveys, our lifestyles would be decidedly different and our food decidedly more expensive. Which is why it's no wonder that these parts have a profound - almost enchanting - impact on those who have called Middle America home.

[...] al, certain [...] a drive [...] winds you [...] were tilled [...] and see what [...] lor. Consider [...] and that [...] God willing, the land will look like this when fate and circumstance collide for you and your children's children's children.

Adam Pitluk
22 June 2013
Dallas, TX

FATE AND CIRCUMSTANCE

ADAM PITLUK

Should fate and circumstance collide in a most cerebral manner, and should you find yourself smack-dab in the middle of America, then take a moment, won't you, to survey your surroundings, breathe deeply, and if you're not en route to a business meeting or a wedding or some other engagement that demands decorum, stick your hand in some Midwestern soil. Plant your fingers in there firmly and clench. Feel the minerals and the loess grip your digits as you slowly squeeze. Let the moist, black, nourishing components engulf your hand until you extract it. Close your eyes. Save for the dirt under your fingernails—a symbolic nod to generations of agrarians who lived their lives and plied their trades on these hallowed grounds—your hand will feel rejuvenated.

Collectively, these parts constitute nothing less than the cradle of American civilization. Were it not for the Midwestern farmer and the crops and livestock he purveys, our lifestyles would be decidedly different and our food decidedly more expensive. Which is why it's no wonder that these parts have a profound—almost enchanting—impact on those who have called Middle America home.

Somehow, in the 21st-century land grab, certain sections of America have remained untouched. A drive through Union County in southern Illinois winds you around the same prairies and farms that were tilled in Lincoln's day. Come and visit, won't you, and see what America looked like in all its Victorian splendor. Consider the visage of this land, the passing of time, and that, God willing, the land will look like this when fate and circumstance collide for you and your children's children's children.

ADAM PITLUK is executive editor of American Way, *the in-flight magazine of American Airlines, and the director of art and editorial for* Celebrated Living *and* AA NEXOS *magazines, the premium class and Spanish/Portuguese magazines of American Airlines, respectively. Pitluk is the author of* Damned to Eternity: The Story of the Man Who They Said Caused the Flood *(DaCapo Press, 2007) and* Standing Eight: The Inspiring Story of Jesus "El Matador" Chavez *(DaCapo Press, 2007), both books, critically acclaimed studies of the human condition. An award-winning journalist, he has reported and written for numerous magazines including* Time, People, Boys' Life, Village Voice Media, *and* Spirit, *the in-flight magazine of Southwest Airlines.*

GENERAL COLIN L. POWELL, USA (RET)
COLIN L. POWELL ASSOCIATES, LLC

In November, 2013, three months after commemorating the 50th Anniversary of Dr. Martin Luther King Jr.'s "I Have a Dream" speech, he commemorated the 150th Anniversary of President Lincoln's "Gettysburg Address."

A century after Lincoln spoke of "the unfinished work" and "that this nation, under God, shall have a new birth of freedom," it fell to Dr. King to remind America that the work was not finished and Lincoln's vision was not yet realized for all Americans.

During that century we saw the rise of segregation and the fiction that "separate but equal" could actually be equal.

... USA (RET)
...ATES, LLC

2

... War was
... to be a war
... would be a
... orals and
... would be a
... erica live up
... of our
... Lincoln
... our score and
... our fathers
... n this
... nation,
... rty and
... e proposition
... that all men are created equal."

Dr. King reaffirmed these hopes in his "I Have a Dream" speech. The "Gettysburg Address" and "I Have a Dream" have gone down in history as the most inspirational speeches in American history.

...LIN L. POWELL, USA (RET)
...OWELL ASSOCIATES, LLC

3

... d of my country
... have done to
... se visions. Both
... be pleased, but
... ed.

... were assassinated
... beliefs. We are
... tors. We must do
... commemorate the
... be harmed by
... We must reach
... se in need so that we all can be "free at last."

The march must continue!

[signature]

16 September 2013

THE MARCH MUST CONTINUE

COLIN L. POWELL

In November 2013, three months after commemorating the 50th Anniversary of Dr. Martin Luther King Jr.'s "I Have a Dream" speech, we commemorated the 150th Anniversary of President Lincoln's "Gettysburg Address."

A century after Lincoln spoke of "the unfinished work" and "that this nation, under God, shall have a new birth of freedom" it fell to Dr. King to remind America that the work was not finished and Lincoln's vision not yet realized for all Americans.

During that century we saw the rise of segregation and the fiction that "separate but equal" could actually be equal. A second Civil War was needed. It was to be a war of protests. It would be a war of ideas, morals, and aspirations. It would be a war to make America live up to the dreams of our forefathers as Lincoln proclaimed in "four score and seven years ago our fathers brought forth on this continent a new nation, conceived in liberty, and dedicated to the proposition that all men are created equal."

Dr. King reaffirmed these hopes in his "I Have a Dream" speech. The "Gettysburg Address" and "I Have a Dream" have gone down in history as the most inspirational speeches in America history.

I am proud of my country and all we have done to realize these visions. Both men would be pleased, but not satisfied.

Both men were assassinated for their beliefs. We are their inheritors. We must do more than commemorate the dates and be warmed by their words. We must reach out to those in need so that we all can be "free at last."

The march must continue!

———

COLIN L. POWELL, U.S. Secretary of State from 2001 to 2005, is a retired General in the United States Army. For more than 50 years, Powell has devoted his life to public service, holding senior military and diplomatic positions across four presidential administrations. Commissioned as an Army second lieutenant in 1958, he served the United States Army for 35 years, rising to the rank of Four-Star General.

From 1987 to 1989 Powell served as President Ronald Reagan's National Security Advisor. From 1989 to 1993 he served as Chairman of the Joint Chiefs of Staff for both Presidents George H.W. Bush and Bill Clinton—the first African American to do so. President George W. Bush appointed Powell the 65th Secretary of State. His military awards and decorations include the Soldier's Medal, Bronze Star Medal, and Purple Heart. His civil awards include two Presidential Medals of Freedom. He has written two bestselling books, My American Journey *(Random House, 1995) and* It Worked for Me *(Harper, 2012).*

OFFICE OF THE GOVERNOR

PAT QUINN
GOVERNOR

December 29, 2014

The will of the people should be the law of the land. I firmly believe that, and I'm fond of saying it. One hundred fifty years ago, someone else said it more eloquently --"that government of the people, by the people, for the people, shall not perish from the earth."

Abraham Lincoln wasn't sure that the young American experiment with democracy would survive the Civil War. But he reminded us in his Gettysburg Address why we should fight to save what he in another famous speech would call "the last best hope of earth." And he admonished us not to waste the sacrifices of those who have fought and died to preserve a nation where a poor sharecropper's son could rise to become one of history's most admired figures.

Lincoln also reminded a nation at war over the issue of equality that all are created equal. Equality is a God-given right, not a human-bestowed gift. A nation of laws like the United States should ensure that gender, race, and physical ability have no bearing on the exercise of individual rights guaranteed by our founding fathers in the Constitution.

With the soul of a poet, a keen legal mind honed on the Illinois prairie, and a conscience steeled in the crucible of America's greatest crisis, Abraham Lincoln reminded us forever why we are the greatest nation on earth, and what it will take to remain so. His immortal words are branded in our hearts and minds. They have guided us for one hundred fifty years, and will continue to reaffirm our founding principles as long as there is a United States of America.

Pat Quinn

Governor of Illinois

THE WILL OF THE PEOPLE
Patrick J. Quinn

The will of the people should be the law of the land. I firmly believe that, and I'm fond of saying it. One hundred fifty years ago, someone else said it more eloquently—"that government of the people, by the people, for the people, shall not perish from the earth."

Abraham Lincoln wasn't sure that the young American experiment with democracy would survive the Civil War. But he reminded us in his Gettysburg Address why we should fight to save what he in another famous speech would call "the last best hope of earth." And he admonished us not to waste the sacrifices of those who have fought and died to preserve a nation where a poor sharecropper's son could rise to become one of history's most admired figures.

Lincoln also reminded a nation at war over the issue of equality that all are created equal. Equality is a God-given right, not a human-bestowed gift. A nation of laws like the United States should ensure that gender, race, and physical ability have no bearing on the exercise of individual rights guaranteed by our founding fathers in the Constitution.

With the soul of a poet, a keen legal mind honed on the Illinois prairie, and a conscience steeled in the crucible of America's greatest crisis, Abraham Lincoln reminded us forever why we are the greatest nation on earth, and what it will take to remain so. His immortal words are branded in our hearts and minds. They have guided us for one hundred fifty years, and will continue to reaffirm our founding principles as long as there is a United States of America.

Patrick J. Quinn is the 41st Governor of the State of Illinois. He took the Oath of Office on January 29, 2009, and was elected to a full term on November 2, 2010. He has served the people of Illinois for more than 30 years as both a citizen and a public official. Quinn was elected Lieutenant Governor in 2002 and re-elected in 2006, serving until his succession to Governor. He also served one term as State Treasurer from 1991 to 1995, commissioner of the Cook County Board of (Property) Tax Appeals, and revenue director for the City of Chicago.

Wheaton North High School
Wheaton, Illinois

Grace Richards
11-14-2013

It is easy to forget that Abraham Lincoln gave the Gettysburg Address to dedicate a graveyard.

The power of the Gettysburg Address has endured through the centuries, words of inspiration and patriotism lifted up time and time again. But these were words offered by a man at the wheel of a shattering ship, endlessly driven against the rocks by the heaving storm of war. The crowd stood upon yet another blood-soaked battleground, and Lincoln spoke to the families of a grieving nation from the fields where their sons had died. And yet, against all odds, the Gettysburg Address is a speech about hope.

Lincoln transformed a memorial to terrible loss into a call to honor the dead, to remember the beauty of the cause for which they fought. He reminded all who listened that death is not a call to sorrow, but a call to action. The only way to truly honor the dead is to finish the work they have left undone, to live as they would have wanted to live. He helped the mourning see through the eyes of the fallen soldiers, shared their hope for a nation united once more and living the ideals on which it was founded: liberty and equality for all.

Today, the Gettysburg Address still holds meaning. Lincoln called not only to those standing on the battlefield, but to all. Until all the wounds of inequality are healed, until the dreams of men like Abraham Lincoln and Martin Luther King Jr. are realized, then the Gettysburg Address will still be a call to action, and a call to remember the origins of this great nation.

FINISHING THEIR WORK

GRACE RICHARDS

It is easy to forget that Abraham Lincoln gave the Gettysburg Address to dedicate a graveyard.

The power of the Gettysburg Address has endured through the centuries, words of inspiration and patriotism lifted up time and time again. But these were words offered by a man at the wheel of a shattering ship, endlessly driven against the rocks by the heaving storm of war. The crowd stood upon yet another blood-soaked battleground, and Lincoln spoke to the families of a grieving nation from the fields where their sons had died. And yet, against all odds, the Gettysburg Address is a speech about hope.

Lincoln transformed a memorial to terrible loss into a call to honor the dead, to remember the beauty of the cause for which they fought. He reminded all who listened that death is not a call to sorrow, but a call to action. The only way to truly honor the dead is to finish the work they have left undone, to live as they would have wanted to live. He helped the mourning see through the eyes of the fallen soldiers, shared their hope for a nation united once more and living the ideals on which it was founded: liberty and equality for all.

Today, the Gettysburg Address still holds meaning. Lincoln called not only to those standing on the battlefield, but to all. Until all the wounds of inequality are healed, until the dreams of men like Abraham Lincoln and Martin Luther King Jr. are realized, then the Gettysburg Address will still be a call to action, and a call to remember the origins of this great nation.

GRACE RICHARDS lives with her family in Wheaton, Illinois. She is a senior at Wheaton North High School where she enjoys playing tennis, serving as an officer in Key Club, and writing and editing for the school newspaper, the Falcon Flyer. *She is a graduate of the Iowa Young Writers' Studio (2013) and the Carleton College Summer Writing Program (2014). She plans to study English, History and Creative Writing in college.*

September 02, 2014

Gettysburg Essay

In November of 1863, when President Lincoln went to Gettysburg to dedicate the new cemetery there, my great-great-grandfather Richard Rutter Ricketts was working the land at his farm in southwestern Iowa. Born in 1802, Richard was too old to fight in the still raging Civil War, but he was hardly indifferent to the struggle. Richard had grown up surrounded by slavery. As an apprentice carpenter in Baltimore, and later in New Orleans (where he made coffins during the terrible cholera epidemic of 1832), he worked alongside slaves, witnessing firsthand the injustice of their plight. Slavery may have been a settled part of his world, but it was not something he could abide, and in the 1840s, after he married my great-great grandmother Charlotte Platt Ricketts, an ardent abolitionist from a family of abolitionists, he joined the anti-slavery cause in earnest. When he and Charlotte moved to Iowa in the 1850s, they became active participants in the Underground Railway, their farm in Civil Bend, near the Missouri River, serving as a well-known transit point for escaping slaves.

Lincoln's speech at Gettysburg was reported widely at the time, and there is little doubt that Richard and Charlotte heard about it. I'm sure its words resonated deeply with them. The proposition that all men are created equal was a defining principle of their lives, as was the notion that the great task of securing freedom remains a continuing obligation for us all. It's a legacy I've spent my life trying to honor, for it remains every bit as pertinent today as it was when Mr. Lincoln first spelled it out back in my great-great-grandparents' time.

Best regards,

J. Joe Ricketts

A CONTINUING OBLIGATION

J. Joe Ricketts

In November of 1863, when President Lincoln went to Gettysburg to dedicate the new cemetery there, my great-great grandfather, Richard Rutter Ricketts was working the land at his farm in southwestern Iowa. Born in 1802, Richard was too old to fight in the still raging Civil War, but he was hardly indifferent to the struggle. Richard had grown up surrounded by slavery. As an apprentice carpenter in Baltimore, and later in New Orleans (where he made coffins during the terrible cholera epidemic of 1832), he worked alongside slaves, witnessing firsthand the injustice of their plight. Slavery may have been a settled part of his world, but it was not something he could abide, and in the 1840s, after he married my great-great grandmother Charlotte Platt Ricketts, an ardent abolitionist from a family of abolitionists, he joined the anti-slavery cause in earnest. When he and Charlotte moved to Iowa in the 1850s, they became active participants in the Underground Railway, their farm in Civil Bend, near the Missouri River, serving as a well-known transit point for escaping slaves.

Lincoln's speech at Gettysburg was reported widely at the time, and there is little doubt that Richard and Charlotte heard about it. I'm sure its words resonated deeply with them. The proposition that all men are created equal was a defining principle of their lives, as was the notion that the great task of securing freedom remains a continuing obligation for us all. It's a legacy I've spent my life trying to honor, for it remains every bit as pertinent today as it was when Mr. Lincoln first spelled it out back in my great-great grandparents' time.

***

J. Joe Ricketts is founder and former Chairman and CEO of TD Ameritrade. He spent more than 35 years building the company into the world's largest online brokerage firm. Ricketts now focuses on a variety of entrepreneurial ventures: premium bison distributor, *Golden Bison; digital neighborhood information source, DNAinfo; feature movie company, The American Film Company; and premiere fly fishing destination, Jackson Fork Lodge. Ricketts also established and directs the charities Opportunity Education Foundation, The Ricketts Conversation Foundation, and The Ricketts Art Foundation.*

We are celebrating The Gettysburg Address, written 150 years ago. What is it about Abraham Lincoln's words that still draw us in today?

Lincoln was a self-made man who hungered for a life of meaning and purpose. No stranger to loss and despair, his pain became the catalyst to his achievements. Ironically, the very experiences he would have liked to escape led to his great compassion and vision for a better United States.

He was a thinker, a shrewd man who thought matters over and after careful deliberation, reached a decision. He had learned that timing was everything. And inside his soul resided a vulnerability that we relate to even today.

Abraham Lincoln was a lot like us. He struggled and felt despair. "Surely there must have been unseen tears rising from the compassion of a heartbroken man."

He vowed: "that we here highly resolve that these dead shall not have died in vain." And he meant it.

The problem ... put someone ... longer see who ... t of the very ... ginally inspired us.

... man. He was ... to be upon a ... alongside

... a funny story ... was a regular ... ecause he cared.

He found the right words to touch hearts.

Lincoln brought hope, and today, we still need that.

Karen Roth
Oct. 3, 2013

272 WORDS OF HOPE

KAREN ROTH

We are celebrating the Gettysburg Address, written 150 years ago. What is it about Abraham Lincoln's words that still draw us in today?

Lincoln was a self-made man who hungered for a life of meaning and purpose. No stranger to loss and despair, his pain became the catalyst to his achievements. Ironically, the very experiences he would have liked to escape led to his great compassion and vision for a better United States.

He was a thinker, a shrewd man who thought matters over and after careful deliberation, reached a decision. He had learned that timing was everything. And inside his soul resided a vulnerability that we relate to even today.

Abraham Lincoln was a lot like us. He struggled and felt despair. Surely there must have been unseen tears rising from the compassion of a heartbroken man.

He vowed: "that we here highly resolve that these dead shall not have died in vain." And he meant it.

He was not a saint or an idol. The problem with hero worship is when we put someone high upon a pedestal, we no longer see who they really are. We lose sight of the very frailties and humanness that originally inspired us.

Lincoln stood with the common man. He was one of us. He would not want to be up on a pedestal. He preferred standing alongside everyone else.

He wanted to laugh with us at a funny story and cry over a sad one. He was a regular man who achieved greatness because he cared. He found the right words to touch hearts.

Lincoln brought hope, and today, we still need that.

Karen Roth is the assistant librarian at Lincoln Elementary School in Ottawa, Illinois. She has resided in Ottawa, the site of the first Lincoln-Douglas debate, since she was twelve years old. In addition to her work in the library, she also teaches an enrichment class on Abraham Lincoln. Roth is the 2009 winner of The History Channel's "Lincoln Lesson Plans" competition and the 2014 recipient of the Robert Doyle Award from the Reaching Forward Conference Committee, which recognizes library workers. She regularly writes columns as part of "The Write Team" for the Times *of Ottawa and has also written for the* Catholic Post.

Little Rock Central High School

The smoke and fog of battle have cleared in the Pennsylvania Piedmont.... The fallen of Gettysburgh have been consecrated. A definition of the moment has been sought and has so eloquently been found in the wisdom of President Abraham Lincoln. His affirmation that all men are created equal is fundamental in the evolution of an emerging America. And the story of our nation with its everlasting struggle to be all we can be continues to propel us forward.

Such was the case at Little Rock Central High in Arkansas' capital city in the mid 1950's. For decades the school district had operated in the framework of a "Separate but equal" system — with one set of schools for white students and another for African Americans. The time had come to desegregate in a world of the Civil Rights Movement, court rulings, political maneuvering and citizen action. The day for change came in September of 1957 when a group of African Americans — labeled by the media as "The Little Rock Nine" — joined the student body.

Spurred by an atmosphere of racial prejudice by in/out-of-state agitators, the threat of possible violence prompted President Dwight Eisenhower to call in federal troops for protection.

At the bottom line, school operations returned to normal and equal rights for students reigned. Today with African Americans composing over 55% of the student population, Central High consistently ranks among the highest in our state for scholarships, academic awards, and numerous other measures.

The words and deeds of President Lincoln remind us all that the battlefields for equal justice always surround us — in war and peace — and indeed represent opportunities to form a more perfect union.

Nancy L. Rousseau, Principal June 23, 2014

BATTLEFIELDS FOR EQUAL JUSTICE

Nancy Rousseau

The smoke and fog of battle have cleared in the Pennsylvania Piedmont. . . . The fallen of Gettysburg have been consecrated—a definition of the moment has been sought and has so eloquently been found in the wisdom of President Abraham Lincoln. His affirmation that all men are created equal is fundamental in the evolution of an emerging America. Add the story of our nation with its everlasting struggle to be all we can be continues to propel us forward.

Such was the case at Little Rock Central High in Arkansas' capital city in the mid 1950s. For decades the school district had operated in the framework of a "Separate but equal" system—with one set of schools for white students and another for African Americans. The time had come to desegregate in a world of the Civil Rights Movement, court rulings, political maneuvering and citizen action. The day for change came in September of 1957, when a group of African Americans—labeled by the media as "The Little Rock Nine"—joined the student body.

Spurred by an atmosphere of racial prejudice by in/out-of-state agitators, the threat of possible violence prompted President Dwight Eisenhower to call in Federal troops for protection.

At the bottom line, school operations returned to normal and equal rights for students reigned. Today with African Americans composing 55% of the student population, Central High consistently ranks among the highest in our state for scholarships, academic awards and numerous other measures.

The words and deeds of President Lincoln remind us all that the battlefields for equal justice always surround us—in war and peace—and indeed represent opportunities to form a more perfect union.

❦

Nancy Rousseau is principal of Little Rock Central High School. Her career in both public and private education spans more than 43 years. She has served as chairperson of the Little Rock Education Commission and on the National Merit Scholarship Foundation Board. In 2007, she cochaired the 50th Integration Anniversary Commission for the City of Little Rock, which featured President Bill Clinton as keynote speaker commemorating the Little Rock Nine who integrated Central High School in 1957. The Little Rock PTA Council and Volunteers in Public Schools, the Arkansas Parent Teacher Association, and the Arkansas Scholastic Press Association each named Rousseau "Administrator of the Year" for her outstanding commitment to education.

Google

Google Inc.

November 19, 2013

In 1858, five years before Lincoln gave his address at Gettysburg and several years before he was even elected President, he delivered a speech in Edwardsville, IL, where he spoke of preserving the "spirit which prizes liberty as a heritage of all men, in all lands, everywhere," and cautioned that without it, "you have planted the seeds of despotism around your own doors."

Lincoln could never have imagined our own new Digital Age, but his calls to protect liberty and fight against despotism echo strongly today. Our modern liberty rests not on the promise of abolition, but on the promise of greater access to information, more transparency, and our new ability to give every person, "in all lands, everywhere" a voice. The Internet has become a platform that helps preserve liberty around the world, decrease the distance between people and power, and enfranchise everyone who uses it. Today, you can speak up, share, learn, debate, and create with nothing more than a WiFi connection and a smartphone. You can spark revolutions, strengthen democracies, and uncover corruption and tyranny wherever it hides.

At Gettysburg, Lincoln dreamed of "a new birth of freedom." 150 years later, his dream still resonates. With the immense potential of technology, and of connection, we can help people everywhere discover, fight for, and exercise new liberties that are rightfully theirs. Human lives can improve greatly. Barriers to opportunity will fall. And new freedoms will be born. We still have a long way to go to see this dream fully realized for everyone, but if we carry this spirit forward, we can, like Lincoln, have high hopes for the future.

Eric Schmidt

THE PROMISE OF GREATER ACCESS

ERIC SCHMIDT

In 1858, five years before Lincoln gave his address at Gettysburg and several years before he was even elected President, he delivered a speech in Edwardsville, IL, where he spoke of preserving the "spirit which prizes liberty as a heritage of all men, in all lands, everywhere," and cautioned that without it, "you have planted the seeds of despotism around your own doors."

Lincoln could never have imagined our own new Digital Age, but his calls to protect liberty and fight against despotism echo strongly today. Our modern liberty rests not on the promise of abolition, but on the promise of greater access to information, more transparency, and our new ability to give every person, "in all lands, everywhere" a voice. The Internet has become a platform that helps preserve liberty around the world, decrease the distance between people and power, and enfranchise everyone who uses it. Today, you can speak up, share, learn, debate, and create with nothing more than a WiFi connection and a smartphone. You can spark revolutions, strengthen democracies, and uncover corruption and tyranny wherever it hides.

At Gettysburg, Lincoln dreamed of "a new birth of freedom." 150 years later, his dream still resonates. With the immense potential of technology, and of connection, we can help people everywhere discover, fight for, and exercise new liberties that are rightfully theirs. Human lives can improve greatly. Barriers to opportunity will fall. And new freedoms will be born. We still have a long way to go to see this dream fully realized for everyone, but if we carry this spirit forward, we can, like Lincoln, have high hopes for the future.

ERIC SCHMIDT is executive chairman of Google. Since joining Google in 2001, he helped grow the company from a Silicon Valley startup to a global leader in technology. From 2001 to 2011, Schmidt served as Google's chief executive officer, overseeing the company's technical and business strategy alongside founders Sergey Brin and Larry Page. Prior to joining Google, Schmidt held leadership roles at Novell and Sun Microsystems, Inc. He is a member of the President's Council of Advisors on Science and Technology and the Prime Minister's Advisory Council in the United Kingdom. He is the coauthor of The New Digital Age: Reshaping the Future of People, Nations and Business *(Knopf, 2013).*

Hubris in 272 Words

It is an act of folly to imitate Lincoln's masterful explanation of self-governance in 272 words. It took Lincoln five drafts and slightly more words before the final text. And even this version may not have been the final one had Lincoln lived to polish it further. The text, like Lincoln's America, was a work in progress recounting past achievements, present imperfections, and infinite possibilities. The maelstrom of events that produced Lincoln's meditation on government recalls our aspirational beginnings in the Declaration of Independence: "that all men are created equal." The terrible Civil War that defined his present tense could only be explained by a transcendent condition for the future. Lincoln believed that the future, under God, was one where the boundaries of liberty and freedom were expanded and self-governance preserved.

Lincoln challenges Americans to know their past, contribute to their present, and have a sense of their future. The preservation of the nation bestows great benefits but often demands individual and collective sacrifice.

Lincoln's expression is concise but his words are timeless. As durable as our democracy appears on its surface, it remains a fragile object at its core. Like any organic system, it requires tending and nurturing. The

n is
wer
never

zing
hallenges.

So we must act. But how? And what if we error? Still, we must try.

Thomas F. Schwartz

August 10, 2013

HUBRIS IN 272 WORDS

Thomas F. Schwartz

It is an act of folly to imitate Lincoln's masterful explanation of self-government in 272 words. It took Lincoln five drafts and slightly more words before the final text. And even this version may not have been the final one had Lincoln lived to polish it further. The text, like Lincoln's America, was a work in progress recounting past achievements, present imperfections, and infinite possibilities. The maelstrom of events that produced Lincoln's meditation on government recalls our aspirational beginnings in the Declaration of Independence: "that all men are created equal." The terrible Civil War that defined his present tense could only be explained by a transcendent condition for the future. Lincoln believed that the future, under God, was one where the boundaries of liberty and freedom were expanded and self-governance preserved.

Lincoln challenges Americans to know their past, contribute to their present, and have a sense of their future. The preservation of the nation bestows great benefits but often demands individual and collective sacrifice.

Lincoln's expression is concise but his words are timeless. As durable as our democracy appears on its surface, it remains a fragile object at its core. Like any organic system, it requires tending and nurturing. The divisiveness among Americans that led to secession is easily dismissed as a unique historical chapter never to be repeated. As Lincoln reminds us, history is never so simple. Try as we might, we cannot escape our historical situation or its later judgments by ignoring unfolding events or denying the reality of life's challenges. So we must act. But how? And what if we error? Still, we must try.

Thomas F. Schwartz, Ph.D., is director of the Herbert Hoover Presidential Library & Museum. He previously served as Illinois State Historian and chief historian for exhibits and content at the Abraham Lincoln Presidential Museum, as well as director of research and the Lincoln Collection at the Abraham Lincoln Presidential Library. An acknowledged authority on the Sixteenth President, Schwartz's honors include Plank Owner, USS Abraham Lincoln (1989), Logan Hay Medal (2000), Studs Terkel Humanities Service Award (2006), Order of Lincoln (2009), and the Civil War Preservation Trust Chairman's Award for Excellence in Education (2009). The author of more than one hundred books, articles, reviews, chapters, and electronic reference entries, Schwartz serves on the advisory boards of Ford's Theatre and The National Civil War Museum.

THE GETTYSBURG ADDRESS Abraham Lincoln, Nov. 19, 1863

4 score and seven years ago our fathers brought forth upon this continent a new nation, conceived in liberty and dedicated to the proposition that all men are created equal.

NOW we are engaged in a great civil war, testing whether that nation, or any nation so conceived and so dedicated can long endure.

WE are met on a great battlefield of that war.

WE have come to dedicate a portion of that field as a final resting place for those who here gave their lives that that nation might live.

IT is altogether fitting and proper that we should do this.

BUT in a larger sense we cannot dedicate, we cannot concecrate, we cannot hallow this ground.

THE brave men, living and dead, who struggled here, _have_ consecrated it, far above our poor power to add or detract.

THE world will little note nor long remember what we say here, but it can never forget what they did here.

IT is for us the living, rather, to be dedicated here to the unfinished work which they who fought here have, thus far, so nobly advanced.

IT is rather for us to be here dedicated to the great task remaining before us:

THAT from these honored dead we take increased devotion to that cause for which they here gave the last full measure of devotion.

THAT we here highly resolve that these dead shall not have died in vain,

THAT this nation, under God, shall have a new birth of freedom.

AND that government of the people, by the people, for the people, shall not perish from the earth.

10 SENTENCES, 4 CLAUSES

PETE SEEGER

> Aug 13, 2013
>
> Dear Friends at the ALPLF —
>
> Since on Nov. 19 it will be 150 years since old Abe gave the Gettysburg Address, I try to get people to memorize it.
>
> Written out as 10 sentences and 4 clauses it's much easier to to memorize than the way it's usually printed, in 2 or 3 paragraphs.
>
> I'm curious to know what you think of it. I'm sorry I cannot visit you in person. But at age 94 my travelling days are over.
>
> Sincerely, Pete Seeger

PETE SEEGER was an American singer, songwriter, and activist. Many of his songs have become American folk music classics and include: "If I Had a Hammer," "Turn! Turn! Turn!" and "Where Have All the Flowers Gone?" In the 1940s, after returning from the Pacific where he served in the Army during World War II, he founded the folk group The Weavers, whose hits included "Kisses Sweeter than Wine," "This Land is Your Land," and "Goodnight, Irene." In the 1950s, Seeger was blacklisted for alleged Communist sympathies during the McCarthy era for his refusal to testify before the House Un-American Activities Committee. In the 1960s, Seeger joined Martin Luther King Jr., in the Freedom Marches in Selma, Alabama, and Washington, DC, adapting the gospel standard "We Shall Overcome" to the Civil Rights movement. In his lifetime, he completed close to three dozen songbooks, instructional instrumental handbooks, and children's stories. Among his many awards and honors, he was the recipient of three Grammys including a Grammy Lifetime Achievement Award, as well as a Harvard Arts Medal, Kennedy Center Award, and the Presidential Medal of the Arts. In 1996, he was inducted into the Rock and Roll Hall of Fame.

11/19/2013

Over a million Americans have given their lives in defense of the principles which form the foundation of this great country. The question to be asked is whether their sacrifice created the country envisioned by our forefathers and where do we go from here?

This country is only as strong as our next generation. Unless we demand from ourselves and our children responsible behavior as citizens of their communities, cities, states and the United States, the greatness that is America will be lost. Finger pointing and excuses for irresponsible behavior have created a generation of people who either never heard the words of JFK or choose to redefine them. The words were simple... "Ask not what your country can do for you, but what can you do for your country."

The freedoms that we enjoy in this country are unrivaled by any other, and the dreams of our children are limited only by a lack of hard work and dedication.

We must demand the best effort from ourselves and our children.

We must demand the best from our government, never forgetting that the government works for us and not the other way around.

We must demand the best from our elected representatives, selecting only the most talented among us to speak for us in the halls of government. If we select mediocrity, we will get what we deserve, and those hundreds of thousands of soldiers will have died for a mediocre country.

A great America means demanding the best from every American and enjoying this wonderful country. Only then will the spirit and sacrifice of those soldiers will be truly honored.

Judith Sheindlin
"Judge Judy"

DEMAND THE BEST

JUDITH SHEINDLIN

Over a million Americans have given their lives in defense of the principles which form the foundation of this great country. The question to be asked is whether their sacrifice created the country envisioned by our forefathers and where do we go from here.

This country is only as strong as our next generation. Unless we demand from ourselves and our children responsible behavior as citizens of their communities, cities, states and the United States, the greatness that is America will be lost. Finger pointing and excuses for irresponsible behavior have created a generation of people who either never heard the words of JFK or choose to redefine them. The words were simple—"Ask not what your country can do for you, but what you can do for your country."

The freedoms that we enjoy in this country are unrivaled by any other, and the dreams of our children are limited only by a lack of hard work and dedication.

We must demand the best effort from ourselves and our children.

We must demand the best from our government, never forgetting that the government works for us and not the other way around.

We must demand the best from our elected representatives, selecting only the most talented among us to speak for us in the halls of government. If we select mediocrity, we will get what we deserve, and those hundreds of thousands of soldiers will have died for a mediocre country.

A great America means demanding the best from every American who enjoys this wonderful country. Only then, the spirit and sacrifice of those soldiers will truly be honored.

JUDITH SHEINDLIN is presiding judge on the Emmy Award–winning Judge Judy, *the top-rated show in daytime television. She began her career prosecuting juvenile delinquency cases for the state of New York. New York Mayor Edward Koch appointed her to the bench in Family Court and later, she was appointed the Supervising Judge in Manhattan. She has heard more than 20,000 cases during her career, credited with pioneering an "open court policy," allowing the public and media to view her daily proceedings. Judge Sheindlin's bestselling books include,* Don't Pee on My Leg and Tell Me It's Raining, Beauty Fades, Dumb Is Forever, *and* Keep It Simple, Stupid: You're Smarter Than You Look. *The recipient of many awards and honors, she was inducted into Broadcasting & Cable Hall of Fame and has a Star on the Hollywood Walk of Fame. She cofounded "Her Honor Mentoring," which seeks to boost self-confidence in young women at the workplace and everyday life.*

Lincoln's Gettysburg Address is the soul of brevity. Not just in the clarity, economy, + musicality of Lincoln's language, but his hard-earned esteem for brevity as a view of life.

The average life expectancy in American in our times hovers around (I dare not put it this way) fourscore. In Lincoln's time, it was not even threescore (+ of course he died ten years shy of that). We are surrounded today by drudgery sparing, timesaving, life-extending technologies —— that wait at the touch of a button! Instantaneous communication over oceans! Open-heart surgery! — that was unfathomable in Lincoln's time. Yet I don't know if it is feel that we have more time.

Lincoln knew life was brief + mean. His mother died when he was a boy. Two of his boys died in childhood. He knew that tens of thousands of people —— so many of them young—had died in a war which, however necessary + noble we deem it now, had unleashed unprecedented + even unimaginable bloodletting by the Lincolns own hand.

The slaughter was senseless. But we could go on hoping if those deaths could breathe life into a more true, just, + moral nation —— "that from these honored dead we take increased devotion to that cause for which they gave the last full measure of devotion."

Lincoln's words remind us at once of the brevity of life + the imperishability of humanity. The clock ticks; the calendar flips. No power exists to slow them down or manufacture more hours + years. And Lincoln reminds us to make as our lives count by filling the hours we have with what's worthy, kind, funny + honorable.

Scott Simon
September 16 - 2013

A TIME-SENSITIVE DOCUMENT

Scott Simon

Lincoln's Gettysburg Address is the soul of brevity. Not just in the clarity, economy, and musicality of Lincoln's language, but his hard-earned esteem for brevity as a view of life.

The average life expectancy of an American in our times hovers around (I dare put it this way) four-score. In Lincoln's time, it was not even three score (and of course he died four years shy of that). We are surrounded today by drudgery-sparing, timesaving, life-extending technologies—hot water at the touch of a button! Instantaneous communication over oceans! Open-heart surgery!—that was unfathomable in Lincoln's time. Yet I doubt many of us feel that we have more time.

Lincoln knew life was often brief and mean. His mother died when he was a boy. Two of his boys died in childhood. He knew that tens of thousands of people—so many of them young—had died in a war which, however necessary and noble we deem it now, had unleashed unprecedented and even unimaginable bloodletting by Abe Lincoln's own hand.

The slaughter was senseless. But we could go on living if those deaths could breathe life into a more free, just, and moral nation—"that from these honored dead we take increased devotion to that cause for which they gave the last full measure of devotion."

Lincoln's words remind us at once of the brevity of life and the imperishability of humanity. The clock ticks; the calendar flips. No power exists to slow them down or manufacture more hours and years. Abe Lincoln reminds us to make our own lives count by filling the hours we have with what's worthy, kind, funny, and honorable.

Scott Simon is the host of NPR's Weekend Edition with Scott Simon *and the series* Backstage With . . . *on PBS stations, and he appears on BBC-TV. He has received numerous awards including the Peabody, Emmy, Columbia-DuPont, and James Beard among others, but the one most meaningful to him is Chicago's Studs Terkel Award. He has contributed to many newspapers including, the* Los Angeles Times, *the* New York Times, *the* Wall Street Journal, *and the* Guardian *and is the author of several books, including* Home and Away: Memoir of a Fan *(Hyperion, 2000)*, Jackie Robinson and the Integration of Baseball *(Wiley, 2007)*, Pretty Birds *(Random House, 2006)*, Windy City *(Random House, 2008)*, *and* Baby, We Were Meant for Each Other: In Praise of Adoption *(Random House, 2010). He has covered ten wars, done stories in all 50 states and every continent, gone swimming with Esther Williams, flown as Peter Pan and aboard the U.S. space shuttle simulator, and danced the role of Mother Ginger in* The Nutcracker.

Remarks on the 150th Anniversary of the Gettysburg Address

Seven score and ten years ago a tall gaunt figure rose on an autumn afternoon to help dedicate the final resting place of Americans who had fought and died so that their nation — and all that it stood for — might live. As his words echoed across the freshly-dug graves of those who had given the last full measure of devotion to that cause, he reaffirmed his commitment to continue the struggle so that those men would not have died in vain.

We today, still remember those words and the man who spoke them. We have never forgotten what he said there on a battlefield of that war. But we must rededicate ourselves to rising to the challenge of meeting the great task remaining before us. Otherwise, those men will have died in vain for a cause that we failed to sustain.

We today must remind ourselves that the struggle continues long after those guns fell silent. If the blood shed during four years of terrible war was necessary to secure a new birth of freedom, achieving that freedom remains our unfinished work. It is not enough to pledge ourselves to ensure that government of the people, by the people, for the people, shall not perish from this earth. We must remain dedicated to ... ual, and we ... that equality ... liberty and ... Let us embrace that proposition completely so that we can be as good as his word and be true to ourselves.

Brooks D. Simpson

November 19, 2013

THE UNFINISHED WORK BEFORE US

BROOKS D. SIMPSON

Seven score and ten years ago a tall gaunt figure rose on an autumn afternoon to help dedicate the final resting place of Americans who had fought and died so that their nation—and all that it stood for—might live. As his words echoed across the freshly-dug graves of those who had given the last full measure of devotion to that cause, he reaffirmed his commitment to continue the struggle so that those men would not have died in vain.

We today still remember those words and the man who spoke them. We have never forgotten what he said there on a battlefield of that war. But we must rededicate ourselves to rising to the challenge of meeting the great task remaining before us. Otherwise, those men will have died in vain for a cause that we failed to sustain.

We today must remind ourselves that the struggle continues long after those guns fell silent. If the blood shed during four years of terrible war was necessary to secure a new birth of freedom, achieving the promise of that freedom remains our unfinished work. It is not enough to pledge ourselves to ensure that government of the people, by the people, for the people, shall not perish from this earth. We must remain dedicated to the proposition that all people are created equal, and we must renew our commitment to realizing that equality is essential to realize fully for all the liberty and freedom we seek to preserve and protect. Let us embrace that proposition completely so that we can be as good as his word and be true to ourselves.

BROOKS D. SIMPSON is Foundation Professor of History at Arizona State University, where he teaches at Barrett, The Honors College as well as the School of Letters and Sciences. A historian of 19th Century U.S. history and the American presidency, he is the author of several books, including Gettysburg, 1873 *(Potomac Books, Inc., 2014);* The Civil War in the East: Struggle, Stalemate, and Victory *(2011);* Ulysses S. Grant: Triumph over Adversity, 1822–1865 *(Houghton Mifflin Harcourt, 2000);* The Reconstruction Presidents *(University Press of Kansas, 1998); and* Let Us Have Peace: Ulysses S. Grant and the Politics of War and Reconstruction, *1861–1868 (The University of North Carolina Press, 1991). He has edited or coedited several collections of documents and essays, including two volumes in the Library of America's series on the American Civil War and has appeared on the History Channel and the PBS series* The American Experience. *Simpson was named a Fulbright Scholar in 1995.*

There is a lot of bloodshed behind American progress. Americans for the most part, are as aware of our legacy of violence as we are of our heritage of reason, and we regard this as a paradox rather than as hypocrisy.

When exploring the four exceedingly bloody and hard years of the Civil War, it is impossible not to see Abraham Lincoln as our very own phoenix, emerging from unimaginable devastation to insist that we can be better than we have been, to show us that it's possible to transform the bloodiest war in American history into a means, even if a tragic means, by which a great proposition, that all are created equal, has been tested and found true. If we regard Lincoln this way, are we worshiping him or do we simply hope to learn from him?

We seem always to have wanted to get close

...ut to better ...ifted and galvanized ...st, this realist, this ...suffering man, who ...the name of

...my peers and I watched ...rejection of the ...the first attempts ...a society truly ...of human equality ...e. As civil rights ...ldiers of Omaha Beach ...offers promises of reason, justice, happiness, liberty, and peace, but often terrible sacrifice is required before those promises can be realized.

Steven Spielberg
9/13/13

THE ATTRACTIVE VISION OF A BETTER WORLD

STEVEN SPIELBERG

There is a lot of bloodshed behind American progress. Americans, for the most part, are as aware of our legacy of violence as we are of our heritage of reason, and we regard this as a paradox rather than as hypocrisy.

When exploring the four exceedingly bloody and hard years of the Civil War, it is impossible not to see Abraham Lincoln as our very own phoenix, emerging from unimaginable devastation to insist that we can be better than we have been, to show us that it's possible to transform the bloodiest war in American history into a means, even if a tragic means, by which a great proposition that all are created equal, has been tested and found true. If we regard Lincoln this way, are we worshiping him or do we simply hope to learn from him?

We seem always to have wanted to get close to him, not to idolize, but to better understand him, to be uplifted and galvanized by this man, this pragmatist, this realist, this openhearted and at times, suffering man, who was a steadfast optimist in the name of freedom and equality.

In the twentieth century, my peers and I watched or participated in a national rejection of the evils of racial segregation and the first attempts to create, at very long last, a society truly dedicated to the realization of human equality and dignity regardless of race. As civil rights workers know, just as the soldiers of Omaha Beach on D-Day knew, democracy offers promises of reason, justice, happiness, liberty, and peace, but often terrible sacrifice is required before these promises can be realized.

STEVEN SPIELBERG is a filmmaker and principal partner of DreamWorks Studios. In 2012 he directed Academy Award winner Daniel Day-Lewis in Lincoln. *The film garnered 12 Academy Award nominations winning two Oscars for Best Actor and Best Production Design. Spielberg is the recipient of the Irving G. Thalberg Memorial and Cecil B. DeMille Awards and a three-time Academy Award winner having received Oscars for Best Director and Best Picture for* Schindler's List, *which received seven Oscars, and a third Academy Award, for Best Director, for* Saving Private Ryan, *which earned four additional Oscars. In addition to his film work, Spielberg devotes his time and resources to many philanthropic causes, having established The Righteous Persons Foundation, as well as the Survivors of the Shoah Visual History Foundation, now the USC Shoah Foundation. He is Chairman Emeritus of the Starlight Children's Foundation. In 2014 Spielberg became the seventh recipient of the Abraham Lincoln Presidential Library Foundation's Lincoln Leadership Prize.*

Midwestern, I'm the dirt of places
Lincoln lived that I've lived too.
His fifteen Indiana years; my
thirty. His twenty-seven in Illinois
pre-D.C., and the twenty-nine I've
notched in the Land of him. I've
knelt at his gravesite with wife and
kids before [spri...]
side trips to dist[...]
dreamt of other [...]
mounted the elo[...]
Lincoln-Douglas de[...]
and read poems [...]
parlor from which [...]
one February morn[...]
In each I've ha[...]
here as he knew [...]
what he imagined [...]
make of it togeth[...]
our common l[...]

No one here frets Lincoln's ancestry.
No one here ponders if the good man's Irish.
No fool worries how "Abraham" hints Jew,
except for one slacker crackpot lurking
the bushes of Internet democracy
Lincoln would've understood as
wired within the veins of you within
the veins of me. This here.

The veins of those ennobled here
forgave us our trespasses; human
and aggrieved chain link lightning
what cleaves us here together is what
they perished to cleave apart —
to sunder not this nation
but the notion one could own another
as if white clouds owned the rain.

Who would fret such dreck of Lincoln?
Who would worry such of our place,
your fine face and mine mingled here
to become us among each other's otherness.
Lincoln repeated "here" seven times at Gettysburg,
blood grounds of and by and for the people,
created equal by one word's equal birth:
American, rainwater upon the tongue.

                    Kevin Stein (9-9-13)

GENEALOGY APOLOGY

KEVIN STEIN

Midwestern, I'm the dirt of places Lincoln lived that I've lived too. His fifteen Indiana years; my thirty. His twenty-seven in Illinois pre-D.C., and the twenty-nine I've notched in the Land of him. I've knelt at his gravesite with wife and kids before Springfield horse shows, side trips to distract the daughter who dreamt of other blue ribbons. I've mounted the eloquent stone steps of a Lincoln-Douglas debate site with my son and read poems in Vachel Lindsay's parlor from which Lincoln departed one February morn for Washington. In each I've hankered to know here as he knew it, to imagine what he imagined you and I might make of it together—his words our common language.

Genealogy Apology

No one here frets Lincoln's ancestry.
No one here ponders if the good man's Irish.
No fool worries how "Abraham" hints Jew,
except for one slacker crackpot lurking
the bushes of Internet democracy
Lincoln would've understood as
wired within the veins of you within
the veins of me. This here.

The veins of those ennobled here
forgave us our trespasses, human
and aggrieved chain link lightning.
What cleaves us here together is what
they perished to cleave apart—

to sunder not this nation
but the notion one could own another
as if white clouds owned the rain.

Who would fret such dreck of Lincoln?
Who would worry such of our place,
your fine face and mine mingled here
to become us among each other's otherness.
Lincoln repeated "here" seven times at
        Gettysburg,
blood grounds of and by and for the people
created equal by one word's equal birth:
American, rainwater upon the tongue.

KEVIN STEIN is Illinois Poet Laureate and Caterpillar Professor of English at Bradley University, where he also directs the Creative Writing Program. He has published eleven books of poetry, literary criticism, and anthology. His collections include Wrestling Li Po for the Remote *(Fifth Star Press, 2013),* Sufficiency of the Actual *(University of Illinois Press, 2009),* and American Ghost Roses *(University of Illinois Press, 2005), winner of the Society of Midland Authors Poetry Award. His* Poetry's Afterlife: Verse in the Digital Age *(University of Michigan Press, 2010). As Illinois Poet Laureate, he succeeds past laureates Gwendolyn Brooks, Carl Sandburg and Howard Austin.*

at&t

Randall L. Stephenson
Chairman and
Chief Executive Officer

October 16, 2013

President Lincoln's Gettysburg Address is one of America's great inspired works. It frames the cost of liberty like no other writing. It portrays the never ending work, pain, and sacrifice required to sustain a free and democratic society.

Lincoln was unapologetic in his conviction that liberty was worthy of a fight, even unto death. And in the end, his conviction was rewarded, democracy and individual freedom were reaffirmed, and the will of the people prevailed.

But today, 150 years later, too often we fight the temptation to doubt. Indeed, as we observe recent events and theatrics in Washington, many have concluded that our democratic process is now broken and dysfunctional. But, the opposite is true. These events don't threaten our democracy, they are democracy. Discerning the will of 300 million people is not easy. It requires the pressure, conflict, and stress of competing ideas and ideologies to force it out.

Our democracy may not always be pretty. In fact, the process is generally messy and, individually, we will not always like the outcome. But we must not forget that this is the system, and these are the freedoms, that those who fought at Gettysburg, and in so many wars since, died to protect. Accordingly, we must never forsake Lincoln's resolve — "that government of the people, by the people, for the people, shall not perish from the earth."

Randall Stephenson

THE WILL OF THE PEOPLE

Randall L. Stephenson

President Lincoln's Gettysburg Address is one of America's great inspired works. It frames the cost of liberty like no other writing. It portrays the never ending work, pain, and sacrifice required to sustain a free and democratic society.

Lincoln was unapologetic in his conviction that liberty was worthy of a fight, even unto death. And in the end, his conviction was rewarded, democracy and individual freedom were reaffirmed, and the will of the people prevailed.

But today, 150 years later, too often we fight the temptation to doubt. Indeed, as we observe recent events and theatrics in Washington, many have concluded that our democratic process is now broken and dysfunctional. But, the opposite is true. These events don't threaten our democracy, they <u>are</u> democracy. Discerning the will of 300 million people is not easy. It requires the pressure, conflict, and stress of competing ideas and ideologies to force it out.

Our democracy may not always be pretty. In fact, the process is generally messy and, individually, we will not always like the outcome. But we must not forget that this is the system, and these are the freedoms, that those who fought at Gettysburg, and in so many wars since, died to protect. Accordingly, we must never forsake Lincoln's resolve—"that government of the people, by the people, for the people, shall not perish from the earth."

Randall L. Stephenson is chairman and chief executive officer of AT&T Inc., a global leader in mobile Internet services and IP-based business communications solutions. He was named to his current position in 2007. During his tenure, AT&T has transformed its nationwide US wireless business with a best-in-class network and more than 100 million subscribers.

Stephenson began his career with Southwestern Bell Telephone in 1982. He formerly served as the company's senior executive vice president and chief financial officer. He was appointed to AT&T's board of directors in 2005. Under his leadership, AT&T launched AT&T Aspire, a philanthropic program to help improve college/career readiness for at-risk students. In addition to his leadership at AT&T, Stephenson chairs the Business Roundtable, is a member of the board of directors of Emerson Electric Co. and the PGA Tour Policy Board, and a National Executive Board member of the Boy Scouts of America.

One hundred fifty years have passed since November 19, 1863. On that day there were President Lincoln's words at the Gettysburg National Cemetery. These words defined our nation. No skin color, birth country, or shared history established the United States. People had come from Europe, Africa, the Caribbean, and Latin America. Soon, they arrived from Asia and Australia as well. Most of the new Americans aspired to citizenship in a nation established to make real the propositions of the Declaration of Independence.

From 1861 to 1865, they fought a war dedicated to preserving that nation & its promise.

In a larger sense, the people of the Union fought for an even greater cause. Their eventual victory proved that a government of the people, by the people, and for the people need not perish in a war for its survival. While battles raged, this republican government did nothing not permanently abolish the liberties that it was founded to protect.

Abraham Lincoln led a United States governed by the consent of its citizens. Its victory brought hope to the republicans around the globe. The Gettysburg Address challenges us to see that his hopes will perish neither from this land, nor from this earth. When we do, no soldier shall ever die in vain. While Lincoln is gone, his words live — to inspire us, and the people of the world.

"The Global Meaning of the Gettysburg Address"

Louise L. Stevenson
Professor, History & American Studies
Franklin & Marshall College.

THE GLOBAL MEANING OF THE GETTYSBURG ADDRESS

LOUISE L. STEVENSON

One hundred fifty years have passed since November 19, 1863. On that day, there were President Lincoln's words at the Gettysburg National Cemetery. Those words defined our nation. No skin color, birth country, or shared history established the United States. People had come from Europe, Africa, the Caribbean, and Latin America. Soon, they arrived from Asia and Australia as well. Most of the new Americans aspired to citizenship in a nation established to make real the propositions of the Declaration of Independence.

From 1861 to 1865, they fought a war dedicated to preserving that nation and perfecting its promise.

In a larger sense, the people of the Union fought for an even greater cause. Their eventual victory proved that a government of the people, by the people, and for the people need not perish in a war for its survival. While battles raged, this republican government did not permanently abolish the liberties that it was founded to protect.

Abraham Lincoln led a United States governed by the consent of its citizens. Its victory brought hope to republicans around the globe. The Gettysburg Address challenges us to see that his hopes will perish neither from this land, nor from this earth. When we do, no soldier shall ever die in vain. While Lincoln is gone, his words live—to inspire us, and the people of the world.

LOUISE L. STEVENSON is professor of history and American studies at Franklin & Marshall College in Lancaster, Pennsylvania, where she is chair of the History Department and Women Studies Program, as well as campus representative for the James Madison Fellowship Foundation scholarship competition. Her scholarship focuses on 19th Century cultural and intellectual life and her books include Lincoln Thought Globally *(Cambridge University Press, 2015),* Scholarly Means to Evangelical Ends: The New Haven Scholars and the Transformation of Higher Learning in America, 1830–1890 *(Johns Hopkins University Press, 1986), and* The Victorian Homefront: American Cultural and Intellectual Life, 1860–1880 *(1991, new ed., Cornell University Press, 2001). Her recent work includes articles published in the* Journal of Southern History *and* A History of the Book in America. *Stevenson serves on the board of directors of the Lancaster County League of Women Voters.*

My Gettysburg
Charles B. Strozier

In my three score and nine years I have lived through far too many American wars that we never should have entered. The results, from Vietnam, to the Gulf, to Iraq and Afghanistan, have left countless soldiers and civilians dead and wounded, and disrupted the lives of millions. Like Barack Obama, I am not against all wars, but I hate stupid wars. Two of my sons fought in the Middle East, one in the Gulf War and the other in Iraq. I love them but hate the wars. It has left me constantly perplexed.

I often turn to Lincoln to try and fathom such contradictions. At Gettysburg he understood not that war is good or glorious but that it can rightly be performed wrong. It mattered that the cause of Union became a fight for human freedom. Slavery was entrenched in American life. It would not simply fade away into the night as he had hoped before the war. It seemed it required a mighty war to give one with hundreds of thousands dead a sacrifice that the wrong itself at the battlefield into a monument of freedom.

I want to believe that was true. It was a century from the battle of Gettysburg to Martin Luther King's "I Have a Dream" speech on the Washington Mall in front of the Lincoln memorial. Another chance forward challenge all Americans now to resolve that that these brave soldiers did not die in vain and that they too can be a new birth of freedom. But I am reminded that King opposed the Vietnam War as wisely and morally wrong. That is where I entered history.

9/1/13

TURN TO LINCOLN

CHARLES B. STROZIER

In my three score and nine years, I have lived through far too many American wars that we never should have entered. The results from Vietnam, to the Gulf, to Iraq and Afghanistan, have left countless soldiers and civilians dead and wounded and disrupted the lives of millions. Like Barack Obama, I am not against all wars, but I hate stupid wars. Two of my sons fought in the Middle East, one in the Gulf War and the other in Iraq. I love them but hate the wars. It has left me constantly perplexed.

I often turn to Lincoln to try to fathom such contradictions. At Gettysburg, he understood not that war is good or glorious but that it can right profound wrongs. It mattered that the cause of Union became a fight for human freedom. Slavery was entrenched in American life. It would not simply fade away into the night, as he had hoped before the war. It seemed it required a mighty war to end, one with hundreds of thousands dead, a sacrifice that the ground itself at the battlefield [was turned] into a monument of freedom.

I want to believe that was true. It was a century from the battle of Gettysburg to Martin Luther King's "I Have a Dream" speech on the Washington Mall in front of the Lincoln memorial. Another blink forward challenges all Americans now to resolve that those brave soldiers did not die in vain and that there can be a new birth of freedom. But I am reminded that King opposed the Vietnam War as wasteful and morally wrong. That is where I entered history.

CHARLES B. STROZIER *is a Professor of History at The City University of New York and a practicing psychoanalyst in New York City. His forthcoming book from Columbia University Press is* Young Man Lincoln: Joshua Speed and the Crucible of Greatness. *He is the author or editor of 12 other books, including* Lincoln's Quest for Union: A Psychological Portrait *(Basic Books, 1982) with a revised edition in paper from Paul Dry Books, 2001.*

People like to eat
by Evelyn Brandt Thomas, with Karl Barnhart

I turned 90 last year and love to come to work.

Why? Because people like to eat. Such a simple -- and obvious -- statement. Yet, such an increasingly difficult thing to satisfy. The global population is exploding. We are loseing arable land every day. And tastes are changing to embrace more high-input proteins.

As a third generation farmer, I have always had a passion to help feed the world. For 60 years, I have help build and shape an agricultural company with one single purpose. Help farmers help feed the world. Simple, I want to help people eat.

We have done that in a breathtaking number of ways -- with new products, innovative technologies and a whole lot of new processes. When I was a girl, we were lucky to get 50 bushels of corn per acre. Now the near-term goal is 300. To do that, we must constantly improve. Abraham Lincoln knew this. He knew we can't improve by doing things the same way.

newest ideas to

billion additional

vanced chemistries,

grower practices.

of the global

we are proud

to be stewards of the land. There's not a farmer alive who would knowingly hurt the land that sustains his family and enable his livelihood. Our job is to help farmers make informed and better decisions by providing agronomic testing, research and information

That means I'll keep coming to work as long as I'm able. Because people like to eat,

PEOPLE LIKE TO EAT

EVELYN BRANDT THOMAS WITH KARL BARNHART

I turned 90 last year and I love to come to work.

Why? Because people like to eat. Such a simple—and obvious—statement. Yet, such an increasingly difficult thing to satisfy. The global population is exploding. We are losing arable land every day. And tastes are changing to embrace more high-input proteins.

As a third generation farmer, I have always had a passion to help feed the world. For 60 years, I have helped build and shape an agricultural company with one single purpose: Help farmers help feed the world. Simple. I want to help people eat.

We have done that in a breathtaking number of ways—with new products, innovative technologies, and a whole lot of new processes. When I was a girl, we were lucky to get 50 bushels of corn per acre: Now the near-term goal is 300. To do that, we must constantly improve. Abraham Lincoln knew this. He knew we can't improve by doing things the same way. Today, we have to bring the newest ideas to bear to fill the predicted three billion additional bellies by 2050.

Those new ideas include advanced chemistries, GMO crops, and innovative grower practices. We are proud to be a part of the global agriculture industry because we are proud to be stewards of the land. There's not a farmer alive who would knowingly hurt the land that sustains his family and enables his livelihood. Our job is to help farmers make informed and better decisions by providing agronomic testing, research, and information.

That means I'll keep coming to work as long as I'm able. Because people like to eat.

Evelyn Brandt Thomas is a businesswoman, philanthropist, and civic leader. She grew up on a small family farm near Pleasant Plains, Illinois. She and her brother, Glen, cofounded a fertilizer business in the early 1950s to supplement the family's income. The business has grown to become BRANDT Consolidated, Inc., a multimillion-dollar international company dedicated to helping farmers adopt new and profitable technologies to enable their success on the family farm. In 2012, the corporation was named to Inc. Magazine's list of 500 Fastest Growing Private Companies. In 2011, Brandt was named an Outstanding Woman in Agriculture by Illinois Agri-Women, and in 2014, she received an honorary doctorate from the University of Illinois–Springfield to recognize her service to the community. An advocate for the 4-H and many other philanthropic causes, the Association of Fundraising Professionals awarded her its 2002 Outstanding Philanthropist Award for her philanthropic leadership.

Several years before his presidency, Abraham Lincoln stood atop the bluffs overlooking the Missouri River and set forth the route for what would become our nation's first transcontinental railroad. Once elected, President Lincoln gave life to the vision he conceived so many years before, signing the Pacific Railway Act of 1862. At a time when the United States was divided north and south by war, he took a step to connect the country east and west, establishing the prosperous nation we salute today.

Ground was broken on the cross-country endeavor, which proved a monumental struggle on scale with history's largest construction projects. Laboring in extreme conditions, soldiers returning from war laid steel alongside immigrants seeking new lives and work in America. On May 10, 1869, the completed railroad was commemorated with the driving of a golden spike in Promontory Summit, Utah – the first event to be announced live, from coast to coast. Travel time from New York to San Francisco had been sheared from six months to 10 days.

Surely President Lincoln would be proud to witness the progress of the company he created. Today, Union Pacific is North America's largest railroad, with more than 32,000 miles of track linking 7300 communities to the global economy. Much of the food we eat, most of the vehicles we drive and many of the consumer goods we use travel along Union Pacific's tracks before reaching our homes.

President Lincoln's vision and leadership united the nation in a way that has proven as innovative and transformative to his time as the Internet is today. More than 150 years later, his enduring legacy continues Building America.

Robert W. Turner
November 6, 2013
Omaha, NE.

LINCOLN'S RAILROAD

ROBERT W. TURNER

Several years before his presidency, Abraham Lincoln stood atop the bluffs overlooking the Missouri River and set forth the route for what would become our nation's first transcontinental railroad. Once elected, President Lincoln gave life to the vision he conceived so many years before, signing the Pacific Railway Act of 1862. At a time when the United States was divided north and south by war, he took a step to connect the country east and west, establishing the prosperous nation we salute today.

Ground was broken on the cross-country endeavor, which proved a monumental struggle on scale with history's largest construction projects. Laboring in extreme conditions, soldiers returning from war laid steel alongside immigrants seeking new lives and work in America. On May 10, 1869, the completed railroad was commemorated with the driving of a golden spike in Promontory Summit, Utah—the first event to be announced live, from coast to coast. Travel time from New York to San Francisco had been sheared from six months to 10 days.

Surely President Lincoln would be proud to witness the progress of the company he created. Today, Union Pacific is North America's largest railroad, with more than 32,000 miles of track, linking 7300 communities to the global economy. Much of the food we eat, most of the vehicles we drive and many of the consumer goods we use travel along Union Pacific's tracks before reaching our homes.

President Lincoln's vision and leadership united the nation in a way that has proven as innovative and transformative to his time as the Internet is today. More than 150 years later, his enduring legacy continues building America.

~ ~

ROBERT W. TURNER is senior vice president, corporate relations of Union Pacific Corporation. He has company-wide responsibility for internal and external communications, corporate advertising and brand management, public affairs, media relations, community and government affairs, and corporate philanthropy. He serves as president of the Union Pacific Foundation and is head of the Union Pacific Railroad Museum. Turner serves as the Private Sector Co-Chair of the National Action Alliance for Suicide Prevention, the public-private partnership established by the Secretaries of Defense and Health and Human Services to advance the National Strategy for Suicide Prevention. He is a board member of the Abraham Lincoln Presidential Library Foundation, Public Affairs Council, Greater Omaha Chamber of Commerce, the railroad industry's national grassroots organization GoRail, U.S. Bank of Nebraska Advisory Board, Durham Museum, and Hiram College.

One and a half centuries ago, Civil War divided these united States of America. Yet in its wake, we would anneal as one Nation, indivisible.

During the bloody year of his Gettysburg Address, President Lincoln chartered the National Academy of Sciences — comprised of fifty distinguished American researchers whose task was then, as now, to advise Congress and the Executive Branch of all the ways the frontier of science may contribute to the health, wealth, and security of its residents.

As a young Nation, just four score and seven years old, we had plucked the engineering fruits of the Industrial Revolution that transformed Europe, but Americans had yet to embrace the meaning of science to society.

Now, with more than two thousand members, the National Academy encompasses dozens of fields undreamt of at the time of Lincoln's charter. Quantum Physics, discovered in the 1920s, now drives nearly one third of the world's wealth, forming the basis of our computer revolution in the creation, storage, and retrieval of information. And as we continue to warm our planet, Climatology may be our only hope to save us from ourselves.

...ses dozens of fields
...Lincoln's charter.
...n the 1920s, now drives
...'s wealth, forming the
...ion in the creation,
...ormation. And as we
...et, Climatology may be
...from ourselves.

...charter, President Kennedy
...bership, noting, "The
...achievement in this
...l of our Nation's future."
...ntury, innovations in
...the primary engines
...most remember
... and Slavery and Freedom,
...come to remember him for setting our Nation on a course of scientifically enlightened governance, without which we all may perish from this Earth.

Neil D. Tyson
November 2013
New York City

THE LINCOLN SEEDBED

NEIL deGRASSE TYSON

One and a half centuries ago, Civil War divided these United States of America. Yet in its wake, we would anneal as one Nation, indivisible.

During the bloody year of his Gettysburg Address, President Lincoln chartered the National Academy of Sciences—comprised of fifty distinguished American researchers whose task was then, as now, to advise Congress and the Executive Branch of all the ways the frontier of science may contribute to the health, wealth, and security of its residents.

As a young Nation, just four score and seven years old, we had plucked the engineering fruits of the Industrial Revolution that transformed Europe, but Americans had yet to embrace the meaning of science to society.

Now with more than two thousand members, the National Academy encompasses dozens of fields undreamt of at the time of Lincoln's charter. Quantum Physics, discovered in the 1920s, now drives nearly one-third of the World's wealth, forming the basis of our computer revolution in the creation, storage, and retrieval of information. And as we continue to warm our planet, Climatology may be our only hope to save us from ourselves.

During the centennial of its charter, President Kennedy addressed the Academy membership, noting, "The range and depth of scientific achievement in this room constitutes the seedbed of our Nation's future."

In this, the twenty-first century, innovations in science and technology form the primary engines of economic growth. While most remember Honest Abe for War and Peace, and Slavery and Freedom, the time has come to remember him for setting our Nation on a course of scientifically enlightened governance, without which we all may perish from this Earth.

～～～

NEIL deGRASSE TYSON, Ph.D., is an astrophysicist and the first occupant of the Hayden Planetarium's Frederick P. Rose Directorship. Since childhood, Tyson has been fascinated with the universe and sharing that fascination with the public. He helped develop the 21st century version of Carl Sagan's television series Cosmos *and also hosted two PBS-NOVA productions,* Origins *and* NOVAScienceNOW. *He has authored numerous books and dozens of professional publications in an effort to write for the public. His book,* Death by Black Hole and Other Cosmic Quandaries *(W. W. Norton, 2007) was a* New York Times *bestseller. President George W. Bush twice appointed Tyson to serve on commissions, the first to study the future of the U.S. aerospace industry and second, to study the implementation of the U.S. space exploration policy. Tyson has led NASA's Advisory Council and has received NASA's Distinguished Public Service Medal, the highest award the agency gives to nongovernment personnel. The International Astronomical Union officially named asteroid 13123 after Tyson for his contributions to the public's appreciation of the cosmos.*

Lech Wałęsa

Budujmy cywilizację na uniwersalnych wartościach

Kiedy zastanawiam się, co „my, Naród," możemy powiedzieć o sobie, o naszej polskiej duszy i historii, dochodzę do wniosku, że niezależnie od epoki, historycznych i politycznych okoliczności łączy i definiuje nas umiłowanie wolności. I zdolność do solidarności. A historycznie – walka o te wartości, bo nadzwyczaj chętnie nas ich pozbawiano. My potrafiliśmy w sobie je znaleźć nawet w najtrudniejszych chwilach. I udawało nam się zaszczepiać je w innych.

To polskie doświadczenie solidarności i marzeń o wolności może stawać się lekcją dla współczesnego świata. Może być podpowiedzią dla ludów i narodów nadal zmagających się ze zniewoleniem czy beznadzieją. Powinno tym bardziej wskazywać kierunek rozwoju globalnej cywilizacji, stając się trwałymi punktami odniesienia. A tego dziś najbardziej nam brakuje. Jak dotąd nie potrafimy jako cywilizacja i globalny świat wskazać wspólnych uniwersalnych dla całej ludzkości wartości, do których moglibyśmy się odwoływać niezależnie od narodowości, koloru skóry czy wyznania. Potrzebny jest naszej cywilizacji pokoju – bo do budowania takiej przecież aspirujemy - katalog wartości niepodważalnych i przyjętych przez wszystkich bez wyjątku, aby na nim budować świat pokoju i bezpieczeństwa. Dlatego chcę, abyśmy ustalili, że nasz świat musimy budować na wartościach uniwersalnych. Widzę wśród nich właśnie solidarność jako fundament życia społecznego w wielu obszarach: w ekonomii, pracy, współdziałaniu globalnym, nierównościach społecznych. To z solidarności oraz mądrej wolności powinniśmy wyprowadzać powszechne poszanowanie dla ludzkiej godności, wolności słowa i wyznania, prawo do sprawiedliwości i równości szans.

Wierzę, że wspólny przecież dla Polski, Europy, Ameryki oraz wszystkich państw i kontynentów gen wolności i solidarności prowadzić będzie nas ku budowie wolnej, otwartej, opartej na wartościach, na międzyludzkim współdziałaniu i na pokoju cywilizacji. I nie pozwoli nam zaznać pełnego wewnętrznego spokoju, dopóki w jakimkolwiek zakątku Ziemi nie będzie jeszcze spełnione pragnienie wolności, bezpieczeństwa i ludzkiej godności.

Instytut Lecha Wałęsy

LET'S BUILD A CIVILIZATION BASED ON UNIVERSAL VALUES

LECH WALESA

TRANSLATED BY WOJCIECH WLOCH

When I think what "We, the People" say about ourselves, our Polish spirit and history, I conclude that what unites and defines us, independent of historical and political circumstance, is love of freedom, capability for solidarity, and, our struggle for those freedoms of which we've been readily deprived. We must be able to find universal values within ourselves even in the most difficult moments, and instill them in others.

Let the Polish experience of solidarity and dreams of freedom become lessons for the modern world. Let them become examples for peoples and nations still struggling with oppression and hopelessness. Let them point the direction for civilization becoming permanent, necessary reference points. Thus far, we haven't found common universal values for all humanity regardless of nationality, color or creed. We aspire to build a civilization of freedom, yet we need a set of irrefutable values accepted by everyone. We need to build upon these universal values to ensure a free and secure world. Among these values, solidarity is the basis of social life in many dimensions: economics, work, global cooperation, combating social inequalities among others. From solidarity and freedom we should grow in regard and respect for human dignity, freedom of speech and religion, right to justice, and equal opportunities.

I trust that the gene of freedom, common to Poland, Europe, America—all countries and continents—will guide us in building a free, open civilization based on values, interpersonal interactions, and peace. This gene won't let us fully experience inner peace until the desire for freedom, security, and human dignity is fulfilled everywhere on Earth.

LECH WALESA is former President of the Republic of Poland and recipient of the Nobel Peace Prize. In the 1980s, he helped lead his country to a new era of freedom and became the first democratically elected leader in Polish postwar history. Walesa's journey as an electrician in the massive Lenin shipyard at Gdańsk, Poland, in the 1970s to his nation's highest office in the 1990s was an arduous one. After witnessing violent government crackdowns ordered by Poland's Communist Party leadership against its own citizens, Walesa took action as a labor leader and activist and was elected the first Solidarity Chairman at the First National Solidarity Congress in Gdañsk. As President of Poland, he helped usher the country into the modern era by laying the foundation for Poland's eventual admission into NATO, and, as a free nation, into the United Nations. He is the fifth recipient of the Abraham Lincoln Presidential Library Foundation's Lincoln Leadership Prize.

A trip to the monuments was a part of my first trip to Washington, D.C. in 1985. Since a number of my counselors at the American Legion's Boys Nation program were Vietnam veterans, our first stop was to the newly opened Vietnam Veterans' Memorial Wall. Many of the names engraved on the walls were friends of my counselors.

Just down from the wall sits the Lincoln Memorial honoring our 16th President. Inside, I read the immortal words of his address on November 19, 1863. Just months after the Battle of Gettysburg, there is no doubt that there were many friends and family of the fallen who heard his words and took comfort that their loved one did not die in vain.

It is somewhat ironic that Abraham Lincoln stated that day that "The world will little note, nor long remember what we say here, but it can never forget what they did here," as he honored the war dead. Just as important as remembering these words is honoring these lives, and countless others, through every generation.

Back in the summer of 1985, I first saw the black slabs of black granite that list the names of those lost in Vietnam. Interestingly, you can see your own reflection behind the names when the sun shines on the wall.

President Lincoln was right. The best way to honor these heroes is to re-dedicate ourselves to protecting the very freedoms they fought to preserve. In a way, we let their lives shine in our own lives as we ensure "that government of the people, by the people, for the people, shall not perish from the earth."

LET THEIR LIVES SHINE

SCOTT WALKER

A trip to the monuments was a part of my first trip to Washington, D.C. in 1985. Since a number of my counselors at the American Legion's Boys Nation program were Vietnam veterans, our first stop was to the newly opened Vietnam Veterans' Memorial Wall. Many of the names engraved on the walls were friends of my counselors.

Just down from the wall sits the Lincoln Memorial honoring our 16th President. Inside, I read the immortal words of his address on November 19, 1863. Just months after the Battle of Gettysburg, there is no doubt that there were many friends and family of the fallen who heard his words and took comfort that their loved one did not die in vain.

It is somewhat ironic that Abraham Lincoln stated that day that "the world will little note, nor long remember what we say here, but it can never forget what they did here," as he honored the now dead. Just as important as remembering those words is honoring those lives, and countless others, through every generation.

Back in the summer of 1985, I first saw the slabs of black granite that list the names of those lost in Vietnam. Interestingly, you can see your own reflection behind the names when the sun shines on the wall.

President Lincoln was right. The best way to honor these heroes is to re-dedicate ourselves to protecting the very freedoms they fought to preserve. In a way, we let their lives shine in our own lives as we ensure "that government of the people, by the people, for the people, shall not perish from the earth."

SCOTT WALKER was inaugurated as the 45th Governor of Wisconsin on January 3, 2011. Governor Walker currently serves as a member of the National Governors Association (NGA) Executive Committee, as well as on the NGA's Education and Workforce Committee. In addition, he is the current Chair of the Midwest Governors Association. Governor Walker served as the County Executive of Milwaukee County from 2002 to 2008, where he worked to reform the county government, cut the county's debt, and protect taxpayers' money. Prior to that, he served in the Wisconsin State Assembly, where he chaired several committees and authored several important pieces of legislation.

The fight for freedom lies within the roots of human nature. The demand for recognition as independent and equal individuals drives humans to challenge establishment and seek new foundations. In 1861, a call for independence rallied in the American South divided the Union through a civil war characterized by brutality and bloodshed. The Battle of Gettysburg illustrated the callous nature of the Civil War and demonstrated one of the greatest decimations of life in American history. However, in spite of the circumstances present, Abraham Lincoln aptly transformed the situation from one of desecration to one of hope and promise.

Lincoln's Gettysburg address represents a keystone in American history in its properties as one of America's greatest speeches and as one of Lincoln's greatest feats. Lincoln proved the power of words by conveying an abstract and moving message in a concise 272 word speech. Surprisingly, Lincoln did not direct his speech at either the Southern Confederacy or the Northern Union but as a single united nation. Instead, he commemorated both sides for their willingness to die for a cause and advocated for the urgency of change to honor the fallen. Lincoln desired for the rebirth of America as a unified power bounded together through nationalism and republicanism. Lincoln's speech revived a disheartened nation with promises of a lasting democracy.

The Gettysburg Address shaped American history and America's perception of Abraham Lincoln. Lincoln's fateful speech carries his legacy along with his famed Emancipation Proclamation and presence in reuniting the Union in desperate times. Lincoln's actions have ensured that a "government of the people, by the people, for the people" still endures to this day.

David Walsec
November 15, 2013

The Early College at Guilford
Greensboro, North Carolina

AN AMERICAN KEYSTONE

DAVID WALSER

The fight for freedom lies within the roots of human nature. The demand for recognition as independent and equal individuals drives humans to challenge establishment and seek new foundations. In 1861, a call for independence rallied in the American South divided the Union through a civil war characterized by brutality and bloodshed. The Battle of Gettysburg illustrated the callous nature of the Civil War and demonstrated one of the greatest decimations of life in American history. However, in spite of the circumstances present, Abraham Lincoln aptly transformed the situation from one of desecration to one of hope and promise.

Lincoln's Gettysburg Address represents a keystone in American history in its properties as one of America's greatest speeches and as one of Lincoln's greatest feats. Lincoln proved the power of words by conveying an abstract and moving message in a concise 272-word speech. Surprisingly, Lincoln did not direct his speech at either the Southern Confederacy or the Northern Union but as a single united nation. Instead, he commemorated both sides for their willingness to die for a cause and advocated for the urgency of change to honor the fallen. Lincoln desired for the rebirth of America as a unified power bounded together through nationalism and republicanism. Lincoln's speech revived a disheartened nation with promises of a lasting democracy.

The Gettysburg Address shaped American history and America's perception of Abraham Lincoln. Lincoln's fateful speech carries his legacy along with his famed Emancipation Proclamation and presence in reuniting the Union in desperate times. Lincoln's actions have ensured that a "government of the people, by the people, for the people" still endures to this day.

DAVID WALSER is a high school senior at the Early College at Guilford. He was born in Feldkirch, Austria, and immigrated to the United States when he was six months old, eventually settling in North Carolina. He is a student of the Advanced Learner program at Florence Elementary, the Very Strong Needs program at the Academy at Lincoln, and the early college curriculum at the Early College at Guilford. Walser participates in a variety of activities from the outdoors to the arts. He plans to pursue a career in architecture as it combines his "love of art, history, science, and mathematics."

United States Department of the Interior

NATIONAL PARK SERVICE
Little Rock Central High School
National Historic Site
2120 W. Daisy L. Gatson Bates Drive
Little Rock, Arkansas 72202

IN REPLY REFER TO:

We are the benefactors of change agents

President Lincoln was a visionary -- a change agent.
He knew the Emancipation Proclamation was inevitable,
just as school desegregation in the 1950s was also
inevitable.
The 1954 landmark decision, Brown versus Board of
Education held separate facilities to be inherently
unconstitutional. Three years after Brown, Little
Rock Central High School became the epicenter of a
direct challenge to federal authority and enforcement not seen
since post-Civil War Reconstruction. In September
1957, wrongly mobed, the governor of Arkansas and the
Arkansas National Guard blocked African American
students from integrating the school. Dubbed "The
Little Rock Nine," they entered classes on September 25,
1957, escorted by the 101st Airborne, ordered by
President Eisenhower to enforce the court ruling.
Despite presence of troops, the Little Rock Nine faced
harassment, verbal and violent, private and public
throughout the school year.

... School National
... story of the
... to maintain
... the Civil Rights

... led back to
... many of
... prevailing
... borders of
... possible!
... agents
... in Central
High School to pursue the American Dream
and an equal education. They are our symbol
of hope, without power, they paved the way for
those yet to come. We are the benefactors
of their sacrifices, dedicated to service to all
mankind to ensure that our social guardians
are prepared to follow their moral compasses.

Robin White
Superintendent

1/1/2014

WE ARE THE BENEFACTORS OF CHANGE AGENTS
ROBIN WHITE

President Lincoln was a visionary—a change agent. He knew the Emancipation Proclamation was inevitable, just as school desegregation in the 1950s was also inevitable.

The 1954 landmark decision Brown versus Board of Education held separate facilities to be inherently unconstitutional. Three years after Brown, Little Rock Central High School became the epicenter of a direct challenge to federal authority and enforcement not seen since post–Civil War Reconstruction. In September 1957, angry mobs, the governor of Arkansas and the Arkansas National Guard blocked African American students from integrating the school. Dubbed "The Little Rock Nine," they entered classes on September 25, 1957, escorted by the 101st Airborne, ordered by President Eisenhower to enforce the court ruling. Despite presence of troops, the Little Rock Nine faced harassment, verbal and violent, private and public throughout the school year.

Today, Little Rock Central High School National Historic Site interprets the heroic story of the Little Rock Nine, the struggle to maintain segregation, and the surging tide of the Civil Rights Movement.

When arriving to work, I am propelled back to 1957, coming to know the true meaning of living history, walking in wisdom, prevailing over fear with courage. The wonders of this world make the impossible, possible! The Little Rock Nine, as change agents with unwavering dignity, enrolled in Central High School to pursue the American dream and an equal education. They are our symbol of hope. Without pause, they paved the way for those yet to come. We are the benefactors of their sacrifices, dedicated to service to all mankind to ensure that our social guardians are prepared to follow their moral compasses.

ROBIN WHITE is the superintendent of Little Rock Central High School National Historic Site in Little Rock, Arkansas. As superintendent, she has worked with a number of the descendants of civil rights pioneers—Homer Plessy, John Ferguson, Crazy Horse, Sitting Bull, and Dred Scott—and civil rights activists—Rev. C. T. Vivian, Harry Belafonte, Myrlie and Reena Evers, Julian Bond, the Freedom Riders, and the Little Rock Nine. An employee of the National Park Service for 25 years, her background is in interpretation and heritage education. White has served at a number of other premier American national parks including Indiana Dunes National Lakeshore, Petroglyph National Monument, Grand Canyon National Park, William Howard Taft National Historic Site, and New Orleans Jazz National Historical Park. White was the first recipient of the Intermountain Region Franklin G. Smith Award honoring her civic engagement and diversity contributions to the National Park Service.

Robert S. Willard

Two-seventy-two. That's the number of words that are in the copy of Abraham Lincoln's Gettysburg speech he wrote out for Edward Everett. They both spoke at the dedication of the cemetery in Pennsylvania — Everett for two hours; Lincoln, two minutes.

"I have never had a feeling politically that did not spring from the sentiments embodied in the Declaration of Independence." Lincoln said that in Independence Hall in February, 1861. His job that day was simply to raise a flag, but his "deep emotion at finding myself standing here" led to his observation that that document "gave liberty, not alone to the people of this country, but, I hope, to the world, for all future time."

The Declaration of Independence, before listing the "abuses and usurpations" by the British monarch, puts forth two great revolutionary ideas — that all people are equal with natural rights, and that government derives its power from the consent of the governed. The Civil War was fought to preserve both ideas. If the Union forces had failed, not only would millions of

e enslaved, but the
xtinguished. What
" might no longer

e of human events"
curity," the Founders' words influenced Lincoln's memorable phrases: "new birth of freedom" and "government of ..., by... and for the people."

Four score and seven years before Lincoln spoke at Gettysburg, the Founders, in their own 272 words, inspired "a few appropriate remarks" we will all long remember.

Bob Willard

July 4, 2014

WORDS THAT COUNT

ROBERT S. WILLARD

Two-seventy-two. That's the number of words that are in the copy of Abraham Lincoln's Gettysburg speech he wrote out for Edward Everett. They both spoke at the dedication of the cemetery in Pennsylvania—Everett, for two hours; Lincoln, two minutes.

"I have never had a feeling politically that did not spring from the sentiments embodied in the Declaration of Independence." Lincoln said that in Independence Hall in February, 1861. His job that day was simply to raise a flag, but his "deep emotion at finding myself standing here" led to his observation that that document "gave liberty, not alone to the people of this country, but, I hope, to the world, for all future time."

The Declaration of Independence, before listing the "abuses and usurpations" by the British monarch, puts forth two great revolutionary ideas—that all people are equal with natural rights, and that government derives its power from the consent of the governed. The Civil War was fought to preserve both ideas. If the Union forces had failed, not only would millions of bondsmen and their descendants continue to be enslaved, but the idea of self-government might have been extinguished. What Lincoln called "the last best hope of earth" might no longer inspire all nations.

From the opening "When in the course of human events" to the concluding "new guards for their future security," the Founders' words influenced Lincoln's memorable phrases: "new birth of freedom" and "government of . . . by . . . and for the people."

Four score and seven years before Lincoln spoke at Gettysburg, the Founders, in their own 272 words, inspired "a few appropriate remarks" we will all long remember.

ROBERT S. WILLARD is a long-time collector of Lincolniana. He is a director and past vice president of the Abraham Lincoln Association, director and past president of the Abraham Lincoln Institute, an advisor to the Lincoln Forum, and past treasurer of the Lincoln Group of the District of Columbia. He was an advisor to the Lincoln Legal Papers project and the Lincoln Digitalization project at Northern Illinois University. In 2005, Willard traveled the Lincoln trail from the 16th President's birthplace in Hodgenville, Kentucky, through southwestern Indiana, ending at Lincoln's tomb in Springfield, Illinois, covering 1,000 miles in a four-week period of time. During his career, Willard served as Executive Director of the National Commission on Libraries and Information Science and senior executive at the Government Printing Office among other positions. He was an officer in the U.S. Army serving in Korea, Vietnam, and at the Pentagon.

Good Work

Abraham Lincoln listened and learned from everything that happened to him. In his pocket he kept a small notebook where he jotted down his thoughts, scribbled ideas, and tucked in between its pages newspaper clippings that spoke to the problems of the day and the issues on his mind. Lincoln struggled to overcome the racism of the era to which he was born. He worked hard to achieve understanding and grow into a better human being.

In an era when children's voices were often discounted, Lincoln was humble enough to pay attention to what they thought and to what they had to say. When eleven-year-old Grace Bedell wrote to suggest he grow whiskers for he would look better and "then he would be President", Lincoln thanked her for her suggestion. And he took her advice! On his way to his inauguration he had his train stop in Westfield, N.Y. where Grace lived, to show her his whiskers and ask, "How do you like the improvement you advised me to make?"

On many mornings citizens came to the White House to seek Lincoln's help. He listened closely to young Hannah Slater, who came

to ask Lincoln
job in a commissary.
the big-hearted,
affairs of
people, as he
listening to

ys willing to
e he understood
unexpected
rew into the
great President

Karen B. Winnick
June 13, 2013

A YOUNG GIRL'S ADVICE

KAREN B. WINNICK

Abraham Lincoln listened and learned from everything that happened to him. In his pockets he kept a small notebook where he jotted down his thoughts, scribbled ideas, and tucked in between its pages newspaper clippings that spoke to the problems of the day and the issues on his mind. Lincoln struggled to overcome the racism of the era to which he was born. He worked hard to achieve understanding and grow into a better human being.

In an era when children's voices were often discounted, Lincoln was humble enough to pay attention to what they thought and to what they had to say. When eleven-year-old Grace Bedell wrote to suggest he grow whiskers for he would look better and "then he would be President," Lincoln thanked her for her suggestion. And he took her advice! On his way to his inauguration he had his train stop in Westfield, N.Y., where Grace lived, to show her his whiskers and ask, "How do you like the improvement you advised me to make?"

On many mornings citizens came to the White House to seek Lincoln's help. He listened closely to young Hannah Slater, who came without her parents' knowledge to ask Lincoln to save her wounded father's job in a commissary. Years later she remembered "the big-hearted, sympathetic man, burdened by affairs of state, beset by hundreds of people, as he sat patiently, unhurriedly, listening to the story of a little girl."

Because he was always willing to listen and learn and because he understood that wisdom often came from unexpected places, Abraham Lincoln grew into the extraordinary man and the great President we remember today.

KAREN B. WINNICK is a children's author, illustrator, and poet. She has published ten picture books, many historically based, including Lucy's Cave *(Boyds Mills Press, 2008) and* Cassie's Sweet Berry Pie *(Boyds Mills Press, 2005), both of which were named* "Best Books of the Year" *by the Children's Book Committee of Bank Street College of Education. Her book,* Mr. Lincoln's Whiskers *(Boyds Mills Press, 1996) was featured by ABC's* Good Morning America *in an American Snapshot segment titled "Girl's Letter Changes Face of Lincoln"(2009). The book tells the fact-based story of young Grace Bedell, who encouraged Abraham Lincoln to grow "whiskers." Winnick is active in the community and is a former member of the board of directors of the Abraham Lincoln Presidential Library Foundation.*

⸺ACKNOWLEDGMENTS⸺

On behalf of the Abraham Lincoln Presidential Library Foundation, I gratefully acknowledge each of the extraordinary essayists who participated in the 272 word project, particularly those whose written and/or photographic essays appear in this book, for without their insightful and thoughtful submissions, this book would not be possible. I also gratefully acknowledge the many individuals associated with the essayists—agents, administrative assistants, parents, teachers, attorneys, chiefs-of-staff—who worked tirelessly with us to attain the essays, photographs, and permissions.

Also I wish to thank Robert Guinsler at Sterling Lord Literistic; Jim Childs, Holly Rubino, James Jayo, Keith Wallman, Julie Marsh, Shana Capozza, Sara Given, Amy Alexander, Jessica DeFranco, Melissa Evarts, Sheryl Kober, and all those at Lyons Press whose vision and perseverance made this publication possible; Scott Saef and Julia Chester at Sidley Austin, who helped us through uncharted waters; and AT&T, the *Chicago Tribune*, GATX, Karl and Heather Barnhart, David Hirsch, and Stephen Young for their support of the 272 Words project.

Last but not least, I wish to thank my colleagues at the Illinois Historic Preservation Agency, Abraham Lincoln Presidential Library and Museum including its advisory board and the board and staff of the Abraham Lincoln Presidential Library Foundation whose support of this project has meant so very much and furthers our vitally important mission of preserving, protecting and advancing Abraham Lincoln's rich legacy for generations to come.

—Carla Knorowski

PHOTO CREDITS